Learn RPGs in GameMaker: Studio

Build and Design Role Playing Games

Ben Tyers

Apress®

Learn RPGs in GameMaker: Studio: Build and Design Role Playing Games

Ben Tyers
Worthing, West Sussex, United Kingdom

ISBN-13 (pbk): 978-1-4842-2945-3   ISBN-13 (electronic): 978-1-4842-2946-0
DOI 10.1007/978-1-4842-2946-0

Library of Congress Control Number: 2017950737

Cover image by www.gamedeveloperstudio.com

Managing Director: Welmoed Spahr
Editorial Director: Todd Green
Acquisitions Editor: Steve Anglin
Development Editor: Matthew Moodie
Technical Reviewer: Dickson Law
Coordinating Editor: Mark Powers
Copy Editor: Mary Behr

Distributed to the book trade worldwide by Springer Science+Business Media New York, 233 Spring Street, 6th Floor, New York, NY 10013. Phone 1-800-SPRINGER, fax (201) 348-4505, e-mail orders-ny@springer-sbm.com, or visit www.springeronline.com. Apress Media, LLC is a California LLC and the sole member (owner) is Springer Science + Business Media Finance Inc (SSBM Finance Inc). SSBM Finance Inc is a **Delaware** corporation.

For information on translations, please e-mail rights@apress.com, or visit www.apress.com/rights-permissions.

Apress titles may be purchased in bulk for academic, corporate, or promotional use. eBook versions and licenses are also available for most titles. For more information, reference our Print and eBook Bulk Sales web page at www.apress.com/bulk-sales.

Any source code or other supplementary material referenced by the author in this book is available to readers on GitHub via the book's product page, located at www.apress.com/9781484229453. For more detailed information, please visit www.apress.com/source-code.

Printed on acid-free paper

Contents at a Glance

Contents

About the Author

Ben Tyers is a freelance programmer and technical writer by day and a sci-fi horror novel writer by night. He made his first computer game way back in 1984, on a ZX Spectrum 48K computer, when he was eight years old. His passion for creation has continued since then. He holds a number of computer-related qualifications. When relaxing, Ben has an infatuation for old-school horror and sci-fi films, particularly 1960s B movies.

About the Technical Reviewer

Dickson Law is a GameMaker hobbyist, commentator, and extension developer with six years of community experience. In his spare time, he enjoys writing general-purpose libraries, tools, and articles covering basic techniques for GameMaker Studio. As a web programmer by day, his main areas of interest include integration with server-side scripting and API design. He lives in Toronto, Canada.

Acknowledgments

Special thanks to

Doug Morrison
&
Wayne Pinnow
&
Vadim
"YellowAfterlife"
Dyachenko

Thanks to the following for allowing use of their assets for the projects in this book

- Main Artwork: GameDeveloperStudio.Com/ Robert Brooks

- Additional Objects: KennyLand

- Main Character: Spyros Kontis

- Zombie Pirates, Card Characters, Main Character: gamedevmarket.net

- Cutscene Backgrounds: Purchased on 123rf.com - Klara Viskova/Roland Warmbier/ Andrei Krauchuk/sergeiminsk/pixxart/Noel Powell/neyro2008/Sergey Breev/Sergey Pigulka/alexmstudio/Roman Dekan

- Ship: millionthvector.blogspot.co.uk

- Human Footsteps Sounds: OwlStorm Yoyodaman234 rocktopus punpcklbw Mikaelfernstrom - FreeSound.org, Creative Commons Attribution

- Fire Audio: midimagician - FreeSound.org

- Water Audio: InspectorJ - FreeSound.org

- Butterfly: GlitchTheGame.Com

- Wooden Pirate Ship: Bleed/OpenGameArt.org, Attribution 3.0 Unported (CC BY 3.0)

- Dice: JamesWhite/OpenGameArt.org, CC0 - Public Domain

- Tree: domsson/OpenGameArt.org

- Appo Paint Font: Grafito Design/Raul Perez

CHAPTER 1

■ ■ ■

Introduction

Some casual-style games may require a fair amount of design time.

RPGs, on the other hand, require copious planning and design. It is advisable to plan out the game in as much detail as possible before starting to code your game.

Designing and programming are two different disciplines. Constantly switching between them can reduce focus and creativity, and can also be mentally draining.

Planning is good for the following reasons:

- Allows you to brainstorm without having to think about programming

- Allows you to focus your creativity and get into the zone

- Provides notes that can be used later when coding

- Can actually be a fun activity in the overall process of design and programming

- Means you don't have to mentally store every idea (and risk forgetting the good ones)

- If you're working as a team, it allows you to share ideas with other team members

Sketching out your ideas on paper can also be beneficial. It allows you to have:

- Some time away from coding on your computer

- A break from having to think about your game

- The option of reviewing your ideas

At any point in the planning process, feel free to throw your notes into the nearest garbage bin, whether one page or all of them. You should think of your notes as a kind of organic life form that can change and adapt over time.

I recommend using one page for each section/element of your game, which makes changing/updating the ideas a slightly less painful affair when you do decide to make changes.

The rest of this introduction covers the main 20 points to consider when making an RPG, and the basic game template that some of the elements use as a template.

The main body of the book covers 40 commonly used RPG elements. I've done it this way so you can clearly understand what is relevant to each element. Some of these elements may be used as a template for other projects; this is indicated at the start of each element. The same game theme will be used throughout.

Hopefully, having each element separate should make it easy to understand what code is relevant to that section.

© Ben Tyers 2017
B. Tyers, *Learn RPGs in GameMaker: Studio*, DOI 10.1007/978-1-4842-2946-0_1

Programming/Source Code Notes

You may reuse the code in your projects.

The code used in this book is made for someone who is relatively new to Game Maker Language (GML). It is assumed that you have already read and learned what is taught in the book *Practical GameMaker: Studio Language Projects* or already have a basic knowledge of GML.

When coding, there is usually more than one method, using different GML or different approaches. The code used in this book is designed so that

- Someone relatively new to GML can understand it

- It's clear and logical

- Otherwise complex code appears clear and easy to read

- It's broken into understandable bite-size blocks

- You can easily reuse it in your projects

- It doesn't take a PhD to understand

- It looks good in print

Coding comments are used to explain what each section does, allowing a newbie to grasp the basics and understand what is going on

The source code is accessible via a download link at www.apress.com/9781484229453.

Story – Plot

Plot: The story of the game

Most RPGs follow some sort of story.

The premise for this one is that a character who lives in a windmill goes to the beach on a hot and sunny day, hires a boat, and gets caught in a storm. The boat sinks and she wakes up on an island run by pirates. She then needs to raise enough cash to get passage off the island.

See the chapter on cutscenes where this premise is made into an animated introduction story.

The story should then continue as the player proceeds in the game. This can be achieved through the following:

- Additional cutscenes

- Dialogue with other game characters

- The collection/use/interaction of objects

- The addition of mini-quests/mini-games

- Changing environments

- Unlockable locations

Locations that the player can visit can help to form part of the plot. When visiting new locations you can gradually provide more info for the player that helps progress the plot, but bear in mind that not all locations need to perform this action.

Having a good story not only engages the player, it sets the scene and gives the player some idea what they need to do. In a pirate-themed RPG, you know you will be treasure hunting and fighting pirates. You're unlikely to be dog-fighting an F-24 attack aircraft.

Most RPGs follow a plot throughout the whole game, for the simple reason that it works and is logical.

Story – Character Design

Character Design: Design of characters used by the story

Character design includes the main characters that the player will interact with; for example, in this story they are a shop-keeper, the ship owner, villains, and allies.

Your main character requires a bit of thought. Whoever plays your game will be spending a lot of time with them. An equal amount of thought should be given to the other main characters in the game. Spending too much time developing your main character can be counterproductive and may unbalance the game.

Consider things such as

- Appearance

- Voice (if they speak, which they probably will in an RPG)

- Quirks: Special things that make your character unique (in the example in this book, there are multiple voice variations when colliding with other objects, or after being static for any length of time)

- Movement: How the player is moved, and whether in four or eight directions or in 360 degrees

- Animation: Pre-rendered, made from separate parts, 3D rendered in real time, or just regular sprites

- Customizable Clothing: Via in-game upgrades or purchasable items

- What Type of Clan: Wizard, human, alien, zombie

- Special Skills: Flying, destroying walls, etc.

- How Much They Can Carry: Three items? Or eight if they find a bag?

At this point you should really decide on your art options. You can

1. Design and draw everything yourself

2. Commission an artist to do it

3. Use free/royalty-based art from the Internet

■ **Note**   Free resources may only be free to use for personal projects. Commercial use may not be permitted under the terms of use. If unsure, it is advisable to check the license or seek permission directly from the creator.

Story – Enemy Design and Minions

Enemy Design: Mainly the design of non-character enemies and "nameless minions"

It is important that the main enemies are unique and have their own traits, such as a shopkeeper who stutters or a villain who chuckles.

Other characters in the game will also require some thought. There are two main types of characters: those that progress the story and plot, and those that don't.

For this example, the main enemy character will be a blue-bearded pirate.

The subcharacters will include a parrot, a pirate with a big nose, a pirate with a dagger, and a pirate with two daggers.

As for the main character, quirks are important. They could be

- A blue beard

- A wooden leg

- A hook

- Random voices and sounds

The parrot could fly randomly around the level. Upon collision with the parrot, the player might have to play a mini-game and win before proceeding.

Equally, there could be mini-games/challenges for the other characters, perhaps with the compensation of some gold coins. Limiting how often a player can play mini-games would be a good idea here.

Additional characters can help develop the plot or just be there for fighting, but the focus should be on the main game characters.

The game should ideally have several boss characters that the player must defeat before being able to proceed. Boss characters are usually strong, dangerous, and sometimes accompanied by nameless minions that also attack. The player should have to learn how the boss moves, where to shoot it, when to shoot it, and how to avoid its arsenal and minions. If it takes fewer than five attempts to learn the boss's movement and defeat it, it isn't tough enough. Make it harder.

As mentioned already, keep to the theme.

Story – Objectives

Objectives: The goals the player must complete to advance the story

The main objective of this game is to collect 1,000 gold coins so the main character can get off the island. Providing a variety of ways to collect gold coins is the key here, such as

- Completing mini-games/quests

- Winning battles/fights

- Finding secret areas

- Small puzzles

- Digging for buried treasure

As before, restricting how often/quickly a player can get gold coins is the key here. For example, you may want to limit battles to once every 20 minutes the player plays the game, or charge the player one gold coin each time they dig (which prevents them trying to dig over the whole level).

Each enemy should have a different battle game with its own mechanics, to create variety.

Mini-quests could include retrieving 10 mushrooms in the level in five minutes or climbing a mountain to retrieve a diamond. The more quests you have, the more variety the player will have when playing your game.

Quests and mini-games can be part of the overall story of your game or independent. Some may require the player to successfully complete them in order to proceed: for example, killing a dragon to get the key that's around its neck, which can then be used to unlock a gate so the player has access to a new game area. A good mix of the two usually works well.

Even for mini-games that aren't part of the story, it's generally a good idea to keep to the theme of the main game. This game is based around a pirates' island, so things involving boats, ropes, sword fights, digging, map reading, exploring the island, building a sandcastle, shooting parrots, and that kind of stuff suit it well.

Story – Setting

Setting: Includes the general theme for graphics

The main theme will pretty much dictate all the graphics and audio used in your game (except for maybe a few mini-games or quests).

For the example in this book, the theme is pirate-based. Backgrounds, objects (both static and interactive), and audio should reflect and reinforce this theme. As the game is based on an isolated island, graphics and locations should reflect that too.

The following objects would be suited for such a pirate theme:

- Anchors

- Old wooden huts

- Wooden signs

- Barrels

- Palm trees

- Flying birds

Sound effects will all help create an immersive environment for the player, such as

- Birds

- Waves from the sea

- Footstep sounds on different surfaces

Themed locations could include

- The beach

- Forests

- Underwater sections

- Mini-platform game on an abandoned ship

Aesthetics – Art Style

Art Style: The style of art the game uses

One of the most important factors to decide upon is the art style of your game. There are tens if not hundreds of art styles and subgenres. The main four are pixel, vector, 3D, and photorealistic. Each has its own positives and negatives, as shown in Table 1-1.

Table 1-1. *The Main Four Types of Art Styles*

	Pixel	Vector	3D/Pre-Rendered	Photorealistic
Positives	Cheap to hire an artist. Lots of resources available for free or low cost. Short learning curve if you go at it alone.	Plenty of talented artists available. Can be adapted for size easily. Huge library online, both free and licensed. Can be pre-rendered to other formats.	Looks cool. Can be pre-rendered so it's quick. Lots of artists offering services. Multiple platforms use 3D.	Awesome eye-candy if done well. Limited by imagination only. Can create a truly immersive experience.
Negatives	If not integrated well, it can make a game look poor. Limited to how much information or detail you can portray. Not suitable for large sprites or backgrounds.	A steep learning curve on making vector graphics. Limited detail. Can be slower to process in real time. Using vectors in GameMaker requires some skill.	Extreme learning curve for modelling and importing into GameMaker. Expensive to hire artists. Minor changes may take days to get new sprites.	Can be extremely expensive. Not really suitable for an indie game developer. Huge game sizes. Requires special graphics cards.

Aesthetics – Choice of Art Style

Choice of Art Style: Must consider how the player sprite is going to be drawn (using either single or multiple layered sprites)

For this project, we're going for vector-style art.

The big question is how to implement it. The two main choices are a single sprite for each frame of animation, or creating the animation using separate parts.

Each has its own benefits and drawbacks.

If your art skills are somewhat limited, then outsourcing your artwork or obtaining pre-rendered sprites is the way to go. This may limit what your characters can do, but it is (usually) a cheap and effective method.

Using separate sprites allows for greater flexibility in what your characters can do, with movement limited only by your imagination. The drawback of this approach is that it requires a good understanding of math and learning other software such as Spine in order to do this in real time in the game.

For single sprites, there are a few options, such as buying custom-made or off-the-shelf sprites, or using specialist sprite creation software. If you choose the latter option, I'd go for one that supports skeletons. Sprite software is the middle road here: the basics can be learned within a day and the results can be visually awesome and very rewarding, but may lack the overall quality you get from hiring a professional or using premade sprites. Another advantage of going it alone is you can create your own animated sequences, rather than just the common walk, run, idle, and jump. If you want your character to do a somersault, you can make that happen. If you want it to rub its belly after eating food, you can also make that happen.

If you want something quickly for a mock-up of a game, then premade sprite packs are the obvious choice. You can always change the sprites to something more suited to your game dynamics as you proceed through your project.

Generating animations in real time has its advantages too. But imagine a highly animated game with 20 characters, each with 20 different animations with 20 frames each; that's 8,000 frames! At a decent quality that could be around 800MB. This is way too much for tablet- or phone-based games. Using skeletal animation could reduce that to around 8MB, which is a much better option.

It all boils down to the target platform and how much time you are prepared to put in to learn the required skills.

Aesthetics – Scening

Scening: How the story progression is going to be implemented in the game (usually via the use of cutscenes)

There are various styles of cutscenes. You can get a breakdown at https://en.wikipedia.org/wiki/Cutscene.

Cutscenes are a great way to provide info to the player. In a RPG it's now expected that there will be several cutscenes. Generally speaking, they are non-interactive animated sequences.

The game for this book will have an opening cutscene that explains how the main character ended up on the pirates' island. (See the chapter on cutscenes for a working example.)

Additional cutscenes could be added to provide extra information or to explain quests/tasks and mini-games.

Cutscenes are also commonly shown at the end of the game, as a kind of a reward to the player for completing it. Sometimes there is more than one possible end scene, depending on decisions made by the player in the game.

In the game for this book, the main task is for the player to acquire enough cash to get passage off the island. A great time to show a cutscene would be when the player finds the buried treasure chest.

Other major events could also warrant a cutscene, such as

- Killing a boss enemy

- Finding their first gold coin

- Visiting the in-game shop

- Conversations between a player and other characters

- A way of explaining complex instructions or tasks

A note of caution: not everyone is a fan of cutscenes. Overdoing them can annoy the heck out of people. You may wish to give players the choice of being able to skip cutscenes.

That said, when done well and at the right times, cutscenes can add a lot to your games.

Aesthetics – Sound Design

Sound Design: Which basic sound effects the game will need (for example, footsteps can be used for a more serious tone, etc.)

I have a great idea! Let's make sound effects for everything:

- Different footsteps on different surfaces (like gravel, grass, water, leaves, snow)

- Make a sound when a player picks up/puts down an object

- Ker-ching noises when collecting coins

- Alarms, bells, and whistles when finding a treasure chest

- Squawking noises when the parrot flies overhead

- Lots of voice instructions

- Voices in dialogues

- Repetitive background music on loop

Repetitive multiple sound effects playing at the same time can be annoying. When used correctly, however, sound effects can add a lot to the game and provide audio feedback based on what is happening on screen. When computers first had the ability to make good quality sound effects, it was pretty cool. (I'm thinking back to Tomb Raider and Alone in the Dark). These days, not so much.

Overusing sound effects is an easy way to alienate your players. Try to use sound effects sparingly and for emphasis. For example, footsteps on grass could be quiet, or some water sounds would be OK.

Provide an options screen where the player can select/deselect/change the volume of various in-game audio effects. They will thank you for that.

When used well, in-game audio can provide an immersive experience for the player. The quality of your sounds and voices is also important. There are plenty of sites out there where you can hire professional voice-over (VO) artists at reasonable prices. If you decide to go the voice route yourself, invest in a quality microphone and DAW (digital audio workstation) software; you can get set up for less than $200 (£150).

Aesthetics – Projection

Projection: The angle from which the player sees the game world (first person, top down, third person, etc.)

Different game genres have different view styles: platform games are usually side-on views. RPGs can be top-down (4/4), isometric, various forms of 2.5D (also known as fake 3D, semi-top, or 3/4 perspective), or full 3D.

Generally speaking,

- Isometric games look pretty cool, but can be a pain to program.

- Top-down looks OK and is quite easy to program.

- Semi-top looks good, is easy to program, and allows you to provide more info than top-down.

As you can see from Figure 1-1, in the top-down view you can see the roof of a building, but you are unable to tell what type of building it is. The semi-top view shows part of the roof and the front of the building; this immediately allows the player to know what the building is. Hey, you could even hang a sign with the word "SHOP" on it. Portraying this information in top-down is trickier.

Isometric views can not only provide the information on the type of building, but also give a feeling of depth and, if done well, look pretty cool.

For the purpose of this book, the project will be using semi-top, for the following reasons:

- A lot of artwork in this style is available, both free and paid.

- Creating your own graphics in this style requires only a gentle learning curve.

- Movement and object interaction is fairly simple (when compared with isometric).

- The math level required for interactions and calculations is reasonably low.

- Low CPU overhead; hey, GameMaker Studio is great for 2D games.

- The player can easily understand what they see on-screen.

- No transparency effects needed (e.g. walking behind a building in isometric view).

Obviously there are also negatives in 3/4 view compared with isometric view, but 3/4 view is a great place to start.

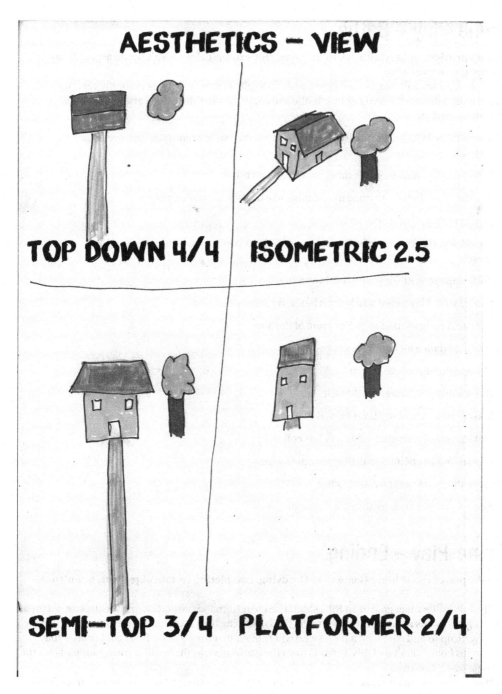

Figure 1-1. *Types of game views*

Core Game-Play – Battle

Battle: The main provider of the challenge in the game (for example, Pac-Man's battle aspect is the avoidance of the ghost creatures)

RPGs are synonymous with battles and fights, with dialogue-driven story lines currently very popular. They are usually a mix of different fighting/battle games; in my view the more variety, the better. The main ones used are

- Boss Battles: Which I won't discuss here because they were mentioned in a previous section

- Turn-Based: Characters take turns attacking each other

- One-On-One: Full-on fighting in real time, like old-school arcade games

- Random: Player just clicks and hopes

- Avoidance: Having to survive an amount of time or reach a goal without hitting an enemy

- JPRG (Japanese RPG): Turn-based variation

- Card-Based: Play a card and hope it beats the enemy's choice

- Hybrid: A combination of one or more of the above

Some general guidance for battle systems:

- Make use of the whole screen

- Use sounds and background music

- Make it clear what the player must do

- Make use of objects that the player has collected

- Have different enemies use different attack styles

- Make the characters face each other

- Allow a skilled player to always be triumphant

Core Game-Play – Ending

Ending: How the player can achieve Game Over (by dying, completing certain objectives, or finishing the story)

Personally, I think the main goal of an RPG should be clear from the onset. The initial cutscene is a great place to put this goal. In this game, this will be reinforced by placing the player near the exit on game start. The player can walk up to and chat with a pirate who will explain that they'll need 1,000 gold coins if they want passage on his boat. I don't feel this distracts from the game-play, as there will be many subplots for the player to uncover on their own.

Exactly how much information you give the player and when is up to you. You may, for example, just give info for the next quest/mini-game, and provide core information later on.

Whether your game takes hours, days, or weeks to complete, reward your player. They've committed their time and money (if they bought it), and they expect something in return. An immersive cutscene is a great way to end the game.

You may wish to throw in a false ending, such as if they've got their 1,000 gold coins, the pirate sails them home. On the way home, they come across another pirate ship and they have a full-on battle with cannon balls, explosions, etc.

Ending credits are also good: you can thank everyone who helped on your game, where you sourced your graphics and audio, and code you got from other places. You could go for simple scrolling text, or full graphics with effects, whichever suits your game style.

Depending on how you planned your game, it may have multiple endings. For example, rather than finding the 1,000 gold coins, your player got together the tools and resources to make a small rowboat. Different endings will get players coming back and playing it more often, which is great if you have an ad-based revenue system.

There is also a school of thought that games should not have multiple endings, as they may somehow punish the player for not doing something or not visiting a location in game.

Core Game-Play – Exploration

Exploration: How players will travel the game world (by exploration or level select screens)

So you've designed the main characters and the basics of your game play. Next is something that is often overlooked or not given enough consideration: how your player gets from A to B.

You can add a little variety without distracting from the fact that it's an RPG.

Mainly the character will be walking, whether on solid ground, grass, or through puddles.

You can also add variety by offering some alternatives.

- Parrot: You catch a parrot that will fly you to isolated locations not accessible by foot

- Swimming: The ability to cross a vast river to otherwise inaccessible locations

- Vehicle/Transport: Perhaps your player can collect items to make a boat or cart. Then they can use it in a mini-quest against another pirate

- Weapons: Starting off the game with a character with no weapons is also a good way to go. Perhaps when they have a sword/cutlass they can cut down bushes or trees to allow access to other areas

- Running: Perhaps for short time after eating food the player can run faster and jump farther, allowing the player to traverse ravines, for example

- Skiing: Perhaps the island has snow-covered mountain peaks. Skiing down them would make a great mini-game: one-on-one against a pirate

Keyboard movement in RPGs is generally done with WSAD (key presses of the keys W, S, A, and D). This is mainly so you can control the character on-screen and still be able to use a mouse; additionally arrow keys are sometimes available.

Core Game-Play – In-Game Text

In-Game Text: How players will receive information from the game (also dialogue)

Text messages are a core component of RPGs. For the purpose of the game made with this book we'll be using the following:

- Text on Scroll: Used during cutscenes to convey information

- Pop-Up Text Box: When conversing with other characters in the game

- Info Text: Kind of a quirk; semi-random sentences when you collide with objects in game. For example, one of ten sentences at random for each object.

- Hints/Tips: Pop-up messages that guide the player through the RPG/story or what they should do next

In RPGs, text is commonly shown in a typewriter-style effect, one letter at a time. For the purposes of this book, I'll be following that convention.

Text is also usually accompanied by spoken words. Each speaking character will have their "own" voice. This is something you can do yourself or outsource it. I recommend going it alone because it can be fun and rewarding. There's plenty of software out there to do this: as a starting point, I recommend Audacity, which is free.

Interactions with main characters should add something to the overall game, such as advancing the plot or giving tips to the player.

Core Game-Play – Scoring

Scoring: How the scoring system of the game will work (this is also used to plan for XP in RPG games)

One way of showing progress to a player in an RPG is their stats/scoring. For example,

- XP (experience points): This stat usually goes up when the player wins a fight or completes a task. It may also be split into levels

- Gold: In the game for this book, the aim is 1,000 gold pieces. Displaying how many the player has will give a good indication of their progress

- Health: As a constant side-plot, the player may need to be on the constant look-out for food or water; otherwise they may die

- Skills: The skills the player currently has, perhaps starting with four and adding extras as they progress through the game

- Time: An indication of how long a player has to complete the current task/challenge/mini-quest

- Mental Well-Being

- Strength, which may be reduced during physical exertion and replenished with rest

- Designing a layout that displays all of this information for a heads-up display (HUD) is a skill unto itself. It is dealt with in its own chapter

Other things that you may want to keep track of, perhaps as a pop-up so as not to overcrowd the HUD, are

- Total distance travelled

- Total gold coins collected/spent/used

- Total battles with some stats

- Total time played

Additional player attributes could include awareness, luck, ego, etc.

Extended Game-Play – Collectables

Collectables: These include secondary objectives that will be used to enhance the game's lifespan

What's a good RPG without collectables? Collectables make an RPG an RPG.
Whether for instant gratification, food or water, or for advancing the story, collectables are it.
For the game designed in this book, the main objects are

- Food and Water: Needs to be constantly sourced and has no effect on the overall story (unless the player dies and needs to restart)

- Gold: The main collectable for this game, the player needs enough gold to leave the island. Gold may also be spent in the shop, reduced if they lose battles, or spent if they want to dig

- Keys: Can unlock areas and help advance the story

- Shovel: Once the player has this item, they can start digging for the buried treasure chest. In this game, each dig will cost one gold coin to prevent cheating by digging everywhere

- Mushrooms: Used in a mini-quest where the player needs to find 10 mushrooms in a set time

- Battle Skills: Certain objects add battle skills

- Sword: Allows the player to participate in battles

- Satchel: A bag that, when collected, allows the player to carry more items

- Birdseed: Allows the player to trap a parrot for hidden areas

An RPG is likely to have tens if not hundreds of separate items. Take time to design/plan each item and how it works within the game.

Having notes to work from is an essential aspect of the design process and will allow for quicker and easier game development.

Extended Game-Play – Further Considerations

Further considerations: This includes the inventory, items, and power-ups that the player can use to increase game depth

The next stage is important. It's how you relate the game back to the player.

Inventory, as mentioned previously, may start with two slots and increase to four when the player finds a bag. Obviously you show two empty slots in the inventory section of your HUD. The other slots could have a big red X in them. On mouse over, you could display the text "Find Bag to Hold More Items," perhaps accompanied by spoken audio, but make sure not to use too much audio at once, or you may alienate the player.

For health, you could use some kind of bar or container that shows current health. In the book's example, we'll use a chemistry bottle with liquid that changes fullness based on health. The player can keep their health up with a constant supply of food and water. A visual bar for each would suffice. Rather than just having items scattered through the level, force the player to give some thought (i.e. running into a tree may drop a coconut, crouching next to a stream may give water).

Showing what battle skills the player has and needs to find can be shown graphically: full colour for current skills, greyscale for those yet to find.

One of the quirks for this game is lots of objects, some of which can be collected, but all of which have multiple sentences that are displayed and spoken when the player collides with them. Some of these sentences will provide hints and tips on how/where to use the item, and other sentences are just for fun and variety. Encouraging the player to collide multiple times is the main aim here.

When it comes to mini-games, variety is the key. Mini-puzzles could be based on anything: flying a parrot through a forest while avoiding branches, crossing a river without being eaten by a crocodile, running across the deck of a ship while avoiding sword fights. For this game, plan to use ancient weapons, like a bow and arrow or a trebuchet.

Extended Game-Play – Mini-Games

Mini-Games: Such as the lock-picking games that many games now use
Here's a rundown of a few mini-game ideas:

- Hunt for Mushrooms: Collect 20 mushrooms from a forest within a set time limit

- Destroy Buildings: Use a trebuchet to throw rocks at a building

- Swimming: Swim in the sea collecting seaweed, but avoiding fish

- Maze: Get out of a maze in a set time limit

- Lock-Picking: Pick a lock using the mathematical clues provided

- Matching Game: Match the cards

- Rowing Race: Race against a pirate over a water-based course

- Find The Treasure: A variation on the classic game Minesweeper

- Tap to Music: A variation on the tap-the-button-to-the-music style game

- Match Three: Swap over objects to get three in a row

As you can see, mini-games are really only limited by your imagination: as long as it has some similarity to the main game, you can't go too far wrong.

Although mini-games are usually distant from the main game story, they should reward the player. For this game, a few gold coins would be sufficient.

You may want to limit how often a player can play each mini-game.

Extended Game-Play – Quirks

Quirks: Unique or strange game-play mechanics that you want to use to make your game stand out from the others
Quirks are things that make your game special. In this game it's going to be the multiple variations in dialogue/text when speaking to in-game characters, colliding with various objects, or when purchasing from the shop. Additionally, sound effects and music will be used for emphasis.

There will also be diversity in the range of the quests and mini-games. I intend to make some so good and engaging that they could stand on their own as a separate game.

Other quirks could include

- Mundane objects as toys (would make good cutscenes)

- Dancing to music if not moved for a time

- Correcting a pirate's speech for not using proper English

- Burping after eating or drinking

Extended Game-Play – Saving

Saving: Saving and loading game files extends game life by allowing the player to return whenever they want.
Saving is an important aspect of RPGs and is relatively easy to do.

With modern devices, players may leave the game part the way through, for example to take a call or check emails. This makes timing when to save a bit of a hit-or-miss affair.

The approach I favor is big signs throughout the game with the words "Save Here" written on them. No mistaking that: on collision with the player, the save script is executed and a message is shown to the player that the game has been saved. Make it so this can only be done when not a mini-game or quest.

I prefer the use of an INI system to save data. In an RPG, this is relatively straightforward because there are only a limited number of things that need to be saved and a limited number of objects in-game.

There is a whole chapter dedicated to saving data in this book.

Basically for an RPG you'll need to store

- Player stats

- Location of objects

- Which mini-games/quests have been played and how often

- Location of player

- Location of other characters

- What items the player has in the inventory

- Location of other in-game objects

Game Base

To make things a little easier, and to prevent me showing the same code in every chapter, most of the RPG topics will use a basic movement code for the player. The GMZ project file for this is in the download resources and is named Game_Base. It's a very basic movement and animation example that will be expanded upon in other sections. For each project, it will be noted whether this or another GMZ file is used as the base template. You could use emums for directions and movement, but the method used allows for easier adaptation of the code in later elements where it is used as a base template. This base will provide four directional movements, controlled by arrow keys. If you prefer movement via WSAD, this is a simple change you can make yourself.

The name of the player object is **obj_player**. The **Create Event** code sets the initial values. It uses a number of variables so you know what direction it is/has been moving in and whether it is currently moving (see Listing 1-1).

Listing 1-1. Setting Up States and Initial Variables

```
///set up
enum player_state {
    idle,
    up,
    down,
    left,
    right
    }

dir= player_state.down;
is_moving=false;
image_speed=0.5;
```

The **Step Event** consists of three blocks. The first block detects keypresses and updates the values accordingly (see Listing 1-2).

Listing 1-2. Changing States Based on Keypresses

```
///keypress code
if (keyboard_check(vk_left))
{
    dir= player_state.left;
    is_moving=true;
}
else
if (keyboard_check(vk_right))
{
    dir=player_state.right;
    is_moving=true;
}
else
if (keyboard_check(vk_up))
{
    dir=player_state.up;
    is_moving=true;
}
else
if (keyboard_check(vk_down))
{
    dir=player_state.down;
    is_moving=true;
}
else
{
    is_moving=false;
}
```

The second block will make the player move if the flag is_moving is true and dir has a value (see Listing 1-3).

Listing 1-3. Moving the Object Based on Its State

```
///movement
if is_moving
{
    switch (dir)
    {
        case player_state.up:
        y -= 4;
        break;

        case player_state.down:
        y += 4;
        break;
```

```
        case player_state.left:
        x -= 4;
        break;

        case player_state.right:
        x += 4;
        break;
    }
}
```

The block used for animation checks whether the player is moving or not and sets the appropriate sprite (see Listing 1-4).

Listing 1-4. Setting the Appropriate Animation Based on Direction and Whether Moving or Not

```
///animation
if is_moving
{
    switch (dir)
    {
        case player_state.up:
        sprite_index=spr_walk_up;
        break;

        case player_state.down:
        sprite_index=spr_walk_down;
        break;

        case player_state.left:
        sprite_index=spr_walk_left;
        break;

        case player_state.right:
        sprite_index=spr_walk_right;
        break;
    }
}
else
{
    switch (dir)
    {
        case player_state.up:
        sprite_index=spr_idle_up;
        break;

        case player_state.down:
        sprite_index=spr_idle_down;
        break;

        case player_state.left:
        sprite_index=spr_idle_left;
        break;
```

```
        case player_state.right:
        sprite_index=spr_idle_right;
        break;
    }
}
```

As you will see from the code, it will animate walking when moving, or show an idle animation if not walking.

There is also a set of four images for each direction, both idle and moving. You can find them in the folder path Resources ➤ Images and Audio ➤ Game Base. The origin for the sprites is 32,60. They can be created by clicking the Create Sprite button, as shown in Figure 1-2.

Figure 1-2. *Creating a sprite*

Next, name your sprite **spr_idle_left**, and click Edit Sprite ➤ File ➤ Create from file, as shown in Figure 1-3.

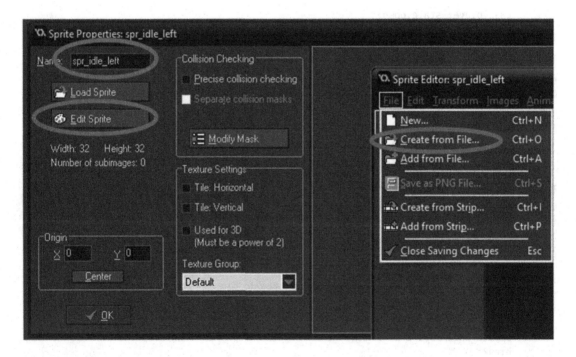

Figure 1-3. *Creating a new sprite from a file*

Next, select the four subimages needed, as shown in Figure 1-4. You can select multiple images by holding down CTRL while clicking each separate image.

Figure 1-4. *Selecting four subimages*

Repeat the process for the other image sets:

spr_idle_right
spr_idle_up
spr_idle_down
spr_walk_left
spr_walk_right
spr_walk_up
spr_walk_down

As mentioned, there is more than one way to skin a cat. The main game base uses switches and enums to make it easy to adapt and modify code for other elements used in this book.

CHAPTER 2

■ ■ ■

The Alert Text Effect

The GMZ file for this element is **Alert_Text_Effect**.

This element uses the **Game_Base.GMZ** as a template.

One of the quirks of this game is that when the player collides with an object, one of many sentences is displayed on the screen and played audibly. This applies both to objects that the player can pick up and not pick up.

Text will be displayed a letter at a time (known as the typewriter effect) when the audio plays.

Upon collision, a random sentence will be chosen and displayed relative to the object.

If your game has lots and lots of objects, then you will have many audio files. You will probably need an audio editor. Audacity is a free software package that is worth checking out and is easy to use from the start, unlike more advanced DAWs (digital audio workstations).

Creating voice audio is skill unto itself. You have the option of doing it yourself or outsourcing. Outsourcing is expensive. Going it alone is a fun way to go, and all you need is a decent microphone and a computer.

For this example, I've done nine sentences. You can, of course, use more or less.

As you will see from the GMZ, keeping the control relative to the object makes it easier. I don't think it's necessary to fix things into a script. Keeping the control in the colliding object will allow for more variation. For example, you may want to

- Play additional sound effects upon collision

- Display graphical effects

- Increase/decrease health, hp (hit points), gold, etc

- Move to a separate room/mini-game

- Save progress

That said, if the object becomes unmanageable due to, for example, lots of collision events, you may wish to delegate some of this to other objects.

RPGs generally have more than one method to display text; other methods and uses are covered in other elements in this book.

Create an object named **obj_mushroom** and set the appropriate sprite from the resources folder. This sprite needs *precise collision checking* set; this is shown in Figure 2-1.

© Ben Tyers 2017
B. Tyers, *Learn RPGs in GameMaker: Studio*, DOI 10.1007/978-1-4842-2946-0_2

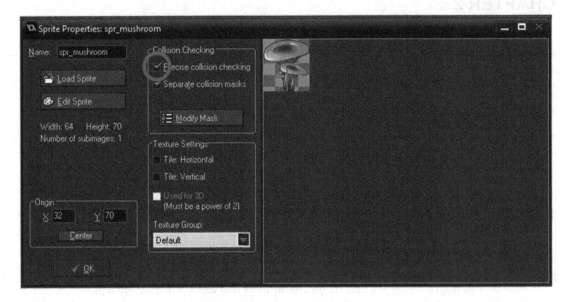

Figure 2-1. *Setting the precise collision checking*

The **Create Event** sets the variables needed, including creating a ds_list to hold the messages. The code is shown in Listing 2-1.

Listing 2-1. Setting Up Initial Variables and a ds_list of Comments

```
///set up mushroom object
is_touching=false; //used to check whether colliding with player
text=""; //initial message state
show_text=""; //start the typewriter text as ""
count=0; //location in show_text
border_size=2;
padding=10;

//add text to ARRAY

mushroom_text[0]="Hmm, mushroom...";
mushroom_text[1]="I'm not touching it#-#it might be poisonous!";
mushroom_text[2]="If only I had some chicken,#I could make soup.";
mushroom_text[3]="It's a mushroom or a toad-stall,#how should I know?";
mushroom_text[4]="This mushroom smells of cheese,#is that normal?";
mushroom_text[5]="Reminds me of my favourite food,#mushrooms on toast.";
mushroom_text[6]="It's just a boring old mushroom.";
mushroom_text[7]="Mushrooms, mushrooms, mushrooms, mushrooms.#Mushrooms, mushrooms,
mushrooms, mushrooms.";
mushroom_text[8]="A mushroom! I've never seen a mushroom before!";
```

The **Alarm[0] Event** clears the message, as shown in Listing 2-2.

Listing 2-2. Changing a Flag for is_touching and Clearing the Text

```
is_touching=false;
text="";
show_text="";
count=0;
```

A **Collision Event** with obj_player chooses a random message and sets up to show the message. It also plays the accompanying audio file; see Listing 2-3. (Note that you could also use a switch/case method instead of multiple if statements.)

Listing 2-3. Choosing a Random Message and Playing the Audio for It

```
if !is_touching
{
    var message=irandom(8);
    show_debug_message(message);
    is_touching=true;
    alarm[0]=room_speed*5;
    text=mushroom_text[message];
    switch (message)
    {
    case 0:
    audio_play_sound(snd_mush_0,1,false);
    break;

    case 1:
    audio_play_sound(snd_mush_1,1,false);
    break;

    case 2:
    audio_play_sound(snd_mush_2,1,false);
    break;

    case 3:
    audio_play_sound(snd_mush_3,1,false);
    break;

    case 4:
    audio_play_sound(snd_mush_4,1,false);
    break;

    case 5:
    audio_play_sound(snd_mush_5,1,false);
    break;

    case 6:
    audio_play_sound(snd_mush_6,1,false);
    break;
```

```
case 7:
audio_play_sound(snd_mush_7,1,false);
break;

case 8:
audio_play_sound(snd_mush_8,1,false);
break;
}
}
```

The object's **Draw Event** draws the mushroom object, any message, and a pop-up background, as shown in Figure 2-3, if there is one present. It draws the message one character at a time, known as the typewriter effect. This code draws relative to the colliding instance. If you want to draw relative to the player, just change all instances of x to obj_player.x and all instances of y to obj_player.y.

The code is shown in Listing 2-4.

Listing 2-4. Drawing the Speech Bubble and Displaying Text Using the Typewriter Effect

```
///drawing stuff

draw_self(); //draw self

///set text to draw
if(string_length(show_text) < string_length(text))
{
show_text = string_copy(text,1,count);
alarm[0] = room_speed*4;
count +=1;
}
if show_text!="" //draw bubble if text present
{

    //set variables
    var width =string_width(text) + padding * 2; // width of message
    Var height = string_height(text) + padding * 2;

    //draw bits below first to create a border
    //round rectangle first
    draw_set_colour(c_blue);
    draw_roundrect(x-(width/2)-border_size,
    y-90-(height/2)-border_size,x+(width/2)+border_size,y-90+(height/2)+border_size,false);

    //triangle outline for triangle
    draw_line_width(x-(width/4)+border_size,y-90+(height/2)-border_size,x+border_size,
    y-25,border_size);
    draw_line_width(x,y-25,x-(width/2),y-90+(height/2),border_size);

    //draw the box
    draw_set_colour(c_white);
    draw_roundrect(x-(width/2),y-90-(height/2),x+(width/2),y-90+(height/2),false);
    //draw_triangle to make it look like speech bubble
    draw_triangle(
```

```
    x-(width/2)+2,y-90+(height/2),
    x-(width/4),y-90+(height/2),
    x,y-25,
    false);

    //draw a message
    draw_set_font(font_message);
    draw_set_halign(fa_center);
    draw_set_valign(fa_middle);
    draw_set_colour(c_black);
    draw_text(x,y-90,show_text);
}
```

■ **Note**   You will see that the alignment of the text is changed to center and middle. If you're drawing text elsewhere, you may wish to set this back to fa_left and fa_top.

Finally, you need to load in the sound files, **snd_mush_0** through **snd_mush_8**.
When done, **obj_mushroom** will look like Figure 2-2.

Figure 2-2. *Showing obj_mushroom*

Figure 2-3 shows the element in action.

25

Figure 2-3. *Showing the alert text in action*

CHAPTER 3

■ ■ ■

Battle System

The GMZ for this element is **Battle_System**.

This element makes use of the **Game_Base**.

An RPG is not an RPG without a battle system. This book covers a couple of battle systems. A battle system is where the player takes on another main character and has a fight with them. This can be achieved in a number of ways.

This battle system is loosely based on Rock, Paper, Scissor, except four options are used:

> Water, Fire, Ground, and Ice

Water beats Fire, Fire beats Ground, Ground beats Ice, and Ice beats Water, as shown in Figure 3-1.

© Ben Tyers 2017
B. Tyers, *Learn RPGs in GameMaker: Studio*, DOI 10.1007/978-1-4842-2946-0_3

BATTLE SYSTEM

Figure 3-1. Battle system

The player can select their choice of play using the appropriate key. The computer then makes a random move. Then either the player wins, the computer wins, or it is a draw. The first to five successful plays wins.

How you reward your player is up to you, but in the context of this book you could award five coins for a win and remove two coins if they lose. This means that over many games, on average, the player will be up on coins. The aim of the game in this book is to acquire 1,000 gold coins. Ideally you don't want the player just playing the battle system over and over, so maybe you limit how many times the player can play each system, or restrict the player from playing more than once every ten minutes, which could be achieved using a global alarm system.

Although this book only deals with a couple of battle systems, there are literally hundreds of variations that you can choose from. Have a look online for free RPG games, play them, and get some more ideas.

Feel free to expand upon this basic battle system. You could add

- Particle effects

- More sounds and music

- A cutscene when the player wins/loses

- Telegraphing (dealt with in this book), such as showing damage to the player or computer

First, create an object named **obj_pirate** and apply the pirate sprite sequence.

obj_player has the additions shown below.

In a **Collision Event** with **obj_pirate** add the code in Listing 3-1.

Listing 3-1. Taking the Player to This Room

```
room_goto(room_battle);
```

Those are the changes for **obj_player**.

Create an object named **obj_setup** and place the code in Listing 3-2 in the **Create Event**. It sets up the initial variables needed.

Listing 3-2. Setting Up Things

```
///set initial variables
global.player_wins=0;
global.computer_wins=0;
global.draws=0;
enum play {
    none,
    water,
    fire,
    earth,
    ice
    }
global.computer_play=play.none;
global.player_play=play.none;
```

Now create an object named **obj_player_play** and in the **Create Event** place the code in Listing 3-3, which just gets things ready for the player to go.

Listing 3-3. Setting the Initial Message

```
///set up
global.text="Player To Go";
```

And finally in a **Step Event** put the code from Listing 3-4. This allows the player to choose which play to make by pressing keys 1 through 4.

Listing 3-4. Allowing the Player to Choose Their Go by Pressing a Number

```
///detect keypress for move
if (keyboard_check(ord('1')))
{
    global.player_play=play.water;
    instance_create(x,y,obj_computer_play);
    instance_destroy();
}
if (keyboard_check(ord('2')))
{
    global.player_play=play.fire;
    instance_create(x,y,obj_computer_play);
    instance_destroy();
}
if (keyboard_check(ord('3')))
{
    global.player_play=play.earth;
    instance_create(x,y,obj_computer_play);
    instance_destroy();
}
if (keyboard_check(ord('4')))
{
    global.player_play=play.ice;
    instance_create(x,y,obj_computer_play);
    instance_destroy();
}
```

There is no sprite for this object. This is all for this object. The code above detects a keypress, sets the player's move as a string, and then destroys itself.

Next, create an object named **obj_computer_play**. In the **Create Event** add the code from Listing 3-5 to choose a random play between 1 and 4 inclusive. This value is then used to set the string for the computer's play.

Listing 3-5. Making the Enemy Choose a Random Play

```
///For Computer Hand
global.text="Computer Playing";
play=irandom_range(1,4); //choose a random number

switch (play)
    {
    case 1:
    global.computer_play=play.water;
    break;
    case 2:
    global.computer_play=play.fire;
    break;
```

```
        case 3:
        global.computer_play=play.earth;
        break;
        case 4:
        global.computer_play=play.ice;
        break;
        }
alarm[0]=room_speed*1;
```

In **Alarm[0] Event**, place the GML from Listing 3-6, which creates an instance of **obj_result** and then destroys itself.

Listing 3-6. Creating the Object to Display the Result and Destroy Itself

///display result
```
instance_create(x,y,obj_result);
instance_destroy();
```

There is no sprite for this object. That is all for this object.

Next, create another object named **obj_global_drawing** and in **Draw Event** put the code from Listing 3-7, which is for the main drawing. It draws the player and computer sprites, the move each makes, and the results.

Listing 3-7. Drawing the Plays as Sprites

///draw stuff

//draw info box
```
draw_sprite(spr_battle_loop,0,400,450);
```
//draw game results
```
draw_set_font(font_text);
draw_set_halign(fa_center);
draw_set_colour(c_white);
draw_text(room_width/2,550,global.text);
draw_text(room_width/2,600,"Player Wins " +string(global.player_wins));
draw_text(room_width/2,650,"Computer Wins "+string(global.computer_wins));
draw_text(room_width/2,700,"Draws "+string(global.draws));

if global.computer_play==play.ice draw_sprite(spr_ice,0,room_width-200,200);
if global.computer_play==play.water draw_sprite(spr_water,0,room_width-200,200);
if global.computer_play==play.earth draw_sprite(spr_ground,0,room_width-200,200);
if global.computer_play=play.fire draw_sprite(spr_fire,0,room_width-200,200);

if global.player_play==play.ice draw_sprite(spr_ice,0,200,200);
if global.player_play==play.water draw_sprite(spr_water,0,200,200);
if global.player_play==play.earth draw_sprite(spr_ground,0,200,200);
if global.player_play==play.fire draw_sprite(spr_fire,0,200,200);
```

//draw the players
```
draw_sprite(spr_player_static,0,100,150);
draw_sprite(spr_pirate_static,0,700,150);
```

Next, create an object named **obj_result**. Not the most compact or the best coding, but the code in Listing 3-8 is relatively clear to understand. It checks each combination, adjusts the score accordingly, sets a text to show the result, and plays the appropriate audio. The final few lines check whether either has reached the target and goes to the appropriate room. This code is for the **Create Event**.

Listing 3-8. Running a Script to Get a Result and Award Points

```
///check result
result=scr_play(global.player_play, global.computer_play);

switch (result)
{
        case -1:
        global.computer_wins++;
        global.text="Computer Wins";
        break;
        case 0:
        global.draws++;
        global.text="Draw";
        break;
        case 1:
        global.player_wins++;
        global.text="Player Wins";
        break;
}
alarm[0]=room_speed*4;

///check score
if global.player_wins==5 room_goto(room_player_win);
if global.computer_wins==5 room_goto(room_computer_win);
```

In an **Alarm[0] Event**, put the code from Listing 3-9, which updates some values and shows that it is the player's move.

Listing 3-9. Resetting Variables for the Next Go and Restarting the Room

```
///done, player to play
global.computer_play=play.none;
global.player_play=play.none;
global.text="";
room_restart();
```

There is no sprite for this object. That is all for this object: This code makes use of a script named **scr_play**, the code for which is shown in Listing 3-10.

Listing 3-10. Comparing Player and Computer Selections, and Returning -1, 0, or 1, Accordingly

```
///scr_play(global.player_play, global.computer_play);
switch (argument0) {
    case play.fire:
        switch (argument1) {
        case play.water: return -1;
```

```
        case play.earth: return 1;
        default: return 0;
    }; break;
    case play.earth:
        switch (argument1) {
        case play.fire: return -1;
        case play.ice: return 1;
        default: return 0;
    }; break;
    case play.ice:
        switch (argument1) {
        case play.water: return -1;
        case play.earth: return 1;
        default: return 0;
    }; break;
    case play.water:
        switch (argument1) {
        case play.ice: return -1;
        case play.fire: return 1;
        default: return 0;
    }; break;
}
```

Next, create an object named **obj_player_win** and put the code from Listing 3-11 in a **Draw Event**. This is used in a Game Over room to show that the player has won.

Listing 3-11. Drawing the Results for a Player Win

///display battle result
```
draw_text(400,400,"Player Wins");
```

That is all for this object.

Next, create an object named **obj_computer_win** and put the code from Listing 3-12 in the **Draw Event**. This will show that the computer won.

Listing 3-12. Drawing the Results for a Computer Win

///display battle result
```
draw_text(400,400,"Computer Wins");
```

That is all for this object.

Next, create three sounds and set as the following, loading in the appropriate sound: **snd_computer_wins**, **snd_player_wins**, and **snd_draw**.

Next, create a font, **font_text**, and set as size 25.

Next, load in the following sprites: **spr_water, spr_fire, spr_ground, spr_ice, spr_pirate_static, spr_player_static**, and **spr_battle_loop**.

Delete any rooms present.

Create a room named **room_start** with a width of 800 and a height of 768 and place one each of **obj_pirate**, **obj_player**, and **obj_setup** into it, as shown in Figure 3-2. That is all for this room.

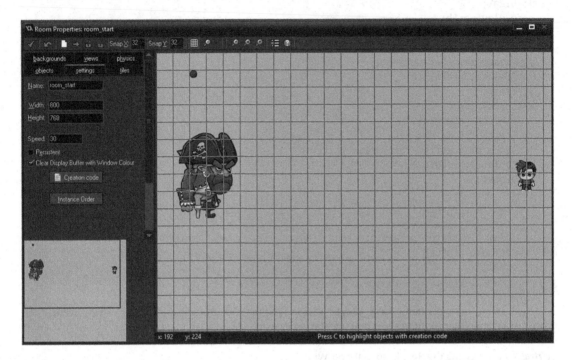

Figure 3-2. *room_start with three objects added*

Next, create a room named **room_battle** with a width of 800 and height of 768 and place one each of **obj_global_drawing** and **obj_player_play**.

Next, create a room named **room_player_win** with a width of 800 and a height of 768, and place one of **obj_player_win**.

Next, create a room named **room_enemy_win** with a width of 800 and a height of 768, and place one of **obj_enemy_win**.

When done, your resource tree will look like that shown in Figure 3-3.

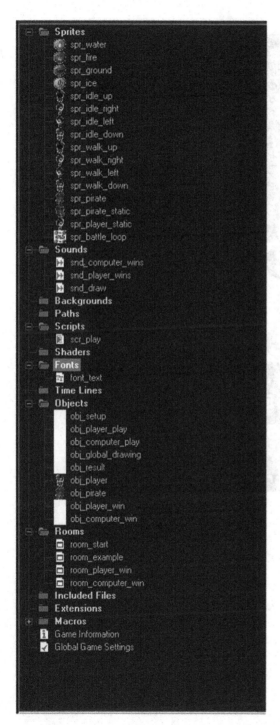

Figure 3-3. *The resource tree*

Figure 3-4 shows this element in progress.

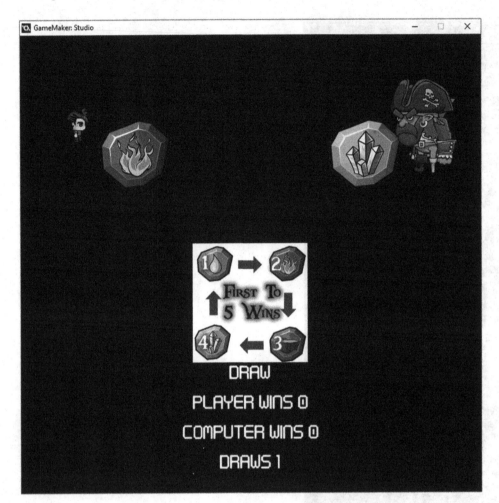

Figure 3-4. *The element in action*

CHAPTER 4

■ ■ ■

Boss Character's Battle

The GMZ file for this element is **Boss_Battle**.

No RPG is complete without at least one boss battle.

A boss battle is generally composed of one or more of the following features:

- It is usually a one-on-one battle, sometimes with minions

- The boss moves in some kind of path, sequence, or pattern

- It has one or more systems of attack

- The boss needs to be beaten for the game to progress

- The boss has a vulnerability that the player must exploit

- The boss is more difficult to defeat than other enemies

- The boss is more formidable than other characters (e.g. larger and scarier)

For the purposes of this book, we'll include all of the above features.

We'll create an enemy that moves left and right at the top of the screen, releases bombs, throws a sword, and drops a big bomb or fruit. Occasionally (actually every 10 seconds), the enemy will jump; this is when it will be vulnerable to the player's sword attack. The dropped bombs of both sizes will damage the player; however, collecting fruit will damage the enemy.

The controls will be simple: left and right, and up to throw a sword, limited to once per second.

I managed to acquire some pirate voices, so we'll throw a few of them in for good measure. (I have added a few too many because I was excited to try them out!)

There are literally hundreds of Boss V player battle methods that can be used: in your own game, try combining some approaches from your favorite games.

Try to keep the elements used in any battle the same as the main game theme.

The first object is **obj_scatter_bomb**, with **spr_mini_bomb** assigned, which needs the *precise collision checking* option set and the origin as center. The **Step Event** destroys the instance as it leaves the room. See Listing 4-1.

Listing 4-1. Destroying Itself When It Reaches the Bottom of the Room

```
///destroy off screen
if y>room_height instance_destroy();
```

The next object is **obj_fruit**. This object has a sprite named **spr_fruit** which has six subimages, each a different fruit, as shown in Figure 4-1. The origin should be set as center.

© Ben Tyers 2017
B. Tyers, *Learn RPGs in GameMaker: Studio*, DOI 10.1007/978-1-4842-2946-0_4

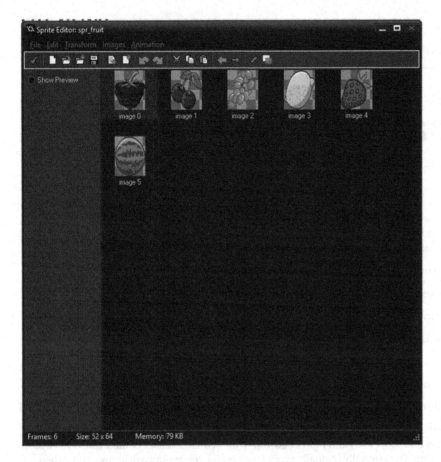

Figure 4-1. *spr_fruit with subimages*

The **Create Event**, which selects a random subimage, is shown in Listing 4-2.

Listing 4-2. Choosing a Random Subimage and Setting the Image Speed to 0, Preventing Animation

```
image_index=irandom(image_number-1);
image_speed=0;
```

The **Step Event** destroys the instance as it leaves the room; see Listing 4-3.

Listing 4-3. Destroying When Off Screen

```
if y>room_height instance_destroy();
```

Next up is **obj_bomb**, which has the sprite **spr_bomb** with the origin as center and *precise collision checking* set.

It has a **Step Event** with the code shown in Listing 4-4.

Listing 4-4. Destroying When Off Screen

```
if y>room_height instance_destroy();
```

The next object is **obj_enemy_sword** with **spr_sword_enemy** assigned and the origin as center. The **Create Event**, which sets it moving and sets up a sine wave, is shown in Listing 4-5.

Listing 4-5. Setting Up Motion and Some Variables to Create a Wobble Effect for the Sword

```
motion_set(180,1);
ang=0; //initial angle
sw=0; //for sine wave
move_angle=40;
```

The **Step Event** applies and updates the sine wave, which makes the sword rotate back and forth. This event also destroys the instance as it leaves the room; see Listing 4-6.

Listing 4-6. Making the Sprite Wobble, and Destroying Itself When Off Screen

```
///rotate && check if outside room
sw += pi/30;//for sine wave - ie speed
angle= sin(sw) * move_angle; //for sine wave
image_angle=angle+45;

if y>room_height instance_destroy();
```

Object **obj_player_sword**, with the sprite **spr_player_sword** assigned and centered, is similar to the enemy sword, although it will destroy itself when it leaves the top of the room. The **Create Event** is shown in Listing 4-7.

Listing 4-7. Making the Sprite Wobble, and Destroying Itself Off Screen

```
    motion_set(180,1);
    ang=0; //initial angle
    sw=0; //for sine wave
    move_angle=40;
Step Event:
    ///rotate && check if outside room
    sw += pi/30; //for sine wave - ie speed
    angle= sin(sw) * move_angle; //for sine wave
    image_angle=angle+225;
    if y<0 instance_destroy();
```

The main player character is **obj_player**. This character can move left and right (staying inside the room) and fire swords toward the enemy. Collisions with instances have different outcomes, depending on whether it's a bomb, sword, or fruit. This makes use of two sprite sheets, **spr_player_left** and **spr_player_right**. Both of these sprites need *precise collision checking* checked in Sprite Properties and have the origin set as center.

The **Create Event** code is shown in Listing 4-8.

Listing 4-8. Setting Up Some Initial Variables for Movement. A Flag Is Set to Allow Shooting.

```
slot=4;
idle=0;
left=1;
right=2;
dir=left;
can_shoot=true;
```

This sets the starting values: slot relates to position on screen, and dir is its starting direction and whether it can shoot (create a flying sword).

The code for the **Alarm[0]**, which resets being able to shoot a sword, is shown in Listing 4-9.

Listing 4-9. Allowing Shooting Again

```
can_shoot=true;
```

The first block in the **Step Event** is shown in Listing 4-10, which will move the character left and right, if able to (i.e. not on the far left or far right), and fire a sword and set the alarm as needed. It will allow the player to move left or right to the next slot, stopping when it reaches the slot.

Listing 4-10. For Movement and Shooting Control

```
///movement && shoot
if keyboard_check_pressed(vk_left) && slot>1
{
    slot--;
    dir=left;
    move_towards_point(64*slot,y,4);
}
if keyboard_check_pressed(vk_right) && slot<11
{
    slot++;
    dir=right;
    move_toward_point(64*slot,y,4);
}


//keep in range
if slot<1 slot=1;
if slot>11 slot=11;


//stop
if x==64*slot
{
    dir=0;
    speed=0;
}


//make a sword
if keyboard_check_pressed(vk_up) && can_shoot
{
    can_shoot=false;
    alarm[0]=room_speed;
    var sword=instance_create(x,y,obj_player_sword);
    sword.direction=90;
    sword.speed=5;
}
```

The second block in the **Step Event** is shown in Listing 4-11, which sets the correct sprite.

Listing 4-11. Setting a Sprite According to Direction

```
///animation
if dir==left sprite_index=spr_player_left;
if dir==right sprite_index=spr_player_right;
```

There are four collision events. The first, **Collision Event with obj_bomb,** checks for a collision with **obj_bomb**. If the player collides with it, they will lose one health point, a choice of sound will be played, and the instance will destroy itself; see Listing 4-12.

Listing 4-12. On Collision with a Bomb, Reduces Player hp, Plays a Sound, and Destroys Other Object Instance

```
global.p1hp-=1;
audio_play_sound(choose(snd_laugh_1,snd_laugh_2),1,false);
with(other) instance_destroy();
```

Collision Event with obj_fruit will reduce the enemy's hp, play a sound, and then destroy itself, as shown in Listing 4-13.

Listing 4-13. On Collision, Reduces Enemy hp, Plays a sound, and Destroys Other Instance

```
global.enemyhp-=1;
audio_play_sound(snd_bonus,1,false);
with(other) instance_destroy();
```

In **Collision Event with obj_scatter_bomb**, when the player collides with it, they will lose one health point, a choice of sound will be played, and the instance will destroy itself. The code is shown in Listing 4-14.

Listing 4-14. On Collision, Reduces Player hp, Plays a Sound, and Destroys Other Object Instance

```
global.p1hp-=1;
audio_play_sound(choose(snd_ouch,snd_ouch_2,snd_ouch_3),1,false);
with(other) instance_destroy();
```

In **Collision Event with obj_sword**, upon collision the player loses five hp points, and it plays a sound and then destroys the sword. See Listing 4-15.

Listing 4-15. On Collision, Reduces Player hp, Plays a Sound, and Destroys Other Object Instance

```
global.p1hp-=5;
audio_play_sound(snd_ouch_4,1,false);
with (other) instance_destroy();
```

The next main object is **obj_pirate**. This object is the boss enemy that the player must beat. It moves left and right, and fires bombs and fruit. This enemy will be vulnerable to the player's attack when it is in the jump animation state. This enemy will get faster over time.

The **Create Event** code sets the starting position, sets the initial alarms, and points randomly left or right. The code is shown in Listing 4-16.

Listing 4-16. Setting Up Initial Variables

```
slot=4;
alarm[0]=global.game_speed; //drop bombs
alarm[1]=room_speed*5; //scatter bombs
alarm[2]=room_speed*8; //throw sword
alarm[3]=room_speed*10; //jump up
dir=choose("left","right");
```

The **Alarm[0] Event** for the enemy consists of three blocks, for clarity. The first, which deals with dropping a bomb or fruit, is shown in Listing 4-17.

Listing 4-17. Randomly Dropping a Bomb or Fruit and Playing a Sound

```
///drop a bomb / fruit & increase speed
global.game_speed--;
if global.game_speed<2 global.game_speed=2;
alarm[0]=global.game_speed;
drop=choose("bomb","fruit","fruit");
if drop=="bomb"
{
    var bomb=instance_create(slot*64,120,obj_bomb);
    bomb.direction=270;
    bomb.speed=2;
audio_play_sound(choose(snd_ar_1,snd_ar_2),1,false);
}
if drop=="fruit"
{
    var fruit=instance_create(slot*64,120,obj_fruit);
    fruit.direction=270;
    fruit.speed=2;
audio_play_sound(snd_bonus_coming,1,false);
}
```

The second block, which resets the alarm, is shown in Listing 4-18.

Listing 4-18. Resetting the Alarm

```
///reset alarm
alarm[0]=global.game_speed;
```

And the third and final block for the **Alarm[0] Event**, which deals with movement, is shown in Listing 4-19.

Listing 4-19. Moving the Object Left or Right

```
///move
//weigh it to move away from edge
if slot==11 dir="left";
if slot==1 dir="right";
//choose next direction - weighted to move in same direction
```

```
dir=choose("left","right",dir,dir);
if dir=="left"
{
    image_xscale=-1;
    slot--;
}
if dir=="right"
{
    image_xscale=1;
    slot++;
}
//keep in range
if slot<1 slot=1;
if slot>11 slot=11;
```

Next is an **Alarm[1] Event**; this event creates the scatter bombs (minions), which are a number of mini-bombs, spread out at 15 degree angles; see Listing 4-20.

Listing 4-20. Creating a Number of Scatter Bombs

```
///send bomb scatter
alarm[1]=room_speed*5;

var loop;
for (loop = 210; loop < 350; loop += 15)
{
    audio_play_sound(choose(snd_ar_3,snd_ar_4),1,false);
    var bomb=instance_create(x,y,obj_scatter_bomb);
    bomb.direction=loop;
    bomb.speed=3;
}
```

The **Alarm[2] Event** shoots a sword instance toward the player's current location; see Listing 4-21.

Listing 4-21. Sending a Sword to the Player's Current Location

```
alarm[2]=room_speed*8; //throw sword
var sword=instance_create(x,y,obj_enemy_sword);
sword.direction=point_direction(x,y,obj_player.x,obj_player.y);
sword.speed=5;
```

The final alarm event is **Alarm[3] Event**, which changes the sprite to jumping; see Listing 4-22.

Listing 4-22. Making the Pirate Jump

```
///jump up
sprite_index=spr_pirate_jump;
image_speed=0.5;
image_index=0;
alarm[3]=room_speed*10;
```

It has a **Step Event** with two code blocks. The first, shown in Listing 4-23, makes the pirate move to the next slot location.

Listing 4-23. Moving to the Next Slot Position

```
///move to position slot
move_toward_point(64*slot,y,4);
//stop
if x==64*slot
{
    dir="idle";
    speed=0;
}
```

The second block, shown in Listing 4-24, deals with the sprite control, which basically changes back to the sprite **spr_pirate_idle** when the jump animation is complete.

Listing 4-24. Resetting to Idle Sprite When the End of Jump Animation Has Been Reached

```
///sprite control
if sprite_index==spr_pirate_jump && image_index>=15
{
    sprite_index=spr_pirate_idle;
    image_index=0;
    image_speed=1;
}
```

Finally for this object there is a **Collision Event with obj_player_sword**, which will reduce the pirate's health if he's hit when the sprite index is **spr_pirate_jump**. The code for this is in Listing 4-25.

Listing 4-25. Damaging the Pirate When Hit by the Player's Sword When Jumping

```
if sprite_index==spr_pirate_jump
{
    global.enemyhp-=5;
audio_play_sound(choose(snd_pirate_ouch_1,snd_pirate_ouch_2),1,false);
}
 with (other) instance_destroy();
```

When done, **obj_pirate** will look like Figure 4-2.

Figure 4-2. obj_pirate all set up

The main control HUD object is **obj_hud**. This displays the player and enemy health as bars and checks if either win.

The **Step Event** for **obj_hud** checks who has won. This won't be present in an actual game, although it is useful for testing purposes. In an actual RPG, you may reward the player with treasure, or allow passage to a new area within the game. See Listing 4-26.

Listing 4-26. Checking If a Player or Enemy Is Dead (No hp Left)

```
if global.p1hp<0
{
    global.message="Enemy Wins"; // for gameover screen
    room_goto(room_game_over);
}
if global.enemyhp<0
{
    global.message="Player Wins"; // for gameover screen
    room_goto(room_game_over);
}
```

It also has a **Draw Event**, which draws a gradient background, as shown in Listing 4-27.

Listing 4-27. Drawing a Rectangle

```
draw_rectangle_colour(0, 0, room_width, room_height, c_blue, c_blue, c_white, c_white, false);
```

A **Draw GUI Event**, which draws the hp of each as bars, and some extra text, is shown in Listing 4-28.

Listing 4-28. Drawing the HUD

```
///draw hp
//hp player
draw_rectangle_colour(334,10,334-(global.p1hp*2),30,c_green,c_red,c_red,c_green,false);
draw_set_colour(c_red);
draw_rectangle(334,10,334-200,30,true);
//draw enemy
draw_rectangle_colour(434,10,434+(global.enemyhp*2),30,c_red,c_green,c_green,c_red,false);
draw_set_colour(c_red);
draw_rectangle(434,10,434+200,30,true);

//draw text
draw_set_font(font_mini);
draw_set_colour(c_black);
draw_set_halign(fa_center);
draw_set_valign(fa_middle);
draw_text(234,20,"Player HP");
draw_text(534,20,"Enemy HP");

draw_text(room_width/2,620,"Arrow Keys To Move And Fire - Shoot Enemy (when jumping)#Collect
Fruit - Avoid Bombs");
```

Next is an object named **obj_splash**, which sets the initial game values. The **Create Event** code is shown in Listing 4-29.

Listing 4-29. Setting Up Initial Variables

```
///set up
global.p1hp=100;
global.enemyhp=100;
global.game_speed=150;
room_goto(room_game);
```

The last object for this element is **obj_game_over**. The **Create Event** that sets an alarm is shown in Listing 4-30.

Listing 4-30. Setting an Alarm for Five Seconds

```
alarm[0]=room_speed*5;
```

The **Alarm[0] Event** code restarts the game, as shown in Listing 4-31.

Listing 4-31. Restarting the Game

```
game_restart();
```

The **Draw Event** code is shown in Listing 4-32.

Listing 4-32. Drawing the Message

```
draw_text(200,200,global.message);
```

This game uses two fonts:

- **font_score**, which is Arial size 20

- **font_mini**, which is Arial size 12

This game has three rooms: **room_splash**, **room_game**, and **room_game_over**. Each room has a height of 640 and a width of 768.

In **room_splash** there is one instance of **obj_splash**.

In **room_game** there is one instance of **obj_hud**, one of **obj_pirate** at the top, and one of **obj_player** at the bottom.

The room **room_game_over** has one instance of **obj_game_over**.

A number of sounds are used. These are in the **resources** folder.

Figure 4-3 shows this element in action.

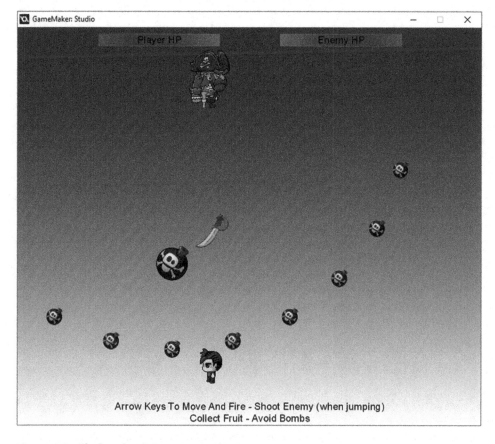

Figure 4-3. The boss battle in action

CHAPTER 5

■ ■ ■

Branching Dialogue

The GMZ file for this element is **Branching_Dialogue**.

An interactive dialogue system is an essential part of an RPG.

When interacting with other characters in-game you want to be able to hold up a decent conversation. Basing the dialogue on the responses that the player makes is the way to go. For example, if the character asks, *"How are you today?"* you may want to answer, *"Yes, I'm fine."* or *"No, I'm having a bad day."*

The other character's next response is based on whether you say yes or no. This branching is pretty logical, and this example includes a diagram (see Figure 5-1). I **strongly** suggest using a chart or other notes when making your own dialogue system, as it can get very complicated very quickly. For each level you add, you'll be doubling the number of options available, so for 5 levels, there will about 32 possible outcomes, which is 63 different sentences including responses!

© Ben Tyers 2017
B. Tyers, *Learn RPGs in GameMaker: Studio*, DOI 10.1007/978-1-4842-2946-0_5

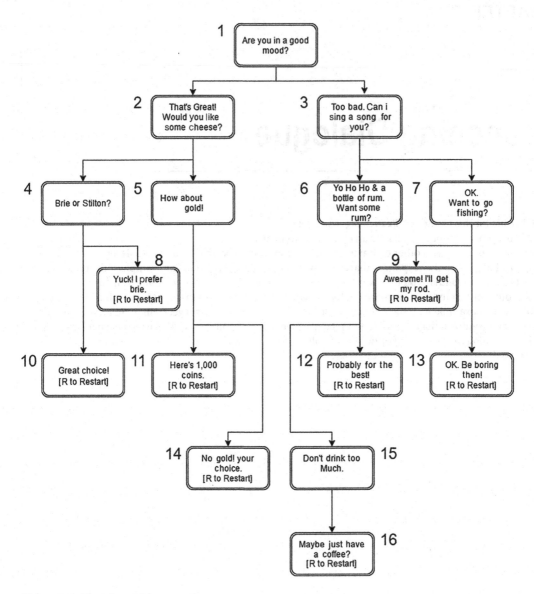

Figure 5-1. Flowchart of conversation

The flow of conversation therefore can be very dynamic and engaging. As well as providing dialogue, you can make other changes. For example, give the player some gold, as in this game; reward with an item; unlock a door; go to a mini-quest/game; and so on, depending on the options.

The approach shown in this section is basic, but allows for easy understanding and customization. The example provides two options for each question, but you could expand to three or more by adding more array elements.

The text is dialogue simply drawn inside boxes. You could add a typewriter effect as used in previous chapters but I'm focusing on certain dynamics here, so I didn't use that effect.

First, you need to know the dialogue options. See Figure 5-1.

As you can see, it's all pretty logical. For clarity, a positive choice (first option) divides to the left and a negative choice (second option) divides to the right.

Create a room named **room_setup** that has a width of 1024 and a height of 768. It has one instance in it, **obj_diag_set_up_and_splash**.

This sets up an array for the data, namely the questions, answers, and number for the next question. It only has a **Create Event**, shown in Listing 5-1.

Listing 5-1. Sets Up Array With Questions, Answers and Target

```
///Set up array to hold data
// 1 Question
// 2 Answer A
// 3 Answer B
// 4 Answer A Target [0 is none]
// 5 Answer B Target [0 is none]
global.diag[1,1]="Are you in a good mood?";
global.diag[1,2]="Yes, I'm in a great mood.";
global.diag[1,3]="No, I'm sad.";
global.diag[1,4]=2;
global.diag[1,5]=3;

global.diag[2,1]="That's great!#Would you like #some cheese?";
global.diag[2,2]="Yes, I love cheese.";
global.diag[2,3]="No. I'll pass.";
global.diag[2,4]=4;
global.diag[2,5]=5;

global.diag[3,1]="Too bad.#Can I sing #you a song?";
global.diag[3,2]="Yes. Sing me a #shanty song.";
global.diag[3,3]="No. I'd rather you didn't.";
global.diag[3,4]=6;
global.diag[3,5]=7;

global.diag[4,1]="Brie or stilton?";
global.diag[4,2]="Brie, please.";
global.diag[4,3]="Stilton, please.";
global.diag[4,4]=10;
global.diag[4,5]=8;

global.diag[5,1]="How about some gold?";
global.diag[5,2]="Yes, I'm after gold.";
global.diag[5,3]="No, I have enough already.";
global.diag[5,4]=11;
global.diag[5,5]=14;

global.diag[6,1]="Yo ho ho &#a bottle of rum.#Want some rum?";
global.diag[6,2]="Yes. Hmm rum.";
global.diag[6,3]="No. I don't drink.";
global.diag[6,4]=15;
global.diag[6,5]=12;
```

```
global.diag[7,1]="OK. Want to go fishing?";
global.diag[7,2]="Yes. Sounds good!";
global.diag[7,3]="No. Fishing is boring.";
global.diag[7,4]=9;
global.diag[7,5]=13;

global.diag[8,1]="Yuck! I prefer brie.##[R to Restart]";
global.diag[8,2]="";
global.diag[8,3]="";
global.diag[8,4]=0;
global.diag[8,5]=0;

global.diag[9,1]="Awesome! I'll get my rod.##[R to Restart]";
global.diag[9,2]="";
global.diag[9,3]="";
global.diag[9,4]=0;
global.diag[9,5]=0;

global.diag[10,1]="Great choice!##[R to Restart]";
global.diag[10,2]="";
global.diag[10,3]="";
global.diag[10,4]=0;
global.diag[10,5]=0;

global.diag[11,1]="Here's 1,000 coins.##[R to Restart]";
global.diag[11,2]="";
global.diag[11,3]="";
global.diag[11,4]=0;
global.diag[11,5]=0;

global.diag[12,1]="Probably for the best!##[R to Restart]";
global.diag[12,2]="";
global.diag[12,3]="";
global.diag[12,4]=0;
global.diag[12,5]=0;

global.diag[13,1]="OK. Be boring then!##[R to Restart]";
global.diag[13,2]="";
global.diag[13,3]="";
global.diag[13,4]=0;
global.diag[13,5]=0;

global.diag[14,1]="No gold! Your choice.##[R to Restart]";
global.diag[14,2]="";
global.diag[14,3]="";
global.diag[14,4]=0;
global.diag[14,5]=0;

global.diag[15,1]="Don't drink too much!##[R to Restart]";
global.diag[15,2]="Continue";
global.diag[15,3]="";
```

```
global.diag[15,4]=16;
global.diag[15,5]=0;

global.diag[16,1]="Maybe just have a coffee.##[R to Restart]";
global.diag[16,2]="";
global.diag[16,3]="";
global.diag[16,4]=0;
global.diag[16,5]=0;

global.message=1;
global.gold=0;
room_goto(room_dialogue);
```

Let's dissect one part for clarity:

```
// 1 Question
// 2 Answer A
// 3 Answer B
// 4 Answer A Target [0 is none]
// 5 Answer B Target [0 is none]
global.diag[1,1]="Are you in a good mood?";
global.diag[1,2]="Yes, I'm in great mood.";
global.diag[1,3]="No, I'm sad.";
global.diag[1,4]=2;
global.diag[1,5]=3;
```

The first element, global.diag[1,1], is the question that is being asked.

The second element, global.diag[1,2], is the first option available (the positive response).

The third element, global.diag[1,3], is the second option available (the negative response).

The fourth element, global.diag[1,4], tells where the target is if the first option, global.diag[1,2], is selected: see the diagram where it shows this.

The fifth element, global.diag[1,5], tells where the target is if the second option, global.diag[1,3], is selected.

This is then repeated for the other elements.

You can offer one option, which is useful if you wish to offer a lot of text in stages, such as going from question 15 to 16:

```
global.diag[15,1]="Don't drink too much!##[R to Restart]";
global.diag[15,2]="Continue";
global.diag[15,3]="";
global.diag[15,4]=16;
global.diag[15,5]=0;
```

You can also offer no options, as in question 14:

```
global.diag[14,1]="No gold! Your choice.##[R to Restart]";
global.diag[14,2]="";
global.diag[14,3]="";
global.diag[14,4]=0;
global.diag[14,5]=0;
```

By setting the text to "", no text or button is shown.

Ensure one instance of **obj_diag_set_up_and_splash** is placed in **room_setup**.

That is all for this object and room.

The next room is **room_dialogue**, which has four objects.

The first object is **obj_show_message**, which has the sprite **spr_message_bg** assigned and centered. It has a **Step Event** with the code shown in Listing 5-2. You won't want to use this in your game, but it will allow you to restart this example quickly for testing purposes.

Listing 5-2. Allowing for Quicker Testing

```
if keyboard_check_released(ord('R'))
{
    game_restart();
}
```

There's also a **Draw Event** with the code shown in Listing 5-3, which draws the sprite, formats the text, and draws the appropriate message.

Listing 5-3. Drawing the Question Message

```
draw_self();
draw_set_font(font_message_big);
draw_set_halign(fa_center);
draw_set_valign(fa_middle);
draw_set_colour(c_black);
draw_text(x,y,global.diag[global.message,1]);
```

That is all for this object.

There are two button objects. The first is **obj_button_one**, which has the sprite **spr_button** assigned. It has a **Left Mouse Button Pressed Event**. I've included an example to show how to make something else happen, such as answer yes to message 5. The click part will update global.message to the next question. See Listing 5-4.

Listing 5-4. Adding Gold If This Option Is Chosen

```
///Example do something - i.e. choose yes to question 5
if global.message==5
{
    global.gold+=1000;
}
//for every click
global.message=global.diag[global.message,4];
```

The **Draw Event** code, which will display an option if present, is shown in Listing 5-5.

Listing 5-5. Drawing the Option Button and Text If There Is Text Present

```
if global.diag[global.message,2]!=""
{
    var width=string_width(global.diag[global.message,2]);
    if width>50 // adjust image size if a long text option
```

```
{
    var size=(250+(width-50))/250
    image_xscale=size;
}
draw_self();
draw_set_font(font_message);
draw_set_halign(fa_center);
draw_set_valign(fa_middle);
draw_set_colour(c_black);
draw_text(x,y,global.diag[global.message,2]);
}
```

The second button, **obj_button_2**, works in a similar way. Duplicate **obj_message_1** and name it **obj_button_2**. There are a few changes. The **Left Mouse Button Pressed Event** code is shown in Listing 5-6, which will update **global.message** to the target held in position 5 of the array.

Listing 5-6. Updating the Message

```
global.message=global.diag[global.message,5];
```

Also the **Draw Event** has changed so that it draws the text for the second option, as shown in Listing 5-7.

Listing 5-7. Drawing the Second Option Button and Text, If Text Is Present

```
if global.diag[global.message,3]!=""
{
    var width=string_width(global.diag[global.message,3]);
    if width>50 // adjust image size if a long text option
    {
        var size=(250+(width-50))/250
        image_xscale=size;
    }
    draw_self();
    draw_set_font(font_message);
    draw_set_halign(fa_center);
    draw_set_valign(fa_middle);
    draw_set_colour(c_black);
    draw_text(x,y,global.diag[global.message,3]);
}
```

Finally there is an object, just as an example, named **obj_gold_hud** with the **Draw Event** code shown in Listing 5-8.

Listing 5-8. A Basic HUD, for Testing the Adding of Gold

```
draw_set_font(font_message_big);
draw_set_halign(fa_center);
draw_set_valign(fa_middle);
draw_set_colour(c_black);
draw_text(room_width/2,room_height-50,"Gold: "+string(global.gold));
```

There are also two fonts, **font_message**, which is Arial size 20, and **font_message_big**, which is Arial size 25. The images are in the downloadable resources.

Figure 5-2 shows **room_dialogue**.

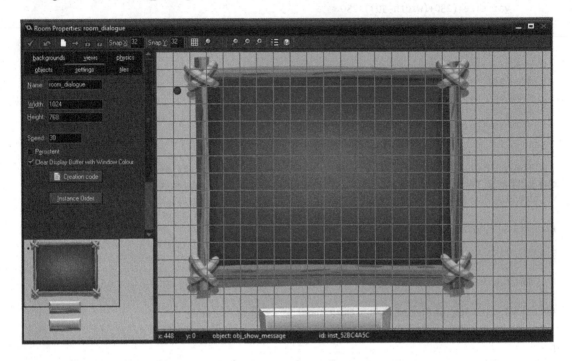

Figure 5-2. *Instances placed in a room*

Figure 5-3 shows this element in action.

Figure 5-3. *Showing branching dialogue in action*

CHAPTER 6

Coin System Shop

The GMZ file for this element is **Coin_Shop**.

It makes use of the **Game_Base** GMZ as a template.

Your player is going to spend a lot of time acquiring loot. It's important to give them something to do with this cash.

A shop is one ideal solution. Having a shop for perishable items or items that the player will require for other quests/interactions is important.

This example gives the player four items to buy:

- Rum

- Banana

- Gun

- Chest

Each has a different price, image, current amount, and maximum amount. This is displayed using a parent object that gets all the info from a global array.

In addition, there is a Buy button, which shows green if the player can buy it or red if they can't. They won't be able to buy if they don't have enough cash, or they have the maximum number of items already.

The programming technique and GML code used in this element is not the most compact, but has been done so it is easy to understand and customize.

The following shows the data as it is used in the array:

		1	2	3	4
1	**Name**	Rum	Banana	Gun	Chest
2	**Sprite**	spr_rum	spr_banana	spr_gun	spr_chest
3	**Cost**	50	12	120	1000
4	**Starting Inventory**	10	4	2	0
5	**Max Inv.**	25	10	100	50

First, load in the **Game_Base** GMZ.

Next, create the shop image. Create an object named **obj_shop** and assign the shop image from the resources. You can keep the origin as 0,0 although this is not important.

In **Collision Event with obj_player** put the code in Listing 6-1.

Listing 6-1. Taking the Player to the Shop Room

```
room_goto(room_shop);
```

That is all for this object.

Next, create an object named **obj_set_up** and put the code from Listing 6-2 in the **Create Event**. This sets up the array needed for the shop, including all info shown above, like cost and maximum inventory. As noted, you load this data from an INI file, but for quickness and clarity of the example, we'll do this in code.

Listing 6-2. Setting Up Array Information

```
///Very basic example
global.cash=10000;
//In the game you may declare gold like here or load from a saved ini file

global.inventory[1,1]="Rum"; //Item Name
global.inventory[1,2]=spr_rum; //Item Sprite
global.inventory[1,3]=50; //Cost
global.inventory[1,4]=10; // Current Inventory
global.inventory[1,5]=25; // Max Inventory

global.inventory[2,1]="Banana"; //Item Name
global.inventory[2,2]=spr_banana; //Item Sprite
global.inventory[2,3]=12; //Cost
global.inventory[2,4]=4; // Current Inventory
global.inventory[2,5]=10; //Max Inventory

global.inventory[3,1]="Gun"; //Item Name
global.inventory[3,2]=spr_gun; //Item Sprite
global.inventory[3,3]=120; //Cost
global.inventory[3,4]=2; //Current Inventory
global.inventory[3,5]=100; //Max Inventory

global.inventory[4,1]="Chest"; //Item Name
global.inventory[4,2]=spr_chest; //Item Sprite
global.inventory[4,3]=1000; //Cost
global.inventory[4,4]=0; //Current Inventory
global.inventory[4,5]=50; //Max Inventory
```

Create a room named **room_village** with dimensions of 800 by 760 and put one instance each of **obj_shop, obj_player**, and **obj_setup in it**, as shown in Figure 6-1.

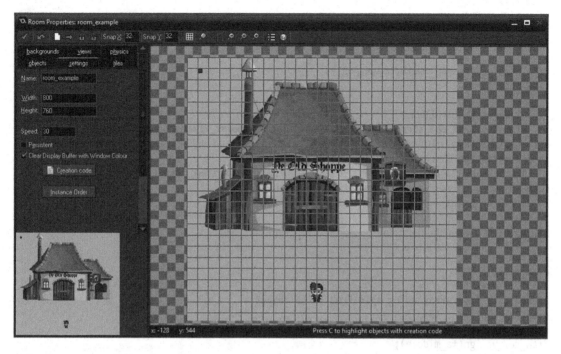

Figure 6-1. *Instances placed in room_village*

That is all for this room. Create a new room named **room_shop**.

Next, create a shopkeeper whose lips move when they speak. This item is made from two sprites: **spr_shop_head** and **spr_shop_mouth**, which consists of 30 subimages and its origin set to center. Load in and assign the appropriate sprites from the resources.

Create an object for this named **obj_shopkeeper** and assign the sprite **spr_shop_head**, setting the origin as center.

The **Create Event** code for this object is what sets the initial value of **img**, which is used for animation and sets the initial state of **is_talking**; see Listing 6-3.

Listing 6-3. Setting Up Initial Values for an Animated Head

```
img=0;
is_talking=false;
```

The **Step Event** code, which will animate over 30 steps if **is_talking** is set to **true**, and reset when **img** reaches 30, is shown in Listing 6-4.

Listing 6-4. Animating the Head

```
if is_talking
{
    img++;
}
if is_talking && img==30
{
    img=0;
    is_talking=false;
}
```

61

The **Draw Event** code is shown in Listing 6-5.

Listing 6-5. Drawing the Head Sprite's Subimage img

```
draw_sprite(spr_shop_mouth,img,x,y+35);
draw_self();
```

That is all for this object.

The next object, **obj_shopkeeper_bg**, has the sprite **spr_keeper_frame** assigned. Its origin is 0,0 although this is not important here. This object has a depth of 10 and will be used as a background for the shopkeeper object. That is all for this object.

The next object is **obj_item_parent**. It has a sprite named **spr_item_frame** assigned. Its origin set as center. This is a parent object that draws the data from the array.

The **Draw Event** code is shown in Listing 6-6.

Listing 6-6. Drawing the Item's Info

```
///draw bg
draw_self();

//draw data from array using myid from child object
draw_set_font(font_shop_mini);
draw_set_halign(fa_center);
draw_set_valign(fa_middle);
draw_set_colour(c_black);
draw_text(x,y-72,global.inventory[myid,1]);
draw_sprite(global.inventory[myid,2],0,x,y-30);
draw_set_colour(c_yellow);
draw_text(x,y+15,string(global.inventory[myid,3])+" Coins");
draw_set_colour(c_black);
draw_text(x,y+40,string(global.inventory[myid,4])+" / "+string(global.inventory[myid,5]));
```

That is all for this object.

Next is **obj_item_1**, with **spr_item_frame** set as the sprite with an origin of center. **my_id** sets which of the buyable instances it relates to. The **Create Event** code is shown in Listing 6-7.

Listing 6-7. Setting Up the Item's Local Reference

```
myid=1;
```

And this object has **obj_item_parent** set as the parent.

That is all for this object.

Next is **obj_item_2**, with **spr_item_frame** set as the sprite, which is again centered. The **Create Event** code is shown in Listing 6-8.

Listing 6-8. Setting Up the Item's Local Reference

```
myid=2;
```

And this object has **obj_item_parent** set as the parent.

That is all for this object.

Next is **obj_item_3**, with **spr_item_frame** set as the sprite. The **Create Event** code is shown in Listing 6-9.

Listing 6-9. Setting Up the Item's Local Reference

```
myid=3;
```

And this object has **obj_item_parent** set as the parent.
That is all for this object.
Next is **obj_item_4**, with **spr_item_frame** set as the sprite. The **Create Event** code is shown in Listing 6-10.

Listing 6-10. Setting Up the Item's Local Reference

```
myid=4;
```

And this object has **obj_item_parent** set as the parent.
That is all for this object.
This example uses just four items, although you could add more as needed.
When set up, it will look like Figure 6-2.

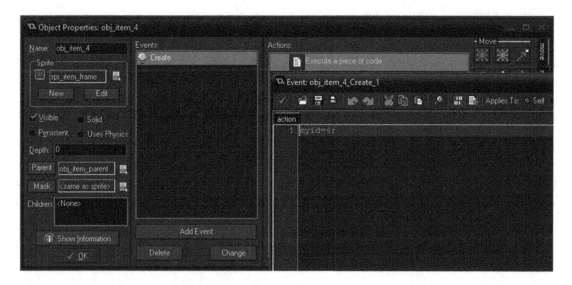

Figure 6-2. *obj_item_4 with create event code and parent set*

The next object is **obj_buy_parent**. This parent object is a button that is clickable when an item is available to buy. It has two subimages, image 0 in green and image 1 in red. Green will show when available and red when not available.

The **Create Event** code is shown in Listing 6-11.

Listing 6-11. Preventing Animation and Setting the Initial Subimage

```
image_speed=0;
image_index=0;
```

The **Step Event** code sets which subimage to show. The first conditional checks whether the player has enough cash and the second checks whether the player has a full allocation of items. See Listing 6-12.

Listing 6-12. Setting the Subimage of the Button, Depending on Whether Available or Not

```
//set as red or green button
if global.cash>=global.inventory[myid,3] //if player has enough cash
{
    image_index=0;
}
else
{
    image_index=1;
}
if global.inventory[myid,4]==global.inventory[myid,5] //if maxed out
{
    image_index=1;
}
```

The **Left Mouse Button Pressed Event** will first check whether the player is maxed out on that item, then check if the player has enough cash, and update the item count and available cash, playing the appropriate audio as required. See Listing 6-13.

Listing 6-13. Allowing the Player to Purchase If Available, and Updating Inventory and Cash Accordingly

```
///basic shop buy
if global.inventory[myid,4]==global.inventory[myid,5] //check if maxed out already
{
    audio_play_sound(snd_overkill,1,false);
    obj_shopkeeper.is_talking=true; //make shopkeeper talk
}

else if global.cash<global.inventory[myid,3] //do this if not enough cash
{
    audio_play_sound(snd_not_enough_cash,1,false);
    obj_shopkeeper.is_talking=true; //make shopkeeper talk
}

//next part for successful purchase
else
{
    audio_play_sound(snd_purchase_complete,1,false);
    obj_shopkeeper.is_talking=true; //make shopkeeper talk
    global.cash-=global.inventory[myid,3];
    global.inventory[myid,4]++;
}
```

That is all for this object.

There are four button objects that make use of this parent object, so each has **obj_buy_parent** as the parent. The sprite is set as **spr_buy**, to make placing it in the room easier. The depth of each is -100.

The first is **obj_buy_1**. The **Create Event** code is shown in Listing 6-14; **event_inherited();** ensures that the code in the parent **Create Event** will also be executed.

Listing 6-14. Setting a Variable and Using Parent Object Code

```
myid=1;
event_inherited();
```

The second is **obj_buy_2**. The **Create Event** code is shown in Listing 6-15.

Listing 6-15. Setting a Variable and Using Parent Object Code

```
myid=2;
event_inherited();
```

The third is **obj_buy_3**. The **Create Event** code is shown in Listing 6-16.

Listing 6-16. Setting a Variable and Using Parent Object Code

```
myid=3;
event_inherited();
```

The last is **obj_buy_4**. The **Create Event** code is shown in Listing 6-17.

Listing 6-17. Setting a Variable and Using Parent Object Code

```
myid=4;
event_inherited();
```

So this, for example, will look like Figure 6-3.

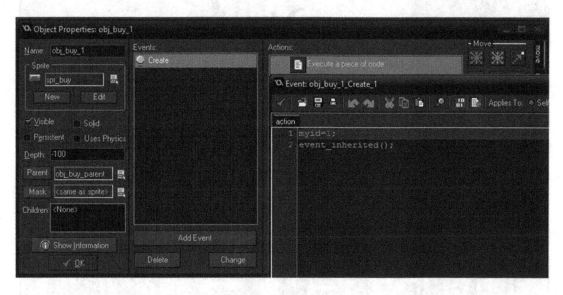

Figure 6-3. A button object with create event code and parent set

The next object is **obj_coin**, which has a coin sprite named **spr_coin** assigned. The depth of this object is -100, and the **Draw Event** code, which draws the value of **global.cash** with a shadow effect by drawing twice at two slightly different locations and in different colours, is shown in Listing 6-18.

Listing 6-18. Drawing the Amount of Cash Available

```
draw_self();
draw_set_font(font_shop_big);
draw_set_halign(fa_center);
draw_set_valign(fa_middle);
draw_set_colour(c_black);
draw_text(x-2,y-122,"Current#"+string(global.cash));
draw_set_colour(c_yellow);
draw_text(x,y-120,"Current#"+string(global.cash));
```

That is all for this object.

Next is **obj_info_bg** with **spr_info_bg** set. There is no code for this object.

Finally there is object **obj_shop_sign** with the sign sprite applied to it.

There is one each of **obj_item_1** with **obj_buy_1** button on it, similarly for the other items and Buy buttons.

There are two fonts needed:

- **font_shop_mini**, which is Arial size 20

- **font_shop_big**, which is Arial size 30

In room **room_shop**, place the objects in it so it looks like Figure 6-4.

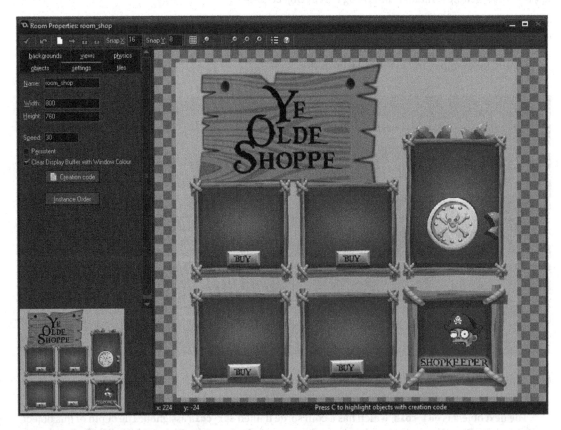

Figure 6-4. *Objects placed in the room*

Figure 6-5 shows the shop in action.

Figure 6-5. *The shop in action*

CHAPTER 7

Cutscene

The GMZ file for this element is **Cutscene**.

Cutscenes are an integral part of any decent RPG.

A cutscene is generally a non-interactive animation that provides information that progresses the story. They are normally shown at the start and end of a game, with additional cutscenes in-game as needed. For example, this could include

- An opening cutscene that explains the premise of the game

- A scene prior to a boss battle, which may or may not explain what the player needs to do

- Special scenes shown when completing a mini-quest

- An end-of-game cutscene showing the conclusion of the story

- Rewarding the player for reaching a goal, like 1,000 gold coins

- When the player dies, showing the death as a cutscene

- Collecting an object and showing how it can be used, such as collecting a shovel and showing how it can be used

Cutscenes vary from game to game: some may use video (either rendered or live action) or real time 3D or 2D animation.

For the purposes of this book, the example will use 2D animation. This will consist of a collection of 11 separate scenes, each having its own room.

The method used is pretty basic, but it demonstrates the rudimentary elements needed to make a cutscene.

It should be noted that overuse of cutscenes is a big no-no. Cutscenes stop the player from playing the game, albeit for a short time. Always consider that the player wants to play, not spend time watching (poorly made) cutscenes.

However, when used sparingly and at the right times, a cutscene can contribute a lot to your game.

For the GML coding for this chapter, I will explain the main GML elements, rather than step-by-step. For full coding, just load in the **Cutscene** GMZ file.

There is a font, **font_text**, which is Arial size 20.

In addition, there are some audio and background files to load in from the **resources** folder.

Fade In/Out

There are two objects that are used in unison to create a fading effect between rooms.

© Ben Tyers 2017

B. Tyers, *Learn RPGs in GameMaker: Studio*, DOI 10.1007/978-1-4842-2946-0_7

The first is **obj_fade_in**, which has the **Create Event** code shown in Listing 7-1.

Listing 7-1. Seting Alpha at 100%

```
alpha=1; //set starting value of alpha
```

The **Step Event** code is shown in Listing 7-2.

Listing 7-2. Reducing Alpha Each Step and Destroying Object When Less Than 0

```
///change and test alpha
alpha-=0.02; //increase alpha
if alpha<=0
{
    instance_destroy(); //destroy when done
}
```

And the **Draw Event** has the code shown in Listing 7-3.

Listing 7-3. Drawing the Rectangle at Current Alpha and Setting Back to 1 So Other Drawing Is Not Affected

```
draw_set_alpha(alpha); //set drawing alpha to value
draw_rectangle(0,0,room_width,room_height,false); //draw a solid rectangle
draw_set_alpha(1);
```

Every room has one instance of **obj_fade_in** in it.
There's also an object to fade out at the end of each room, which is created by the room's control object. This is **obj_fade_out**. It has the **Create Event** code shown in Listing 7-4.

Listing 7-4. Starting Alpha at 0%

```
alpha=0; //set starting value of alpha
```

A **Step Event** uses the code in Listing 7-5.

Listing 7-5. Going to Next Room When Alpha Is Above 1

```
///change and test alpha
alpha+=0.02; //increase alpha
if alpha>=1 room_goto_next(); //goto new room when done
```

Finally, the **Draw Event** uses the code in Listing 7-6.

Listing 7-6. Drawing the Rectangle at Current Alpha and Setting Back to 1 So Other Drawing Is Not Affected

```
draw_set_alpha(alpha); //set drawing alpha to value
draw_rectangle(0,0,room_width,room_height,false); //draw a solid rectangle
draw_set_alpha(1);
```

Common Elements

The bubble effect object, **obj_bubble**, makes use of the sprites **spr_bubble_1** and **spr_bubble_2**, both of which have their origin as center. The **Create Event** code is shown in Listing 7-7.

Listing 7-7. Creating a Bubble, Setting Up Variables, and Starting Movement

```
sprite_index=choose(spr_bubble_1,spr_bubble_2);
ang=0; //initial angle
sw=0; //for sine wave
move_angle=5+irandom(10);
base=irandom_range(100,700);
x=base;
y=room_height+32;

scale=irandom_range(1,20);
scale*=0.1;
image_xscale=scale;
image_yscale=scale;
motion_set(90,1+scale);
depth=choose(6,-7);
```

And the **Step Event** code is shown in Listing 7-8.

Listing 7-8. Making the Bubble Wobble

```
sw += 0.1; //for sine wave - i.e. speed
angle= sin(sw) * move_angle; //for sine wave
x=base+angle;
```

To add a bit of movement, a few clouds are placed in the room. A sine wave is used to make them wobble. This is **obj_cloud**, which has the sprite **spr_cloud** assigned with the origin at the center.

The **Create Event** of **obj_cloud** is shown in Listing 7-9.

Listing 7-9. Making the Cloud Move and Setting Up Some Variables

```
motion_set(0,2+irandom(2));
ang=0; //initial angle
sw=0; //for sine wave
move_angle=5+irandom(10);
```

This code sets initial values.

The **Step Event** is shown in Listing 7-10.

Listing 7-10. Making the Cloud Wobble

```
if x>room_width+64 x=-64;
sw += 0.1; //for sine wave - i.e. speed
angle= sin(sw) * move_angle; //for sine wave
image_angle=angle;
```

This code allows the cloud to wrap the room and sets the **image_angle** to the sine wave.

71

The **Draw Event** is shown in Listing 7-11.

Listing 7-11. Drawing Self

```
image_alpha=1;
draw_self();
```

This is added because other elements may have a lower alpha value; this ensures it is set to 1.
Next is a fish object named **obj_fish_2** with **spr_fish_2** assigned.
The **Create Event** code is shown in Listing 7-12.

Listing 7-12. Creating an Instance Just Outside the Room and Starting Movement

```
x=room_width+96;
motion_set(180,4);
```

There is a fish object named **obj_fish_4** with the fish animation **spr_fish_4** sprite with subimages applied and the origin centered. This fish swims from right to left.
The fish **Create Event** code is shown in Listing 7-13.

Listing 7-13. Starting Movement

```
motion_set(180,2);
```

Next is the lightning effect called **obj_lightning**. The sprite is **spr_lightning**, which has an origin at the top of the forking at 310,2. The **Create Event** for **obj_lightning** is shown in Listing 7-14.

Listing 7-14. Creating an Initial Location and Playing a Sound

```
alarm[0]=8;
x=irandom(room_width);
y=-5;
audio_play_sound(choose(snd_storm_1,snd_storm_2,snd_storm_3),1,false);
```

Its **Alarm[0] Event** code is shown in Listing 7-15.

Listing 7-15. Alarm Triggers a Change in Size and Location, and Plays a Sound

```
alarm[0]=8;
x=irandom(room_width);
image_xscale=choose(1,-1);
image_yscale=random_range(0,1);
x=irandom(room_width);
audio_play_sound(choose(snd_storm_1,snd_storm_2,snd_storm_3),1,false);
```

Obviously the code will change the sprite every alarm event and play a sound.
Next is **obj_moon**, which has the sprite **spr_moon** applied and again the origin is the center. There is no code for this object.
The next object is **obj_sails**, which has the sprite **spr_sails** assigned and the origin as center.
The **Step Event** code for this object is shown in Listing 7-16.

Listing 7-16. Changing Angle Every Step

```
image_angle+=2;
```

That is all for this object.

The next object is **obj_sails_small** with sprite **spr_sails_small** assigned at the origin at 32,32, which is the center. The **Step Event** is shown in Listing 7-17.

Listing 7-17. Changing Angle Every Step

```
image_angle+=2;
```

The next object, **obj_sea_5**, has the sprite **spr_sea_5** assigned with the origin as center.

The next object, **obj_sea_9**, has the sprite **spr_sea_9** assigned; the origin for this sprite can be left at 0,0.

The next object is **obj_ship_4**, which has the sprite **spr_ship_4** assigned and the origin of 0,0. The **Create Event** code is shown in Listing 7-18.

Listing 7-18. Creating a Wobble Effect

```
ang=0; //initial angle
sw=0; //for sine wave
move_angle=5;
```

The **Step Event** code is shown in Listing 7-19.

Listing 7-19. Making It Wobble

```
sw += 0.1; //for sine wave - i.e. speed
angle= sin(sw) * move_angle; //for sine wave
image_angle=angle;
```

Next up is object **obj_ship_5**, which has the sprite **spr_ship_5**. This origin should be set at 97,142, which will be the point that rotation uses.

The **Create Event** code for this object is shown in Listing 7-20.

Listing 7-20. Starting Motion and Creating Variables for Wobble

```
motion_set(180,1);
ang=0; //initial angle
sw=0; //for sine wave
move_angle=5+irandom(10);
```

And its **Step Event** is shown in Listing 7-21.

Listing 7-21. Making It Wobble

```
sw += 0.1; //for sine wave - i.e. speed
angle= sin(sw) * move_angle; //for sine wave
image_angle=angle;
```

There is one use of object **obj_fade_out_white**. It has the **Create Event** code shown in Listing 7-22.

Listing 7-22. Setting Alpha at 0%

```
alpha=0; //set starting value of alpha
```

The **Step Event** code is shown in Listing 7-23.

Listing 7-23. Increasing Alpha and Going to Next Room When Above 1

```
///change and test alpha
alpha+=0.02; //increase alpha
if alpha>=1 room_goto_next(); //goto new room when done
```

Finally, a **Draw Event** uses the code in Listing 7-24.

Listing 7-24. Drawing with Alpha

```
draw_set_alpha(alpha); //set drawing alpha to value
draw_set_colour(c_white);
draw_rectangle(0,0,room_width,room_height,false); //draw a solid rectangle
draw_set_alpha(1);
```

The next object is **obj_star** with **spr_star** assigned. There is no code for this object.

The next object is **obj_sub**, which has the sprite **spr_sub** assigned. The **Create Event** code is shown in Listing 7-25.

Listing 7-25. Creating Offscreen and Starting Motion

```
x=-96;
motion_set(0,3);
```

Next up is **obj_sun** with the sprite **spr_sun**, and if you guessed origin as center you'd be correct. There is no code for this object.

The next object is **obj_sunk_boat** with sprite **spr_sunk_boat**. The default origin 0,0 can remain.

The next is object **obj_windmill** with **spr_windmill**. The origin should be the middle of the roof at 64,16. This is the point the windmill sails will rotate on. There is no code for this.

The final object is **obj_windmill_small** with the sprite **spr_windmill_small** with origin at 64,78.

Base Code

The cutscenes display text on the screen. To facilitate this we'll use an object dedicated to just messaging. Basically the object is created and a string is sent to it. This string is shown after a short pause and then faded out.

This object is called **obj_message**.

The **Create Event** is shown in Listing 7-26.

Listing 7-26. Setting Initial Variables

```
x=200;
y=650;
typewriter_out = ""; //string that will be drawn
i = 1; //start position
alarm[0] = 1; //set alarm
destroy=false;
fading=1;
```

As you can see, the coordinates are set, the initial text to display is set to " ", and the alarm is created. It sets destroy to **false**, which will be used later when fading out. The variable **fading** is used to change the alpha value (its transparency).

The **Alarm[0] Event** code is shown in Listing 7-27.

Listing 7-27. Drawing Text as a Typewriter Effect

```
typewriter_out += string_copy(text_to_write, i, 1); //add new character to string
i += 1;
if ((i - 1) != string_length(text_to_write)) //if not end of text
{
    alarm[0] = 2; //restart alarm
    //audio_play_sound(snd_keyboard,1,false);//play click
}
else if alarm[1]< 0 alarm[1]=room_speed*4;
```

This block will set the text and add a letter at a time.
The **Alarm[1] Event** code is shown in Listing 7-28.

Listing 7-28. Setting a Flag

```
destroy=true;
```

This sets destroy to **true**, so it can start fading in the **Step Event** in Listing 7-29.

Listing 7-29. Fading After the Text Has Fully Appeared and Destroying It When Less Than 0

```
if destroy
{
    fading-=0.02;
}
if fading<0 instance_destroy();
```

This will make it fade out gradually. When fading is less than 0, it will destroy itself.
The **Draw GUI Event**, which will draw the background and text, is shown in Listing 7-30.

Listing 7-30. Drawing the Typewriter Effect Text

```
draw_set_alpha(fading);
draw_sprite(spr_parchment,0,400,700);
draw_set_font(font_text);
draw_set_colour(c_white);
draw_text(x+1, y+1, typewriter_out); //draw string to screen
draw_text(x+1, y-1, typewriter_out); //draw string to screen
draw_text(x-1, y+1, typewriter_out); //draw string to screen
draw_text(x-1, y-1, typewriter_out); //draw string to screen
draw_set_colour(c_black);
draw_text(x, y, typewriter_out); //draw string to screen
draw_set_alpha(1);
```

Most of the control objects for the scene follow the example above, but with some minor changes. The full code for each is shown for each scene for clarity purposes.

There is a screenshot after each section showing each cutscene in action.

Scene 1

Scene 1, shown in Figure 7-1, has an instance of the control object for it and **obj_fade_in**.

Figure 7-1. *Scene 1*

In addition, there is one each of **obj_windmill** and **obj_sails**.

The main code is in **obj_cs_1_cont**. The **Create Event** code is shown in Listing 7-31.

Listing 7-31. Setting Up the View and Initial Alarm, Which Is Used to Spawn Alarms 0 and 1

```
view_wview[0]=100;
view_hview[0]=100;
alarm[2]=room_speed*10;
```

The **Step Event** code is shown in Listing 7-32.

Listing 7-32. Increasing the View Size to Give the Effect of Zooming Out

```
view_wview[0]+=1;
view_hview[0]+=1;
```

Alarm[0] Event code is shown in Listing 7-33.

Listing 7-33. Creating obj_message and Sending the Message as a String

```
text=instance_create(x,y,obj_message);
text.text_to_write = "Alice Lived In A Windmill. #Up High On A Hill."; //text to  write - #
for line break
```

This object has an **Alarm[1] Event**, which creates a fade out object, as shown in Listing 7-34.

Listing 7-34. Creating the Fade Out Object Instance

```
instance_create(x,y,obj_fade_out_white);
```

Alarm[2] Event sets the other alarms and plays the audio music for the scene. See Listing 7-35.

Listing 7-35. Starting a Couple of Alarms and Playing the Audio for the Scene

```
alarm[0]=room_speed*3;
alarm[1]=room_speed*21;
audio_play_sound(snd_scene_1,1,0);
```

This room is named **cs_1**. This room has a background, and one instance each of the windmill and sails. The view is set in the room properties to follow the windmill object. See Figure 7-2.

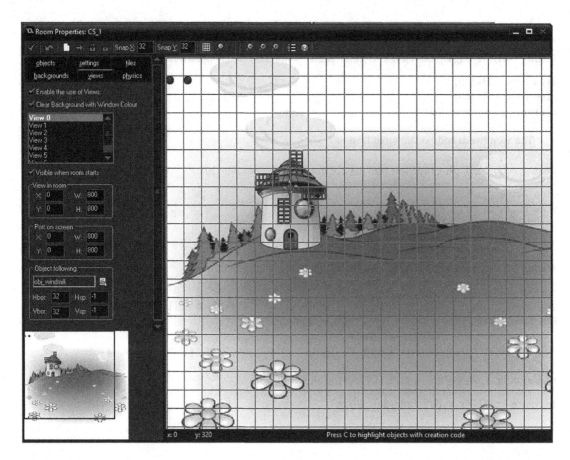

Figure 7-2. *room cs_1 all set up*

Scene 2

Scene 2, shown in Figure 7-3, has an instance of the control object for it and **obj_fade_in**.

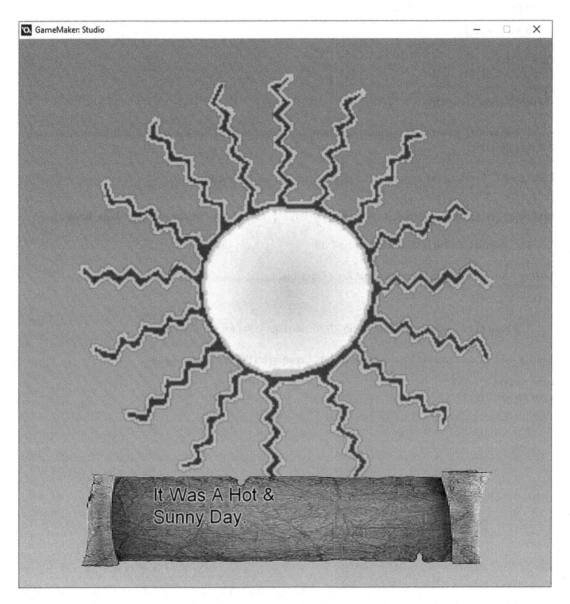

Figure 7-3. Scene 2

In addition, there is one of **obj_sun**, **obj_windmill_small**, and **obj_sails_small**.

This is basically the same as scene 1, with the addition of an animated sun. The view is set to follow this sun object. This room is **cs_2**.

The control object for this scene is **obj_cs_2_cont**. **The Create Event** is shown in Listing 7-36.

Listing 7-36. Stopping Any Sound, Playing the Audio for the Scene, and Setting Initial View. Also StartingTwo Alarms.

```
audio_stop_all();
audio_play_sound(snd_scene_2,1,false);
view_wview[0]=50;
view_hview[0]=50;
alarm[0]=room_speed*3;
alarm[1]=room_speed*20;
```

The **Alarm[0] Event** code is shown in Listing 7-37. The # forces a line break, which draws the following text on a new line.

Listing 7-37. Creating obj_message and Sending the Message as a String

```
text=instance_create(x,y,obj_message);
text.text_to_write = "It Was A Hot &#Sunny Day."; //text to  write - # for line break
```

The **Alarm[1] Event** is shown in Listing 7-38.

Listing 7-38. Creating an Instance of the Fade Out Object

```
instance_create(x,y,obj_fade_out);
```

The **Step Event** code is shown in Listing 7-39. See Figure 7-4 for room setup.

Listing 7-39. Increasing the View Size Each Step, Creating an Effect of Zooming Out

```
view_wview[0]+=1;
view_hview[0]+=1;
```

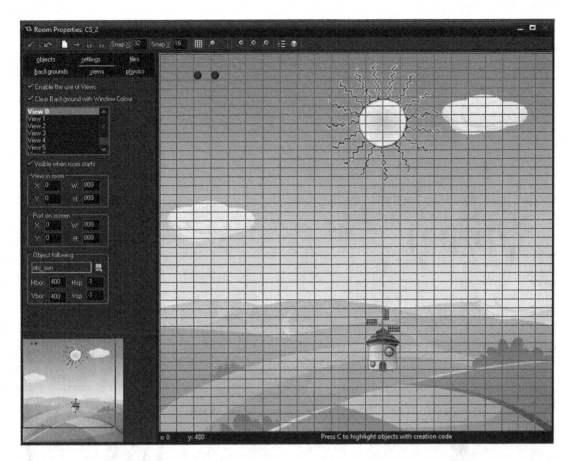

Figure 7-4. *Room cs_2 all set up*

Scene 3

Scene 3, shown in Figure 7-5, has an instance of the control object for it and **obj_fade_in**. The room name is **cs_3**.

Figure 7-5. *Scene 3*

The control object for this scene is **obj_cs_3_cont**.

The **Create Event** code is shown in Listing 7-40.

Listing 7-40. Stoping Any Sound, Setting Initial View, and Starting Two Alarms

```
audio_stop_all();
audio_play_sound(snd_scene_3,1,false);
view_wview[0]=1000;
view_hview[0]=1000;
alarm[0]=room_speed*3;
alarm[1]=room_speed*14;
```

The **Alarm[0] Event** is shown in Listing 7-41.

Listing 7-41. Creating an Instance of the Message Object and Sending the Text for It to Use

```
text=instance_create(x,y,obj_message);
text.text_to_write = "So She Went Down#To The Beach."; //text to  write - # for line break
```

The **Alarm[1] Event** code is shown in Listing 7-42.

Listing 7-42. Creating an Instance of the Fade Out Object

```
instance_create(x,y,obj_fade_out);
```

The **Step Event** code is shown in Listing 7-43. See Figure 7-6 for room setup.

Listing 7-43. Changing the View Every Step by Reducing It to Create a Zoom-In Effect

```
view_wview[0]-=1;
view_hview[0]-=1;
```

Figure 7-6. *Room cs_3 all set up*

Scene 4

Scene 4, shown in Figure 7-7, has an instance of the control object for it and **obj_fade_in**.

Figure 7-7. Scene 4

In addition, there is one each of **obj_ship_4** and **obj_fish_4**.
This is a static view with a moving fish and boat.
The control object for this scene is **obj_cs_4_cont**.
This room is **cs_4**.

The **Create Event** code is shown in Listing 7-44.

Listing 7-44. Playing Audio

```
audio_stop_all();
audio_play_sound(snd_scene_4,1,false);
view_wview[0]=1000;
view_hview[0]=1000;
alarm[0]=room_speed*3;
alarm[1]=room_speed*20;
```

The code for the **Alarm[0] Event** is shown in Listing 7-45.

Listing 7-45. Sending a Message

```
text=instance_create(x,y,obj_message);
text.text_to_write = "There She Hired#A Small Boat."; //text to  write - # for line break
```

The **Alarm[1] Event** code is shown in Listing 7-46.

Listing 7-46. Fading Out

```
instance_create(x,y,obj_fade_out);
```

And the **Step Event** code is shown in Listing 7-47. Figure 7-8 shows the results.

Listing 7-47. Changing The View

```
view_wview[0]-=1;
view_hview[0]-=1;
```

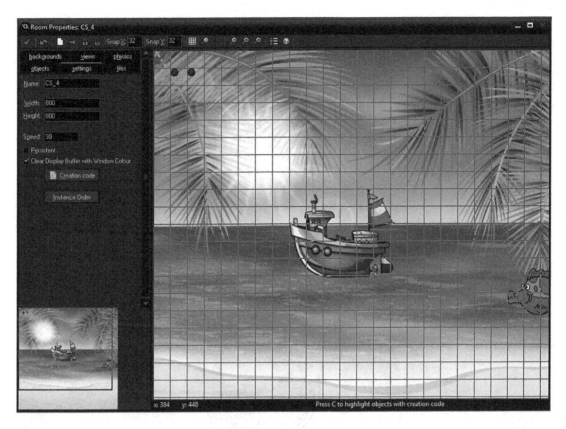

Figure 7-8. *Room cs_4 all set up*

Scene 5

Scene 5 in Figure 7-9 has an instance of the control object for it and **obj_fade_in**.

Figure 7-9. *Scene 5*

In addition, there is one each of **obj_ship_5** and **obj_sea_5** and a couple of **obj_cloud**.
In this scene, a boat moves across the screen, and some clouds also move across the screen.
This room is **cs_5**.
The main control object for this scene is **obj_cs_5_cont**.

The **Create Event** code is shown in Listing 7-48.

Listing 7-48. Stopping Audio, Setting View, and Starting Two Alarms

```
audio_stop_all();
audio_play_sound(snd_scene_5,1,false);
view_wview[0]=1000;
view_hview[0]=1000;
alarm[0]=room_speed*3;
alarm[1]=room_speed*20;
```

The code for the **Alarm[0] Event** is shown in Listing 7-49.

Listing 7-49. Creating the Object Instance for Text and Sending the Text It Needs

```
text=instance_create(x,y,obj_message);
text.text_to_write = "She Was Enjoying Herself,#When..."; //text to write - # for line break
```

And the **Alarm[1] Event** code is shown in Listing 7-50.

Listing 7-50. Creating the Instance to Fade Out

```
instance_create(x,y,obj_fade_out);
```

Finally for this object is the **Step Event** code is shown in Listing 7-51. See Figure 7-10 for the room setup.

Listing 7-51. Changing View Each Step by Zooming In

```
view_wview[0]-=1;
view_hview[0]-=1;
```

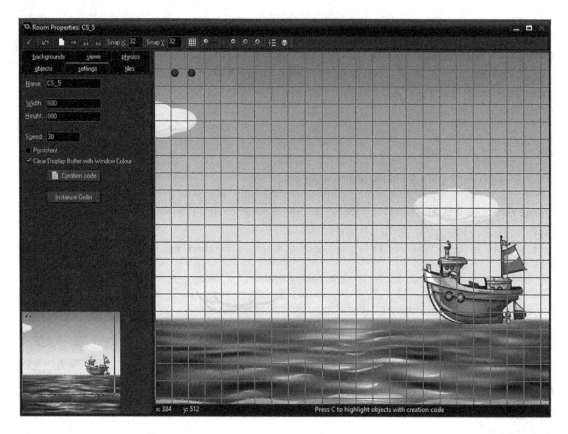

Figure 7-10. *Room cs_5 all set up*

Scene 6

Scene 6, shown in Figure 7-11, has an instance of the control object for it and **obj_fade_in**.

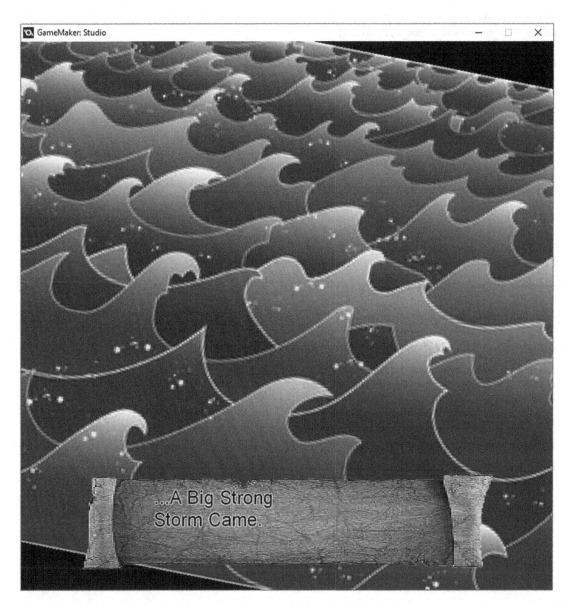

Figure 7-11. *Scene 6*

It consists of a moving ocean. The room name is **cs_6**.

The **Create Event** for this control object, **obj_cs_6_cont**, is shown in Listing 7-52.

Listing 7-52. Setting Up, Including Values to Create a Wobble Effect

```
audio_stop_all();
audio_play_sound(snd_scene_6,1,false);
alarm[0]=room_speed*3;
alarm[1]=room_speed*20;
ang=0; //initial angle
sw=0; //for sine wave
move_angle=5+irandom(10);
```

Alarm[0] Event is shown in Listing 7-53.

Listing 7-53. Creating the Object Instance for Text and Sending the Text It Needs

```
text=instance_create(x,y,obj_message);
text.text_to_write = "...A Big Strong#Storm Came."; //text to  write - # for line break
```

Alarm[1] Event is shown in Listing 7-54.

Listing 7-54. Creating the Instance to Do the Fade Out Effect

```
instance_create(x,y,obj_fade_out);
```

And the **Step Event** is shown in Listing 7-55.

Listing 7-55. Setting the View to Wobble Back and Forth

```
sw += 0.1; //for sine wave - i.e. speed
angle= sin(sw) * move_angle; //for sine wave
view_angle[0]=angle;
```

As you can see, it's the same as other control objects, with the addition of a sine wave to change the angle of the view. See Figure 7-12 for the results.

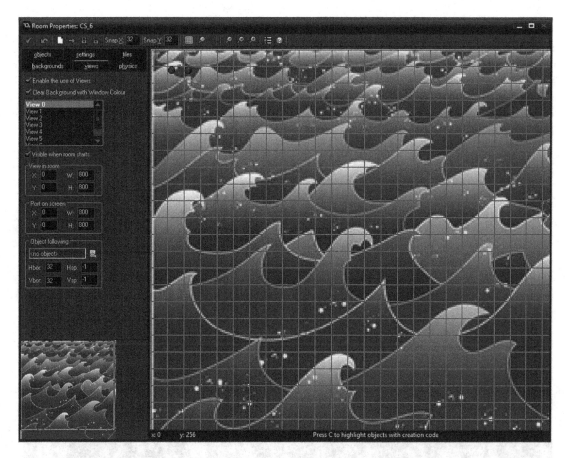

Figure 7-12. *Room cs_6 all set up*

Scene 7

Scene 7, shown in Figure 7-13, has an instance the control object for it and **obj_fade_in**.

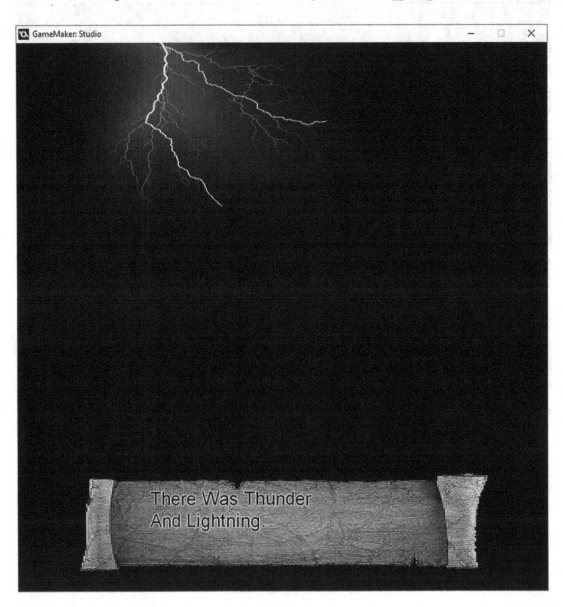

Figure 7-13. *Scene 7*

In addition, there is one instance of **obj_lightning**.
This room's name is **cs_7**.
This scene consists of lightning sprite images and loud audio.
The main control object for this scene is **obj_cs_7_cont**.

The **Create Event** is shown in Listing 7-56.

Listing 7-56. Setting Up and Starting Three Alarms

```
audio_stop_all();
audio_play_sound(snd_scene_7,1,false);
alarm[0]=room_speed*3;
alarm[1]=room_speed*20;
alarm[2]=irandom(room_speed*2);
```

The **Alarm[0] Event** is shown in Listing 7-57.

Listing 7-57. Creating the Object Instance for Text and Sending the Text It Needs

```
text=instance_create(x,y,obj_message);
text.text_to_write = "There Was Thunder#And Lightning."; //text to  write - # for line break
```

The **Alarm[1] Event** code is shown in Listing 7-58.

Listing 7-58. Creating the Instance to Fade Out

```
instance_create(x,y,obj_fade_out);
```

An **Alarm[2] Event** is also used; its code is shown in Listing 7-59. See Figure 7-14 for the results.

Listing 7-59. Reseting the Alarm, Deleting Existing Lightning, and Creating More

```
alarm[2]=irandom(room_speed*2)
if instance_exists(obj_lightning)
{
    with obj_lightning instance_destroy();
}
instance_create(x,y,obj_lightning);
```

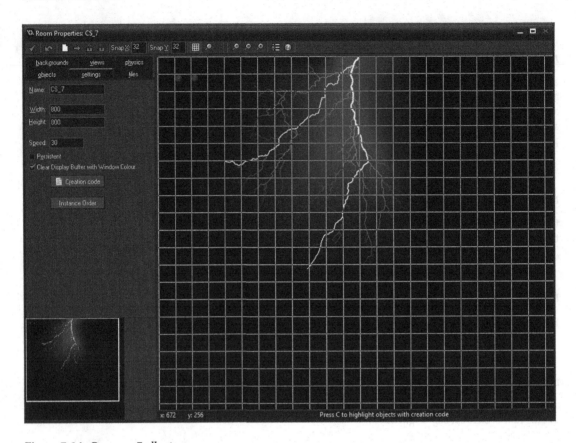

Figure 7-14. *Room cs_7 all set up*

There is no **Step Event** on this object.

Scene 8

Scene 8, shown in Figure 7-15, has one instance of the control object for it and **obj_fade_in**.

Figure 7-15. *Scene 8*

In addition, there is one instance each of **obj_sub**, **obj_sunk_boat**, and **obj_fish_2**.
This scene is an underwater scene with a fish and submarine.
The name of this room in **cs_8**.
The main control object for this scene is obj_**cs_8_cont**.

The **Create Event** is shown in Listing 7-60.

Listing 7-60. Setting Up and Starting Three Alarms

```
audio_stop_all();
audio_play_sound(snd_scene_8,1,false);
view_wview[0]=1000;
view_hview[0]=1000;
alarm[0]=room_speed*3;
alarm[1]=room_speed*20;
alarm[2]=room_speed;
```

The **Alarm[0] Event** is shown in Listing 7-61.

Listing 7-61. Displaying Text and Sending It

```
text=instance_create(x,y,obj_message);
text.text_to_write = "The Stormy Seas#Sank Her Ship."; //text to  write - # for line break
```

The **Alarm[1] Event** code is shown in Listing 7-62.

Listing 7-62. Creating an Instance to Fade Out

```
instance_create(x,y,obj_fade_out);
```

The **Alarm[2] Event** is shown in Listing 7-63. See Figure 7-16 for the result.

Listing 7-63. Making a Bubble and Restarting the Alarm

```
instance_create(x,y,obj_bubble);
alarm[2]=room_speed;
```

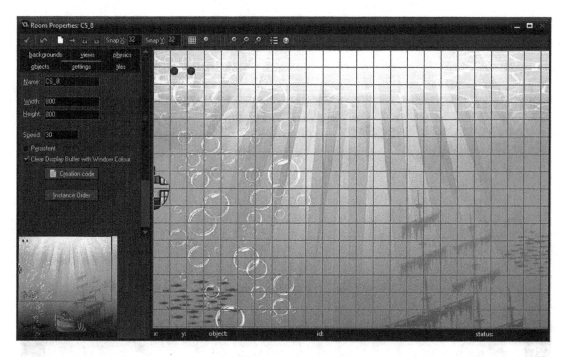

Figure 7-16. *Room cs_8 all set up*

Scene 9

Scene 9, shown in Figure 7-17, has an instance of the control object for it and **obj_fade_in**.

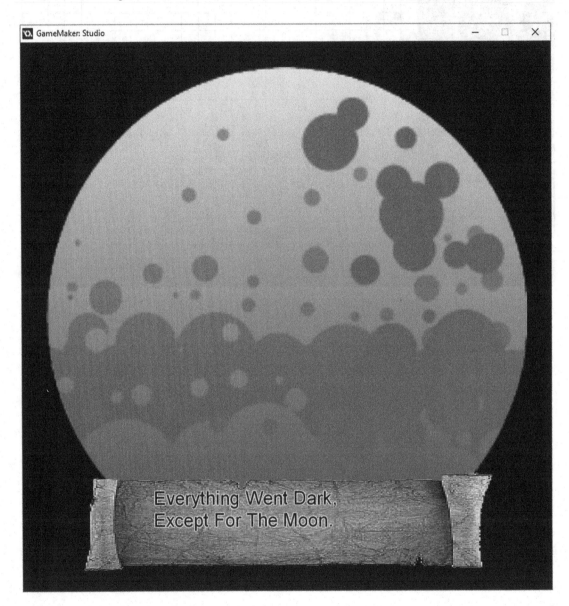

Figure 7-17. Scene 9

In addition, there is one instance **obj_moon** and **obj_sea_9**.
This scene zooms out from the moon to show a dark night scene with the ocean below.
Objects in this room are just static objects, **obj_moon** and **obj_sea**, with a sprite applied.
The control event for this scene is **obj_cs_9_cont**.
The name of this room is **cs_9**.

Its **Create Event** code is shown in Listing 7-64.

Listing 7-64. Setting Initial Values and Starting Two Alarms

```
audio_stop_all();
audio_play_sound(snd_scene_9,1,false);
view_wview[0]=1000;
view_hview[0]=1000;
alarm[0]=room_speed*3;
alarm[1]=room_speed*20;
view_wview[0]=50;
view_hview[0]=50;
```

The **Alarm[0] Event** is shown in Listing 7-65.

Listing 7-65. Creating the Object for the Message and Sending the Text for It

```
text=instance_create(x,y,obj_message);
text.text_to_write = "Everything Went Dark, #Except For The Moon."; //text to write - # for
line break
```

The **Alarm[1] Event** code is shown in Listing 7-66.

Listing 7-66.

```
instance_create(x,y,obj_fade_out);
```

And finally the **Step Event** code is shown in Listing 7-67. See Figure 7-18 for the result.

Listing 7-67. Changing the View Every Step by Zooming Out

```
view_wview[0]+=1;
view_hview[0]+=1;
```

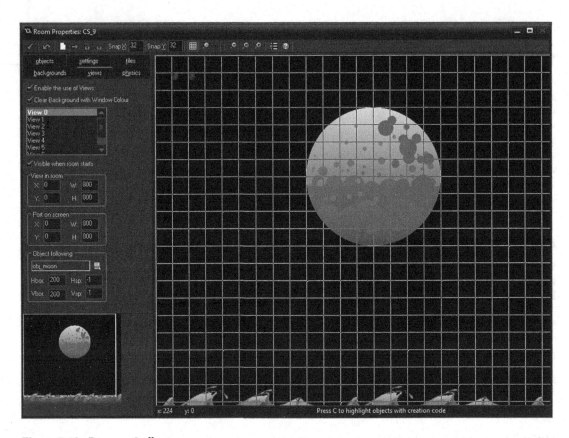

Figure 7-18. *Room cs_9 all set up*

Scene 10

Scene 10, shown in Figure 7-19, has an instance the control object for it and **obj_fade_in**.

Figure 7-19. *Scene 10*

In addition, there are a few instances of **obj_cloud**.
It is just a basic zoom view.
The control object is **obj_cs_10_cont**.
The room is **cs_10**.

The **Create Event** code is shown in Listing 7-68.

Listing 7-68. Stop Audio, Start New Music, and Set Alarms

```
audio_stop_all();
audio_play_sound(snd_scene_10,1,false);
alarm[0]=room_speed*3;
alarm[1]=room_speed*20;Sets everything up.
```

The **Alarm[0] Event** is shown in Listing 7-69.

Listing 7-69. Sending the Text to the Created Instance

```
text=instance_create(x,y,obj_message);
text.text_to_write = "She Woke Up On#An Island."; //text to  write - # for line break
```

And the **Alarm[1] Event** is shown in Listing 7-70. See Figure 7-20 for the result.

Listing 7-70. Creating the Instance to Fade Out

```
instance_create(x,y,obj_fade_out);
```

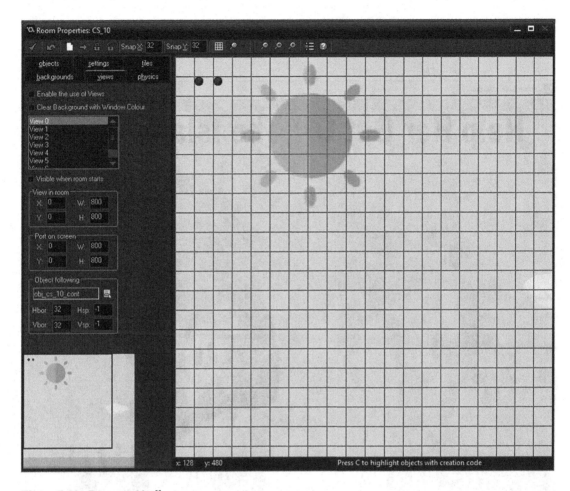

Figure 7-20. *Room cs_10 all set up*

Scene 11

The final scene, shown in Figure 7-21, is a static image, no special code. This room is cs_11.

Figure 7-21. *The final scene*

CHAPTER 8

■ ■ ■

Depth-Based Graphics

The GMZ for this element is **Depth_Based**.

It makes use of the **Game_Base** GMZ file.

Keeping things looking good visually is important in any game. Making sure things behave like they would in the real world is another matter. This element employs a trick to make sure that the player and in-game objects are drawn in the correct place, and prevents the player from being able to walk through objects.

This is done by changing the depth of the player and in-game objects relative to the y-position on screen. This technique also creates an additional object that is used to prevent the player moving through the base of an object.

First, create a sprite named **spr_solid_base** and set it as 15 by 9 pixels in solid red and set the origin as center.

Next, create an object named **obj_solid_base** and set the sprite you just created.

Instances of this object will be placed at certain points in the room and the main player object will be programmed to prevent it walking through instances of this object. This object needs the visible option turned off; this is shown in Figure 8-1.

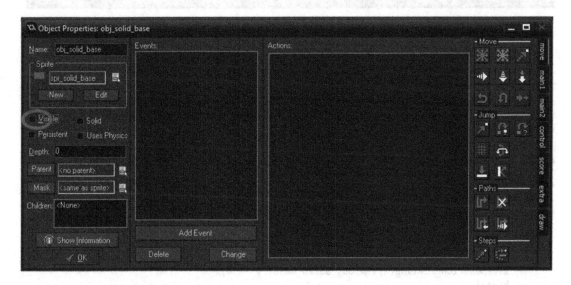

Figure 8-1. *Visible box unticked*

That is all for this object.

Next, create an object named **obj_elements_parent** and in the **Create Event** put the code in Listing 8-1.

Listing 8-1. Creating an Instance of a Solid Base for All Objects That Have the Parent obj_elements_parent

```
instance_create(x,y,obj_solid_base);
depth=-y;
```

There is no sprite for this object. That is all for this object.

Next, create an object named **obj_cactus** and load and set the sprite **spr_cactus**. The origin should be set as 32,64. Set the parent of this object to **obj_elements_parent**, as shown in Figure 8-2.

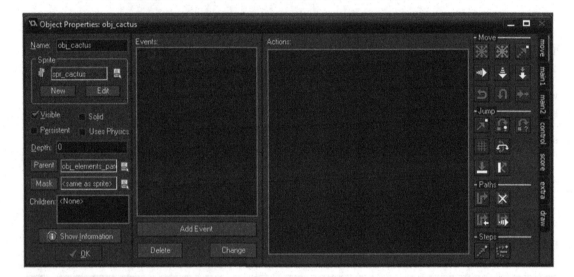

Figure 8-2. *obj_cactus with sprite and parent set*

Repeat this process for **obj_flag**, with its origin as the base of the flag pole, and **obj_mushroom**, setting the origin as bottom middle.

Open up **obj_player** and change the code block for movement in the **Step Event** to the code in Listing 8-2, which will only allow a player to move if it will not collide with **obj_solid_base** in the direction it is travelling.

Listing 8-2. Allowing Movement Only If No Instance of obj_solid_base Is in the Direction of Travel

```
///movement
if is_moving
{
    switch (dir)
    {
        case player_state.up:
        if !position_meeting(x,y-4,obj_solid_base) y -= 4;
        break;

        case player_state.down:
        if !position_meeting(x,y+4,obj_solid_base) y += 4;
        break;
```

```
        case player_state.left:
        if !position_meeting(x-4,y,obj_solid_base) x -= 4;
        break;

        case player_state.right:
        if !position_meeting(x+4,y,obj_solid_base) x += 4;
        break;
    }
}
depth=-y;
```

Place a few instances each of **obj_cactus**, **obj_flag**, and **obj_mushroom** in the room and test them; this will look like Figure 8-3. Obviously, you must uncheck the visible option in **obj_solid_base** for your own game.

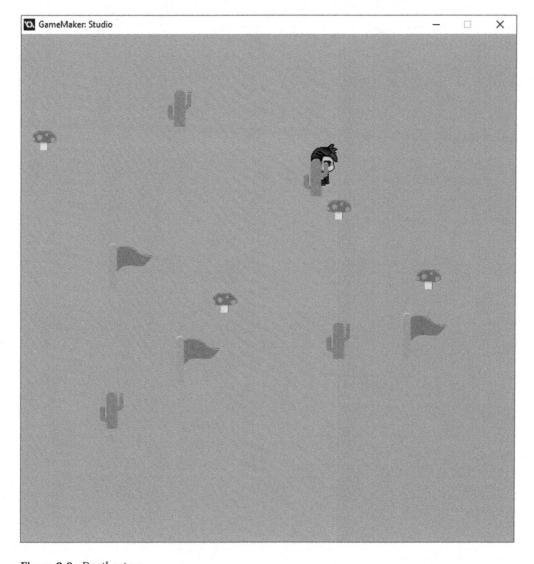

Figure 8-3. Depth set up

CHAPTER 9

Downloading Bonus Levels from a Website

This example uses the **Game_Base**. The GMZ for this element is **Download_Bonus**.

Adding longevity to your games is important, whether an RPG, a casual game, or something puzzle-based. Allowing your players to access extra and new levels is one approach. It is possible to create text files that can be downloaded and processed with GameMaker. How you represent your bonus content in text form is up to you. This chapter shows a very basic and easy-to-understand example.

You could allow access and use bonus content when

- Your player makes an in-game purchase

- Your player completes a special challenge

- Your player enters a code

- It is Monday and a level is updated

For this example, we'll use a simple grid system. The file that is downloaded from my website in this example looks something like this:

```
WWWWWWWWWWWWWWWWWWWWWWW
W     LLLLL           W
W     LLLLL   B       W
W      LLL            W
W       L       T     W
W                     W
W   B                 W
W         P           W
WWWWWWWWWWWWWWWWWWWWWWW
```

Each letter represents a different object. W is a wall, L is a lake, B is a bush, T is a tree, and P is the player. Blanks are just a space character and indicate that there is no object present in that slot.

The file is downloaded asynchronously and saved locally as a text file. This text file is then opened, each line is saved as a string, and this is then processed to place an instance of the required objects in the room.

Open the Game_Base and create four objects, each with a 32x32 sprite assigned, the origin of which can be set as center:

- **obj_wall** with a red sprite assigned

- **obj_lake** with a light blue sprite

© Ben Tyers 2017
B. Tyers, *Learn RPGs in GameMaker: Studio*, DOI 10.1007/978-1-4842-2946-0_9

- **obj_tree** with a light green sprite

- **obj_bush** with a dark green sprite

You can set the depth of the above four objects to 1.

Next, create an object named **obj_get_from_net**. In the **Create Event** put the block of code from Listing 9-1. This code shows a message that it is getting the level and it sets up an asynchronous event (which is an event that takes place in the background and sets a variable change when complete). A flag and an alarm will be set; the alarm will trigger after 10 seconds. Using the function http_get_file, it attempts to access the given URL. A ds_map holds information related to this call, such as status that is monitored in the asynchronous code block further below.

Listing 9-1. Retrieving level1.txt from the Given Address. An Alarm Is Used to Timeout After 10 Seconds.

```
//Next part sets file path and target
show_message("Getting Level");
file = http_get_file("http://gamemakerbook.com/example.txt",working_directory +"level1.txt");
//save locally as level1.txt
str[0]=""; //initiate array
done=false; //this will be used as a flag to detect if file is downloaded
//prevent pc hanging - assume failed after 10 seconds
alarm[0]=room_speed*10;
```

In **Alarm[0] Event** put the code from Listing 9-1, which lets us know that the download failed.

Listing 9-2. Failed Retrieval

```
show_message("Download Failed. Exiting");
file=-1;
game_end();
```

In a **Step Event** put the code from Listing 9-3, which takes the player to another room as soon as done returns as true.

Listing 9-3. Taking the Player to Another Room When Done

```
if done room_goto(room_from_file); //when saved goto game room
```

Then finally make an **HTTP Asynchronous Event**. This can be done via Add Event ➤ Asynchronous ➤ HTTP. The code in Listing 9-4 checks on the status of the asynchronous event created previously. The status changes to <0 for failure or 0 when it is completed successfully. It may also be a status of 1 for *in progress*. In this case, it will set the flag done to true.

Listing 9-4. Returning Done as True When Successfully Downloaded

```
if ds_map_find_value(async_load, "id") == file //sets up map
{
    var status = ds_map_find_value(async_load, "status"); //gets status
    if status == 0 //status 0 means file is finished downloading
    {
        show_message("Downloaded Level");
        done=true;
    }
}
```

That is all for this object. It does not have a sprite assigned. It will look like Figure 9-1 when completed.

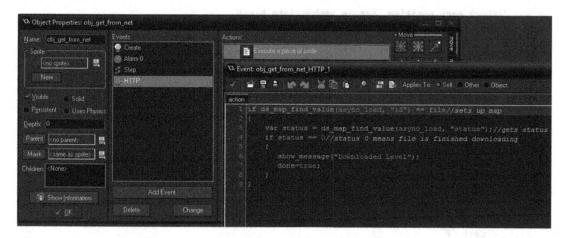

Figure 9-1. *The completed obj_get_from_net object*

Next, create an object named **obj_create_from_file**. This has a **Create Event** with two code blocks. The first reads each line of the file that was created previously, and puts it all into an array named str.

Listing 9-5. Opening the File and Reading Each Line into an Array

```
///read lines to an array
lines=0;
var file=file_text_open_read(working_directory+"level1.txt"); //open file for reading
while (!file_text_eof(file)) //loops until end of file
{
    sentence[lines] = file_text_read_string(file);
    file_text_readln(file);
    lines++;

}
file_text_close(file); //closes file
```

The second block reads the characters from each line and places instances of the appropriate object accordingly, as shown in Listing 9-6.

Listing 9-6. Going Through Each Character on Each Line and Creating an Object Based on the Letter

```
///read characters and create objects
//size of grid
grid_size=32;

//create a loop for however many lines
for ( var loop = 0; loop < lines; loop += 1)
{
    var line=(str[loop]);
    line_width=string_length(line);
```

```
for (var position = 1; position <= line_width; position+= 1)
{
    //check each position, create appropriate block
    switch (string_char_at(line, position))
    {
        case "P":
        instance_create(16+(position-1)*grid_size,16+loop*grid_size,obj_player);
        break;
        case "W":
        instance_create(16+(position-1)*grid_size,16+loop*grid_size,obj_wall);
        break;
        case "L":
        instance_create(16+(position-1)*grid_size,16+loop*grid_size,obj_lake);
        break;
        case "T":
        instance_create(16+(position-1)*grid_size,16+loop*grid_size,obj_tree);
        break;
        case "B":
        instance_create(16+(position-1)*grid_size,16+loop*grid_size,obj_bush);
        break;
    }
}
}
```

Next, create a room named **room_get_file_from_net**. Set it as 800x768 in size. Place one instance of **obj_get_from_net** in it.

Finally, create another room named **room_from_file** with the same dimensions and place one instance of **obj_create_from_file** in it.

That is all for this element.

When the run and download is completed, it will look like Figure 9-2.

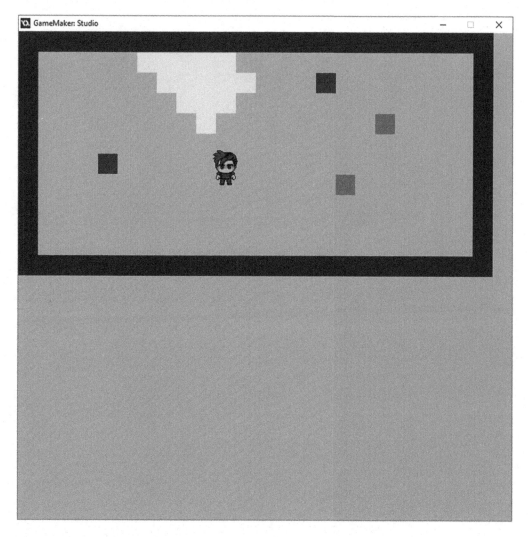

Figure 9-2. *The level created from a downloaded file*

CHAPTER 10

■ ■ ■

Drivable Vehicles

The GMZ for this element is **Drivable_Vehicle**.

It makes use of the **Depth_Based** GMZ file as a base engine.

As well as having a main player character, you may want other controllable items, such as a car or other vehicle, a horse, a bird, a boat, etc.

You could set it up so certain areas can only be traversed by a vehicle. For example, you could have an island in the middle of the lake that can only be accessed by boat. It could also be used for mini-quests/games.

Providing some variation in how the player interacts with the game is important, although you should make sure you don't veer off from it being an RPG and step into an arcade game style.

For this example, a horse is used.

The example makes use of one additional object, **obj_boat**, and a HUD object. Collisions are calculated using a script, **scr_CollisionMoveAwaySelf**. This uses a mass-based system, which also prevents the horse getting "stuck" over other objects. A slight change is made to **obj_elements_parent** to set up the mass of the **obj_solid_base**. This is detailed later in the chapter.

This example uses a script, **scr_CollisionMoveAwaySelf**, which prevents objects from getting stuck, as shown in Listing 10-1.

Listing 10-1. Allowing Objects to Bump into Each Other Without Getting Stuck

```
///scr_CollisionMoveAwaySelf (factor)
//CollisionMoveAway (1) is standard for AI
//call in collision event
//objects should have am_Mass variable, >0 Could be pounds or kg
//pushes each other out of the way while moving each other out of contact
//Origins must be centered
//argument0 is the max rewind step (4 for fast, .5 for slow and accurate)

var a,xoff,yoff,maxcheck;
a = point_direction( x,y,other.x,other.y)
xoff = lengthdir_x( argument0,a);
yoff = lengthdir_y( argument0,a);
var om,mm;
om = other.m_Mass/m_Mass;
mm = m_Mass/other.m_Mass;
var mag; mag=sqrt((om*om)+(mm*mm))
om/=mag;
mm/=mag;
maxcheck = ((speed+other.speed)/argument0)*2 + 100;
```

© Ben Tyers 2017
B. Tyers, *Learn RPGs in GameMaker: Studio*, DOI 10.1007/978-1-4842-2946-0_10

```
while( place_meeting( x,y,other.id) and maxcheck>=0)
{
    x -= xoff * om;
    y -= yoff * om;
    maxcheck-=1;
}
```

That is all for this script.

That is all for this object.

There is also an object named **obj_hud**. The **Create Event**, which will prevent any error if global.active is not yet initiated, is shown in Listing 10-2.

Listing 10-2. Using a Flag to Check the State of the Player

```
global.active="Walking";
```

And the **Draw GUI Event** code, which is mainly here for testing purposes, is shown in Listing 10-3.

Listing 10-3. Drawing Info

```
draw_set_font(font_data);
draw_set_halign(fa_center);
draw_set_valign(fa_middle);
draw_set_colour(c_black);
draw_text(640,600,"Active "+global.active+"#Arrow Keys Move Player#WSAD Move Boat#X To Get
In Car#Z To Get Out of Boat");
```

The boat object, **obj_boat**, utilizes one sprite named **spr_boat**.

The **Create Event** for **obj_boat** sets the initial variables needed, as shown in Listing 10-4.

Listing 10-4. Setting Up Initial Variables, Maxiumum Speed, and Mass

```
///Set variables
max_speed=4;
m_Mass = 100;
direction=0;
```

The **Step Event** has four blocks.

The first, which deals with movement if player object **obj_player** is not present, is shown in Listing 10-5.

Listing 10-5. Allows Movement If in Ship

```
///movement code
if instance_exists(obj_player)
{
    speed=0;
    exit; //prevent move if player present
}

if keyboard_check(ord('A'))
{
    direction+=10;
}
```

```
if keyboard_check(ord('D'))
{
    direction-=10;
}
direction=direction mod 360;
if keyboard_check(ord('W'))
{
    speed+=0.5;
}
if speed>max_speed speed=max_speed;
//friction
speed-=0.2;
if speed<0 speed=0;
```

The second block deals with image speed and sprite control, and is shown in Listing 10-6.

Listing 10-6. Keeps The Instance Pointing In The Direction of Travel

```
///sprite control
//Main Sprite Control
image_angle=direction;
```

The third block sets the boat as active or not, depending on whether **obj_player** is present, and is shown in Listing 10-7.

Listing 10-7. Allowing a Player to Get Out of the Vehicle by Pressing Z

```
///Get out of boat
if instance_exists(obj_player) exit; //Prevent creation if player already present
if keyboard_check_pressed(ord('Z'))
{
    instance_create(x,y+32,obj_player);
    global.active="Walking";
}
```

There is also a **Collision Event with obj_player**, with the code shown in Listing 10-8.

Listing 10-8. Allowing a Player to Get in the Boat If Touching It

```
///Get in boat
if instance_exists(obj_player) && keyboard_check_pressed(ord('X')) //Check keypress &&
player present
{
    with (obj_player) instance_destroy(); //Destroy player
    global.active="Boat";
}
```

Next, there is a **Collision Event with obj_solid_base**, with the code shown in Listing 10-9.

Listing 10-9. Running the Script for Movement

```
scr_CollisionMoveAwaySelf(1);
```

Finally, assign a sprite, **spr_boat**, with the origin at 67x60.
When done, **obj_boat** will look like Figure 10-1.

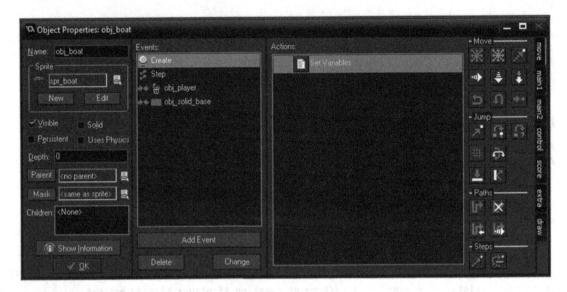

Figure 10-1. *obj_boat all set up*

There is one font, **font_data**, which is Arial size 20.

The room, **room_ship_example**, has one of each of **obj_hud**, **obj_player**, and **obj_horse**, and a few elements of the mushroom, flag, and cactus. An example is shown in Figure 10-2.

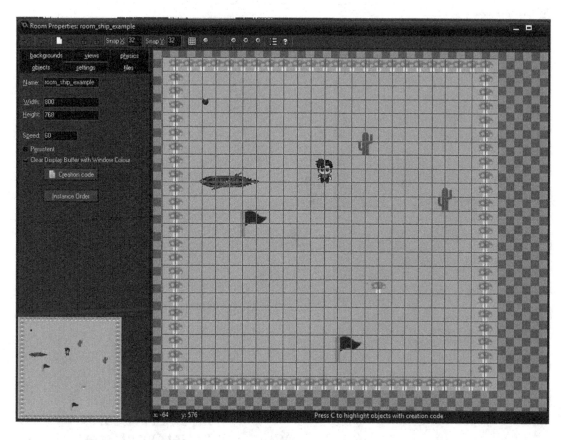

Figure 10-2. *The room all set up*

Figure 10-3 shows the boat being moved.

Figure 10-3. The drivable vehicle element in action

CHAPTER 11

███

Enemy Path Finding

The GMZ for this element is **Enemy_Path_Finding**.

It uses **Depth_Based** as a base.

AI (artificial intelligence) is an import aspect of an RPG. Creating characters that have path finding is a basic form of AI. The ability to get from point A to B while avoiding objects is AI at its most basic.

You could have a character

- Move between two points

- Move to random points in the room

- Move toward the player

- Constantly follow a set path

For the purpose of this example, we'll create a character that moves toward the player's location.

The math behind path finding is quite complex. Fortunately, this is quite easy to do in GameMaker's GML because it has a number of functions that can be combined to achieve this task.

First up a grid is created that covers the room in invisible cells where a path may be considered. Then cells in this grid are flagged where the path finding cannot go. A path start and end point are then set. The path-finding algorithm creates a path between these two points, while avoiding cells that it cannot go through.

This is achieved in only a few lines of code, and for the most part is pretty fast and accurate.

Load up the **Depth_Based_Graphics** GMZ.

This element has one additional object, **obj_enemy**.

The sprite for this is **spr_pirate** and it has 12 subimages. The sprite origin is 22,61.

The **Create Event** for this object is shown in Listing 11-1. First, this code creates a grid that will be used for path finding. It then adds **obj_solid**, which is created by **obj_elements_parent**; and it marks places (cells) that the path cannot go through. The final part then creates a path between itself and the player, and then starts this path.

Listing 11-1. Setting Up the Path-Finding Grid, Wall Objects, and the Initial Path

```
///Create grid
size = 16;
grid = mp_grid_create(0,0,ceil(room_width/size),ceil(room_height/size),size,size);

///Add walls to grid
mp_grid_add_instances(grid,obj_solid_base,1);
```

© Ben Tyers 2017
B. Tyers, *Learn RPGs in GameMaker: Studio*, DOI 10.1007/978-1-4842-2946-0_11

```
//create initial path
path=path_add();

mp_grid_path(grid,path,x,y,obj_player.x,obj_player.y,1);
path_start(path,2,path_action_stop,true);
```

The **Step Event** has two blocks. The first block checks if the end of the path is reached; if it is, it creates a new path between itself and the player object, and starts moving along this path (see Listing 11-2).

Listing 11-2. Runs when Half Path is Down, Creates New Path Toward the Player

```
///reset path at end
if path_position>=0.5
{
    path_clear_points(path);
    mp_grid_path(grid,path,x,y,obj_player.x,obj_player.y,1);
    path_start(path,2,path_action_stop,true);
}
```

The second block in the **Step Event** makes the sprite point in the direction it's moving (left/right); see Listing 11-3.

Listing 11-3. Makes the Instance Point Left or Right, Depending on Movement

```
///face direction moving
if direction>90 and direction<270
{
    image_xscale=-1;
}
else
{
    image_xscale=1;
}
```

Finally there is a **Draw Event** with the code in Listing 11-4, which draws the path and the enemy. You could omit this whole event, but I have left it in for testing and visualization purposes.

Listing 11-4. Drawing the Path as a Series of Lines

```
///For drawing grid
draw_path(path,x,y,true);
draw_self();
```

When done, it will look like Figure 11-1.

Figure 11-1. obj_enemy all set up

The room has several instances of **obj_cactus**, **obj_flag**, and **obj_mushroom**, plus one each of **obj_player** and **obj_enemy**.

Figure 11-2 shows an example of this element.

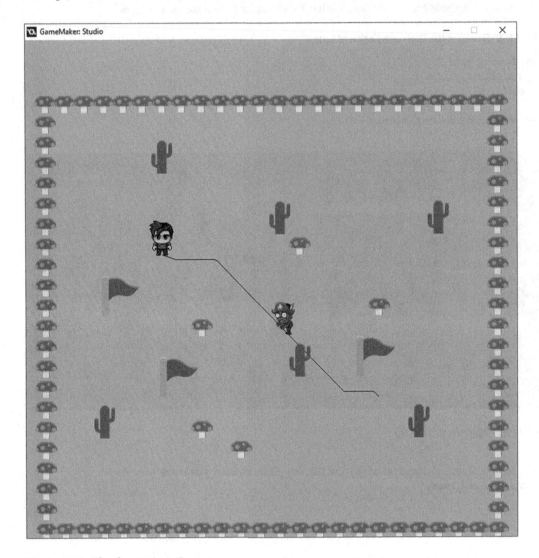

Figure 11-2. *The element in action*

CHAPTER 12

Footstep Sounds

This example uses the **Game_Base** GMZ as a template.

The GMZ for this element is **Foot_Steps**.

Audio, both sound and music, can add a lot to a game. The style of music and sound effects can drastically affect the ambience of a game/level. When used sparingly and for emphasis, the result can be an immersive experience for the player.

However, it is important not to overdo sound effects. Too much too often can be overkill and can detract from the overall experience.

Using sounds at important points is the way to go, such as

- When collecting treasure

- Entering a door

- Walking on a different surface

- Buying/collecting/picking up an object

This example demonstrates how to use different sounds when walking on different things such as water, leaves, wood, and solid floors.

It's a very simple method: you set an alarm. If the player is moving, the alarm triggers, checks what they are walking on, and plays the appropriate sound. Then the alarm is reset. Using an alarm prevents constant playing of the walking sound. Playing once every ½ second is enough to give the player enough feedback to let them know the surface they are walking on has changed.

The GMZ for this completed element is **Foot_Steps**.

There is an additional code block added to the **Step Event** of **obj_player**. This code deals with setting the correct sound effect and the playing of the audio if the player is moving; see Listing 12-1. Note that it will only play if no sound is already playing.

Listing 12-1. Playing the Appropriate Sound Effect

```
///select walking fx
var soundfx;
if position_meeting(x,y,obj_water) soundfx=snd_water;
else if position_meeting(x,y,obj_leaves) soundfx=snd_leaves;
else if position_meeting(x,y,obj_wood) soundfx=snd_wood;
else if position_meeting(x,y,obj_solid) soundfx=snd_solid;
else soundfx=snd_normal;
//play the sound
if is_moving && !audio_is_playing(soundfx) audio_play_sound(soundfx,1,false);
```

© Ben Tyers 2017

B. Tyers, *Learn RPGs in GameMaker: Studio*, DOI 10.1007/978-1-4842-2946-0_12

Additional objects are

- **obj_water** with a blue 32x32 sprite assigned

- **obj_leaves** with a light brown 32x32 sprite assigned

- **obj_wood** with a dark brown 32x32 sprite assigned

- **obj_solid** with a dark green 32x32 sprite assigned

The origin of the sprites for the above four objects is not important, so either 0,0 or 32,32 will suffice. The sound resources you need to load in are **snd_water**, **snd_leaves**, **snd_wood**, **snd_solid**, and **snd_normal.** When done, the resources tree will look like Figure 12-1.

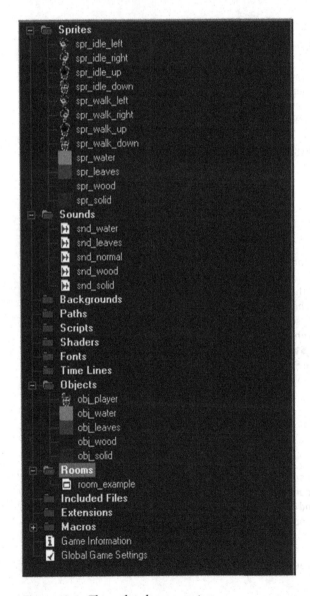

Figure 12-1. *The updated resources tree*

Figure 12-2 shows an example room layout to test the walking sound effects.

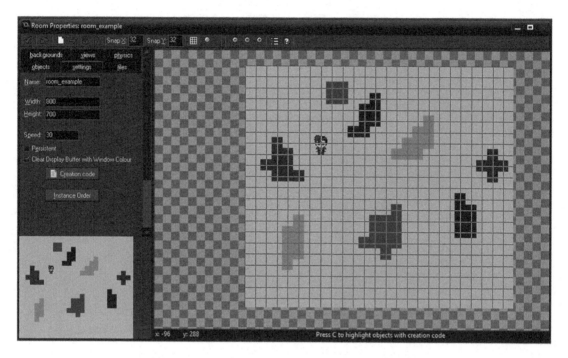

Figure 12-2. *Example room setup*

CHAPTER 13

Hints and Tips

The GMZ for this element is **Hints_and_Tips**.

It uses **Game_Base** as a starting point.

There will be times when you'll want to convey information to the player, such as

- What key to press to make something happen

- Tutorial/guide information

- Instructions for a quest/mini-game

- To guide the player on what to do next

You may want to provide more than one sentence at a time, which could prove problematic. This element deals with this issue by queuing messages in a **ds_list** and showing each message for an amount of time.

Each message is shown and deleted; if there is another message in the queue, it will show that one next.

This is achieved through the use of one script and one object, and with a minor change to **obj_player**. Some additional objects are added to show how to use this in practice. Since messages are queued easily through a script you can add them at any time; it doesn't have to be through a collision event.

First up is a parent object, **obj_message_item**. Create this object. There is no code or sprite for this. That is all for this object.

Next is an object named **obj_door** with the door sprite **spr_door** assigned and having the origin as center. The **Create Event** code is shown in Listing 13-1.

Listing 13-1. Setting a Message to Be Shown

```
message="You Need A Key To Open This";
```

This object has **obj_message_item** as the parent.

Next is an object named **obj_banana** with **spr_banana** assigned with the origin as center. The **Create Event** code is shown in Listing 13-2.

Listing 13-2. Setting Another Message to Be Shown

```
message="Press P To Pick Up Banana";
```

This object has **obj_message_item** as the parent.

Next is object **obj_rum** with the rum bottle sprite **spr_rum** assigned and the origin as center. The **Create Event** code is shown in Listing 13-3.

Listing 13-3. Setting a Message to Be Shown

```
message="Press M To Drink The Rum";
```

This object has **obj_message_item** as the parent.

Next is an object named **obj_chest** with the sprite **spr_chest** assigned and the origin as center. The **Create Event** code is shown in Listing 13-4.

Listing 13-4. Setting a Message to Be Shown

```
message="Press K To Use The Key";
```

This object has **obj_message_item** as the parent.

These messages are shown as examples; pressing the keys won't actually do anything. This has been omitted to keep it easy to understand.

Figure 13-1 shows **obj_rum** with the sprite and parent object assigned.

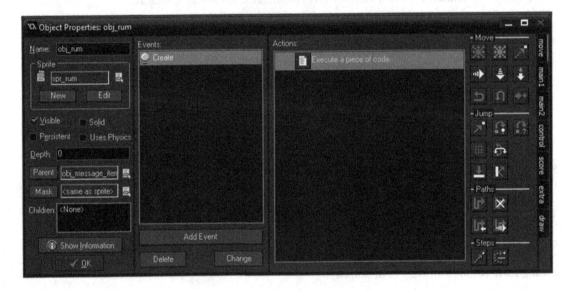

Figure 13-1. *Sprite and parent assigned*

There is a slight addition to the **obj_player**.

The **Create Event** has been changed to the code in Listing 13-5. This code sets up a state for the player as originally there, plus the addition of a flag to show a message.

Listing 13-5. Setting Up As Usual and Adding a Flag to Show a Message

```
///set up
enum player_state{
    idle,
    up,
    down,
    left,
    right
    }
```

```
dir=player_state.down;
is_moving=false;
image_speed=0.5;
can_show_message=true; //allows message to be shown
```

It also has a **Collision Event with obj_message_item** with the code, which queues a message, as shown in Listing 13-6. If a message can be shown, this code sets a flag to false, runs the script to process this message, and starts an alarm.

Listing 13-6. Setting Responses If a Message Can Be Shown

```
if can_show_message
{
    can_show_message=false;
    scr_message(other.message);
    alarm[0]=room_speed*3;
}
```

Next is the object that will show the messages, if any. The object is **obj_message**. The **Create Event** that sets the required starting values is shown in Listing 13-7.

Listing 13-7. Setting Up a List and Flag, and Defining Initial Values

```
global.message=ds_list_create(); //create a ds_list to hold messages
can_show=true; //set that a message can show
to_draw=""; //set text to draw to ""
show_text="";
count=0;
```

The **Alarm[0] Event** is shown in Listing 13-8. This clears any current message.

Listing 13-8. Clearing the Message and Setting an Alarm for One Second

```
///alarm0 set alarm1
alarm[1]=room_speed*1; //create a short pause
to_draw=""; //remove text to show
show_text="";
count=0;
```

The **Alarm[1] Event** sets the flag so a message can be shown, as shown in Listing 13-9.

Listing 13-9. Changing the Flag Back to True

```
///set as able to show
can_show=true;
```

The **Step Event** checks the **ds_list** for any content. If there is content, it adds it to **to_draw** and then deletes it. Then it adds a letter of the message **to_draw** each step to **show_text**. See Listing 13-10.

Listing 13-10. Looks for a Message, Saves It in a Variable, and Shows It a Letter at a Time

```
///check if message waiting
if !ds_list_empty(global.message) && can_show //do this if one or message and can_show
flag is true
{
    to_draw=ds_list_find_value(global.message,0); //get message from top of ds list
    ds_list_delete(global.message,0); //destroy this message    can_show=false; //prevent showing
    alarm[0]=room_speed*4; //create a pause
}
if(string_length(show_text) < string_length(to_draw))
{
show_text = string_copy(to_draw,1,count);
alarm[0] = room_speed*5;
count +=1;
}
```

Finally, the **Draw Event** draws the border and text if **to_draw** is not equal to "". It does this by drawing an appropriately sized background and places the text over it, as shown in Listing 13-11.

Listing 13-11. Drawing Background and Message If One Is Present

```
///draw message

if to_draw!="" //do if there is a message waiting
{
    var xx=350;
    var yy=600;
    var padding=10;
    var border_size=2;
    var width =string_width(to_draw) + padding * 2; // width of message
    var height = string_height(to_draw) + padding * 2; //draw border
    draw_set_colour(c_blue);
    draw_roundrect(xx-(width/2)-border_size,
    yy-(height/2)-border_size,xx+(width/2)+border_size,yy+(height/2)+border_size,false);
    //draw main message background
    draw_set_colour(c_aqua);
    draw_roundrect(xx-(width/2),
    yy-(height/2),xx+(width/2),yy+(height/2),false);
    //draw a message
    draw_set_font(font_message);
    draw_set_halign(fa_center);
    draw_set_valign(fa_middle);
    draw_set_colour(c_red);
    draw_text(xx+1,yy+1,show_text);
    draw_set_colour(c_black);
    draw_text(xx,yy,show_text);
}
```

Finally there is a **Game End Event** with the GML shown in Listing 13-12.

Listing 13-12. The Game End Event

```
ds_list_destroy(global.message);
```

Then comes the script, **scr_message**, with the code in Listing 13-13. This adds the message (**argument0**) to the **ds_list** ready to be used.

Listing 13-13. Queuing the Message

```
///scr_message(message);
ds_list_add(global.message,argument0);
```

Finally there is the font, **font_message**, which is Arial size 12.
Place a few of the items in the room, and one of **obj_message**.
Figure 13-2 shows this element in action.

Figure 13-2. Showing the hints and tips element in action

135

CHAPTER 14

HUD

This element uses the GMZ named **HUD**.

It uses **Hints_and_Tips** as a template.

HUDs (heads up display) are important in lots of game genres, particularly in an RPG. The player needs access to a whole menagerie of information, such as

- Health

- HP

- HP Level

- Mana

- Inventory

- Selected Weapon/Weapon Power

- Spells

As you can see, that's a lot info to combine into a small area.

A HUD is usually a non-interactive element of a game, although inventory and spells are often selectable and useable.

The HUD is usually drawn separately from the view. In GameMaker Studio, this is relatively easy because you can draw a GUI above and independent from the main game view.

The example for this element draws the seven elements listed above. In your own game, you may choose to display more or less. This is your choice.

This uses the **Hints_and_Tips** GMZ with the following changes.

First, a sprite named **spr_message_bg** is used as a pop-up for the hints and tips message. Note that the origin is set as 230, 250 and is not assigned to an object.

Second, the **Draw GUI Event** in **obj_message** has been updated to the code in Listing 14-1.

Listing 14-1. Combining Various Drawings to Make a HUD Layout

```
///draw message

if to_draw!="" //do if there is a message waiting
{
    draw_set_alpha(0.5);
    //set up
var xx=350;
    var yy=250;
    var padding=10;
```

```
var border_size=2;
var width =string_width(to_draw) + padding * 2; // width of message
var height = string_height(to_draw) + padding * 2;
//draw background sprite
draw_sprite(spr_message_bg,0,xx,yy);

//draw border of message
draw_set_colour(c_blue);
draw_roundrect(xx-(width/2)-border_size,
yy-(height/2)-border_size,xx+(width/2)+border_size,yy+(height/2)+border_size,false);
//draw main message background
draw_set_colour(c_aqua);
draw_roundrect(xx-(width/2),
yy-(height/2),xx+(width/2),yy+(height/2),false);
//draw a message
draw_set_font(font_message);
draw_set_halign(fa_center);
draw_set_valign(fa_middle);
draw_set_colour(c_red);
draw_text(xx+1,yy+1,show_text);
draw_set_colour(c_black);
draw_text(xx,yy,show_text);
draw_set_alpha(1);
}
```

These are all of the changes.

There are some fonts:

- **font_info**, which is Arial size 16

- **font_info_small**, which is Arial size 10

- **font_message**, which is Arial size 12

In addition, there are other sprites.

- **spr_popup_spells** has an origin of center

- **spr_inv_rum** has an origin of center

- **spr_inv_chest** has an origin set of center

All the other HUD graphics are done within the following object, **obj_hud**.

obj_hud has a sprite named **spr_hud** with the origin at 0,0. In fact, this is never drawn in a **Draw Event**, but is present so you can place the room at the correct position.

This routine utilizes extra code for example purposes, which is indicated in the comments of the applicable code. Your actual game would omit these additions.

The **Create Event** code is shown in Listing 14-2.

Listing 14-2. Setting Up Initial Variables with Starting Values

```
///Set up variables for testing/example
//In your own game you'd set initial values
//in a splash screen or load saved data spells
can_show_spells=false; // flag as to whether pop-up shows
```

```
global.ice_spell=5;
global.earth_spell=2;
global.fire_spell=8;
global.water_spell=1;
//hp and xp
global.hp=80;
global.xp=35;
//gold
global.gold=1150;
//weapon
global.weapon=0; //starts at 0 as using subimages start at index 0
```

The **Step Event** has two code blocks. The first code block checks for keyboard input, as shown in Listing 14-3.

Listing 14-3. Changing Flags Between True and False on Keypress

```
///Keyboard control
//show/hide spells pop-up
if keyboard_check_pressed(ord('S'))
{
    can_show_spells=!can_show_spells;
}
//show/hide inventory pop-up
if keyboard_check_pressed(ord('I'))
{
    can_show_inventory=!can_show_inventory;
}
```

The second block uses the code in Listing 14-4.

Listing 14-4. Just for Testing, Allowing You to Change Various Values

```
///Following for testing - to allow changing of variables
if keyboard_check(ord('Q'))
{
    global.hp++;
}
if keyboard_check(ord('A'))
{
    global.hp--;
    if global.hp<0 global.hp=0;
}
if keyboard_check(ord('E'))
{
    global.xp++;
}
if keyboard_check(ord('D'))
{
    global.xp--;
    if global.xp<0 global.xp=0;
}
```

```
if keyboard_check(ord('R'))
{
    global.gold++;
}
if keyboard_check(ord('F'))
{
    global.gold--;
    if global.gold<0 global.gold=0;
}
if keyboard_check_pressed(ord('W'))
{
    global.weapon++;
    if global.weapon==3 global.weapon=0;
}
```

Listing 14-5 shows the **Draw Event** code, in which we simply put a comment line to turn off default drawing.

Listing 14-5. The Draw Event

///this comment prevents default drawing

Next there is the **Draw GUI Event**. This has eight code blocks.
The first block draws the sprite for the object, on the GUI layer, as shown in Listing 14-6.

Listing 14-6. Drawing the Assigned Sprite

///draw self - frame
```
draw_self();
```

The second block formats the text, as shown in Listing 14-7.

Listing 14-7. Formatting the Text

///format text
```
draw_set_font(font_info);
draw_set_halign(fa_left);
draw_set_valign(fa_middle);
draw_set_colour(c_yellow);
```

The third block draws the spell pop-up if **can_show_spells** is **true**; see Listing 14-8.

Listing 14-8. If the Flag Is True, This Element Will Be Drawn

///draw spell pop-up
```
if can_show_spells
{
    draw_set_alpha(0.5); //set as half transparent
    draw_sprite(spr_popup_spells,0,350,200);
    draw_set_alpha(1); //reset transparency
    draw_text(142,180,global.earth_spell);
    draw_text(274,180,global.fire_spell);
    draw_text(416,180,global.ice_spell);
    draw_text(551,180,global.water_spell);

}
```

The fourth block draws the hp, xp, and level, as shown in Listing 14-9.

Listing 14-9. Drawing the Main HUD Info

```
///Draw hp, xp, and level
draw_hp=global.hp mod 100;
draw_xp=global.xp mod 100;
draw_level=(global.xp div 100)+1;
//hp
draw_text(60,552,"HP:"+string(global.hp));
for (var loop = 0; loop < draw_hp; loop += 1)
{
    draw_line(135+loop,547,135+loop,557);
}
draw_set_colour(c_black);
draw_roundrect(135,547,230,557,true);
draw_roundrect(134,546,231,558,true);
draw_set_colour(c_yellow);
//xp

draw_text(60,582,"XP: "+string(draw_xp));

draw_set_colour(c_teal);
for (var loop = 0; loop < draw_xp; loop += 1)
{
    draw_line(135+loop,577,135+loop,587);
}
draw_set_colour(c_black);
draw_roundrect(135,577,230,587,true);
draw_roundrect(134,576,231,588,true);
draw_set_colour(c_yellow);
//level
draw_set_halign(fa_center);
draw_text(150,524,"Level: "+string(draw_level));
draw_set_halign(fa_left);
```

The fifth draws the player's gold; see Listing 14-10.

Listing 14-10. Drawing the Gold as Text

```
///draw gold
draw_text(100,638,"Gold: "+string(global.gold));
```

The sixth block draws the chosen weapon; see Listing 14-11.

Listing 14-11. Drawing the Sprite for the Selected Weapon

```
///draw weapon
switch (global.weapon)
{
  case 0:
  weapon_name="Cutlass";
  break;
```

```
  case 1:
  weapon_name="Gun";
  break;

  case 2:
  weapon_name="Hook";
  break;
}
draw_set_halign(fa_middle);
draw_text(350,522,"Weapon");
draw_text(350,540,weapon_name);
draw_sprite(spr_weapon_1,global.weapon,350,600);
draw_set_halign(fa_left); //reset to preferred default
```

The seventh block draws an example inventory if **can_show_inventory** is **true**, as shown in Listing 14-12.

Listing 14-12. Drawing the Inventory Element If the Flag Is True

```
///Draw inventory
//For example purposes, see the Inventory section in the book for a full working example

if can_show_inventory
{
    draw_sprite(spr_inv_bg,0,0,400);
    draw_set_halign(fa_center);
    draw_text(350,420,"Pop Up Inventory System Would Go Here");
    draw_set_font(font_info_small);
    //draw example
    draw_sprite(spr_inv_rum,0,300,450);
    draw_sprite(spr_inv_chest,0,400,450);
}
```

The eighth and final block is shown in Listing 14-13.

Listing 14-13. Draw Control Info

```
///info
draw_set_font(font_message);
draw_set_halign(fa_left);
draw_text(100,200,"S to show spells - I to show inventory#
Q A change hp#
E D change xp#
R F change gold#
W change Weapon");
Mainly just for testing purposes.
```

When done, the **Draw GUI Event** will look like Figure 14-1.

Figure 14-1. Eight blocks in a GUI event

One instance of **obj_hud** is placed in the room, as shown in Figure 14-2.

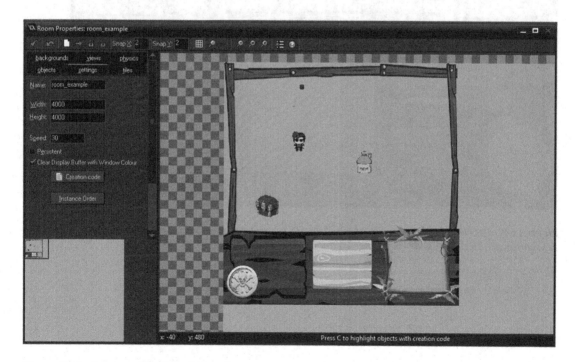

Figure 14-2. A room with obj_hud placed

When you run the game, it will look like Figure 14-3. You can use the keyboard to change the variable for testing, and show and hide the spells and inventory pop-ups.

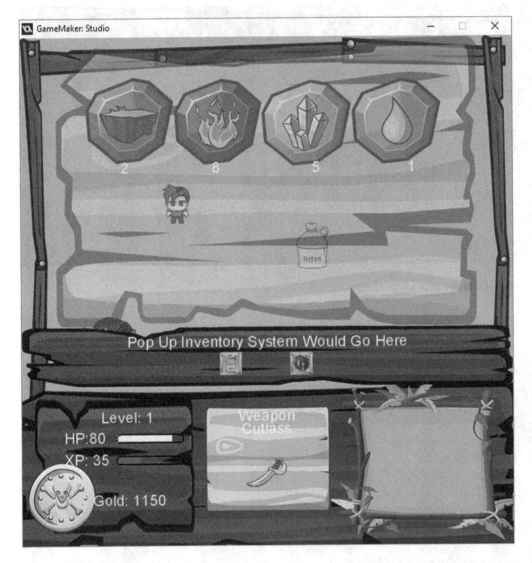

Figure 14-3. *The element in action. S to show spells - I to show inventory QA change hp, ED change xp - RF change gold - W change Weapon*

CHAPTER 15

■ ■ ■

Inventory

This element uses the GMZ **Inventory**.

It uses **Game_Base** as a template.

An RPG must have some form of inventory system. Collecting items is one of the main focuses for a player. For example, in the RPG in this book, the player needs to collect items and use them appropriately to get cash so she can get off of the island she has been marooned upon.

Acquired items are generally stored visually so the player can see what items they have. In this example, this is achieved by using a pop-up that the player can show/hide with a single keypress.

The example shown is very basic, but simple enough to understand and expand upon. The inventory has a number of slots for placing items in, which the player can then drag around and place into other slots. This example allows the player to collide with an instance of an object and pick it up using a keypress, if there is a free slot available.

Each slot holds a value of -1 if empty; otherwise, it holds a number that represents the object to be shown. We will use four items. Each item has a mini-sprite as a subimage that is shown on the inventory. Adding additional items is pretty straightforward.

As an example, in-game items that can be picked up will be generated randomly. In your own game, you'll probably want separate items.

This element uses **Game_Base** as a template, with no changes made.

First up is a sprite named **spr_border**, which is 32x32 with the origin set as center.

Next is a sprite that will hold the images used in the inventory. This is also 32x32 with the origin set as center. The name is **spr_items**. It consists of five subimages, but we'll only be using subimages 1 through 4. Note that 0 is not used but needs to be present. This is shown in Figure 15-1.

Figure 15-1. *Subimages of spr_items, with a null first image*

The next sprite is **spr_pickup**, which is used in this element for objects that can be picked up. It is 64x64 in size and the origin is center. It also consists of five subimages, again with a null first image, as shown in Figure 15-2.

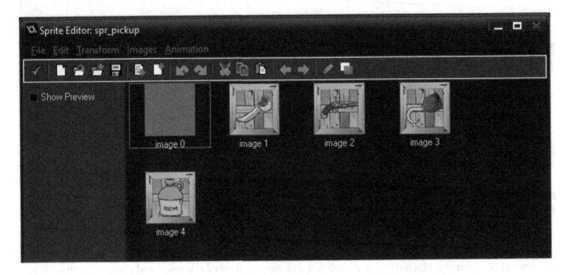

Figure 15-2. spr_pickup with subimages and a null first image

The final sprite is used as a background when the inventory is visible. It is named **spr_inv_bg**. Its size is 650x52. The origin is 0,0.

There are a few objects. The first is **obj_bag**, which has the sprite **spr_bag** with the origin set as center. There is a **Collision Event with obj_player**, with the code in Listing 15-1. This code will increase the size of the inventory (**global.maxItems**) by four slots and then destroy itself.

Listing 15-1. Increasing Size of Inventory on Keypress of P

```
///detect keypress
if keyboard_check_pressed(ord('P'))
{
    global.maxItems+=4; //add four inventory slots
    instance_destroy();
}
```

That is all for this object. In your own game, you may want to provide the bag as a reward for completing something in-game, or have it available for purchase in the shop.

The next object is **obj_pickup** with sprite **spr_pickup** that you created previously.

The **Create Event** code sets a random value for **my_id** between 1 and 4. This value is used to show the item's subimage and is also used when it's being picked up. In your own games, you'll probably want to use separate items each with their own **my_id** value, but this is used here as concise example; see Listing 15-2.

Listing 15-2. Randomly Set Up

```
///set up
my_id=irandom_range(1,4);
image_speed=0;
image_index=my_id;
```

146

Next is a **Collision Event with obj_player**. The code in Listing 15-3 checks for a keypress and checks whether there is an empty slot. The script **scr_itempickup** checks for an empty slot and adds the item if there is one. There is a more thorough inventory example in the element Usable Items.

Listing 15-3. Checking for an Empty Slot

```
///detect keypress and check for empty slot
if keyboard_check_pressed(ord('P')) && scr_itempickup(my_id) //if slot available, add to slot
{
    instance_destroy(); //then destroy instance
}
```

There are five scripts. These scripts work together to allow you to add items to the inventory and to click and drag items.

The first one is **scr_itemcheck**; see Listing 15-4.

Listing 15-4. Checking for an Item and Returning True or False Accordingly

```
for (var i = 0; i < global.maxItems; i += 1)
{
    if (global.inventory[i] == argument0) //if slot "i" contains argument 0
    {
        return true;
    }
}
return false;
```

The second is **scr_itemdrop**; see Listing 15-5.

Listing 15-5. Allowing for Dropping an Item, Returning True or False

```
for (var i = 0; i < global.maxItems; i += 1)
{
    if (global.inventory[i] == argument0) //if slot "i" contains argument0
    {
        global.inventory[i] = -1;
        return true;
    }
}
return false;
```

The third is **scr_itemdrop_slot**; see Listing 15-6.

Listing 15-6. Checking If a Slot Is Empty and Returning True If It Is

```
//scr_itemdrop_slot(slot);

if (global.inventory[argument0] != -1)
{
    global.inventory[argument0] = -1;
    return true;
}
return false;
```

The fourth is **scr_itempickup_slot**; see Listing 15-7.

Listing 15-7. If Slot Is Empty, Adding the Item and Returning True

```
//scr_itempickup_slot(item,slot);
if (global.inventory[argument1] == -1)
{
    global.inventory[argument1] = argument0;
    return true;
}
return false;
```

The fifth is **scr_itempickup**. This script will check if a slot is available. If it is, it will add it and return **true**; otherwise **false** is returned. See Listing 15-8.

Listing 15-8. Checking All Slots for Empty Space and Adding If Available

```
for (var i = 0; i < global.maxItems; i += 1)
{
    if (global.inventory[i] == -1) //if slot "i" is empty
    {
        global.inventory[i] = argument0;
        return true;
    }
}
return false;
```

Then there is object **obj_mouseitem**, which has a **Draw Event** with the code shown in Listing 15-9.

Listing 15-9. Setting the Sprite at Mouse Position If Held

```
if (global.showInv)
{
    var item = global.mouseItem;
    if (item != -1)
    {
        x = mouse_x;
        y = mouse_y;
        draw_sprite(spr_items,item,x,y);
    }
}
```

Next up is object **obj_invbutton,** with the **Draw Event** shown in Listing 15-10.

Listing 15-10. Drawing Inventory Buttons

```
if (global.showInv)
{
    var item = global.inventory[slot];
    var click = mouse_check_button_pressed(mb_left);

    if (abs(mouse_x - x) < 16) && (abs(mouse_y - y) < 16)
    {
```

```
        draw_set_colour(c_white);
        draw_rectangle(x-16,y-16,x+16,y+16,0);
        if (click)
        {
            if (item != -1)
            {
                scr_itemdrop_slot(slot);
            }
            if (global.mouseItem != -1)
            {
                scr_itempickup_slot(global.mouseItem,slot)
            }
            global.mouseItem = item;
        }
    }


    if (item != -1)
    {
        draw_sprite(spr_items,item,x,y);
    }
}
```

Last up is the main inventory object, **obj_inventory**. It has the **Create Event** shown in Listing 15-11.

Listing 15-11. Setting Up and Creating Mouse Item

```
///set up
global.showInv=true; //display the inventory?
global.maxItems=4; //total item slots

for (var i = 0; i < 12; i += 1)
{
    global.inventory[i] = -1;
    button[i] = instance_create(0,0,obj_invbutton)
    button[i].slot = i;
}

global.mouseItem=-1;
instance_create(0,0,obj_mouseitem);
```

It has a **Step Event** that toggles **global.showInv** between **true** and **false** when V is pressed. This variable is used to show or hide the inventory; see Listing 15-12.

Listing 15-12. Toggling Between True and False

```
///visible switch - switches between true and false, used to show/hide inventory
if keyboard_check_pressed(ord('V'))
{
    global.showInv=!global.showInv;
}
```

And finally a **Draw Event** will draw the inventory if **global.showInv** is **true**; see Listing 15-13.

Listing 15-13. Drawing the Inventory

```
///draw the inventory
if (global.showInv)
{
    var x1,x2,y1,y2;
    x1 = view_xview[0]+75;
    x2 = x1 + view_wview[0];
    y1 = view_yview[0]+30;
    y2 = y1 + 64;

    draw_set_colour(c_black);
    draw_set_alpha(0.8);
    draw_sprite(spr_inv_bg,0,x1-50,y1+15);

    for (var i = 0; i < global.maxItems; i += 1)
    {
        var ix = x1+24+(i * 40);
        var iy = y2-24;

        draw_sprite(spr_border,0,ix,iy)
        button[i].x = ix;
        button[i].y = iy;
    }
    draw_text(x1+100,y1+100,"V to show/hide - Click and Drag Items With Mouse##Pick Up Bag
    For Extra Room To Store Items");
}
```

In the room, place one of **obj_inventory**, one of **obj_bag**, and a few of **obj_pickup**, as shown in Figure 15-3.

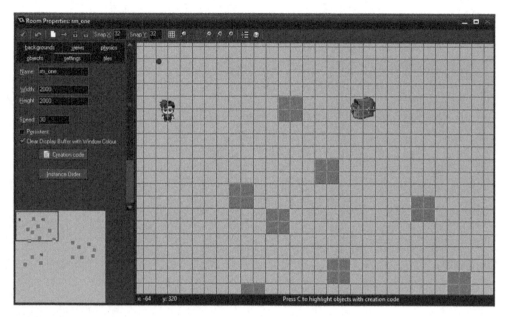

Figure 15-3. *The room all set up*

When tested, it should look like Figure 15-4.

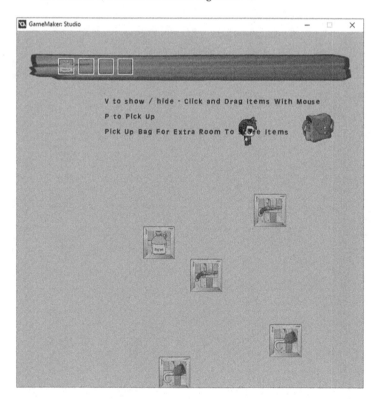

Figure 15-4. *Inventory example in action*

CHAPTER 16

■ ■ ■

Invincibility

This element uses the GMZ **Invincibility**.

It uses **Game_Base** as a template.

Providing info to the player using various messages, pop-up messages, spoken sentences, and so on does have its place. However, too much can be overkill.

Another method worth considering is changing the colour of the player sprite. Don't worry; you won't need to make a new set of sprites because GameMaker Studio has a colour-blend function.

You could use this method to convey information to the player. In this example, it will show the invincibility of the player by flashing red. It will also draw a bar above the player to show how much invincibility the player has remaining, which will replenish over time.

This example uses **Game_Base** with the following changes.

The **Create Event** of **obj_player** has changed to the code in Listing 16-1. The additions set up the variables needed.

Listing 16-1. Updating the Player Object Code

```
///set up
enum player_state{
    idle,
    up,
    down,
    left,
    right
    }

dir=player_state.down;
is_moving=false;
image_speed=0.5;

col=0; //initial value
sw=0; //for sine wave
move_col=5;
invincible=false;
invincible_timer=100;
alarm[0]=20; //to replenish
```

An **Alarm[0] Event** has been added with the code in Listing 16-2, which replenishes the timer once every 20 steps and keeps it at a maximum value of 100.

Listing 16-2. Setting the Timer and Starting an Alarm

```
invincible_timer++;
if invincible_timer>100 invincible_timer=100;
alarm[0]=20;
```

An additional block has been added to the **Step Event**. This first part allows the player to turn on/off the invincibility; the second part sets the colour blend if active. The last line turns off invincibility if there is no timer left. See Listing 16-3.

Listing 16-3. Checking for Keypress of I to Switch Between Invincible and Normal

```
///invincibility
if keyboard_check_released(ord('I')) //switch between true/false on keypress
{
    invincible=!invincible;
}

if invincible
{
    sw += 0.1; //for sine wave - i.e. speed
    col= sin(sw) * move_col; //for sine wave
    image_blend = make_colour_rgb(125+(col*20), 100, 100);
    invincible_timer-=1;
}
else
{
    image_blend = make_colour_rgb(255,255,255);
}

//check if player has invincible_timer
if invincible_timer<1 invincible=false;
```

And finally a **Draw Event** has been added, which draws the player's sprite and coloured bars showing available invincibility; see Listing 16-4.

Listing 16-4. Drawing the Player's Sprite and Available Invincibility

```
///draw self and box showing invincible_timer
draw_self();
//background
draw_set_colour(c_red);
draw_rectangle(x-50,y-70,x+50,y-65,false);
//bar
draw_set_colour(c_green);
draw_rectangle(x-50,y-70,x-50+invincible_timer,y-65,false);
```

When done, the player object named **obj_player** will look like Figure 16-1.

Figure 16-1. The obj_player with additions made

When you test this element, it will look like Figure 16-2.

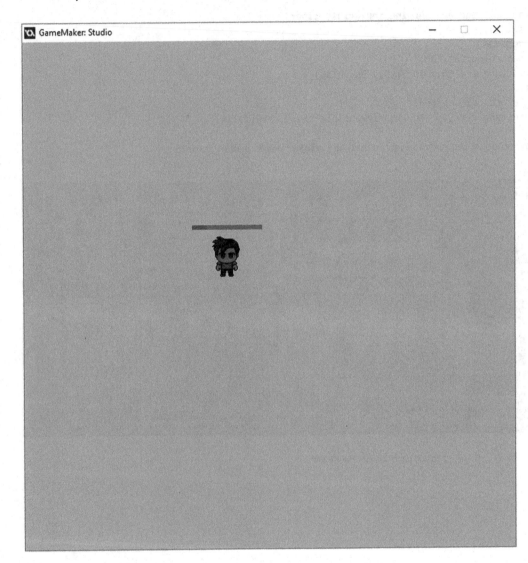

Figure 16-2. *This element in action*

CHAPTER 17

■ ■ ■

Mini-Quests

This GMZ for this element is **Mini_Quest**.

It uses **Game_Base** as a template. The room size needs to be changed to 2000x2000.

Mini-quests that the player must complete, either to progress the story, unlock something, or get a reward, provide variety within your game.

Quests should ideally be themed so that they match the overall game theme.

This example challenges the player to collect all treasure chests before time runs out.

First up is a change to the **Game_Base** template.

The room size needs to be 2000x2000.

The movement block in the **Step Event** of **obj_player** is changed to the code in Listing 17-1, which prevents the player from walking through any walls.

Listing 17-1. Updating the Player Object

```
///movement
if is_moving
{
    switch (dir)
    {
        case player_state.up:
        if !position_meeting(x,y-4,obj_wall) y -= 4;
        break;

        case player_state.down:
        if !position_meeting(x,y+4,obj_wall) y += 4;
        break;

        case player_state.left:
        if !position_meeting(x-4,y,obj_wall) x -= 4;
        break;

        case player_state.right:
        if !position_meeting(x+4,y,obj_wall) x += 4;
        break;
    }
}
depth=-y;
```

These are the only changes.

This element makes use of a few additional objects and sprites.

There is an object called **obj_wall** with the 32x32 sprite **spr_wall** assigned and the origin set as center. There is no code for this object.

Next is an object that draws a mini-map of certain object instances in the room.

It uses two sprites. The first is **spr_map_wall** which is 5x5, solid red, and has an origin of center.

The second sprite is **spr_map_chest**, which is solid yellow, 5x5 pixels, and also has an origin set as center.

These two sprites are not assigned to any object.

The main object for drawing the mini-map is **obj_map**, which does not have any sprite assigned. The **Draw GUI Event** code is in Listing 17-2. This will draw a background and the sprite **spr_map_wall** with it. The section for drawing the chest blips, **spr_map_chest**, will draw on the outside edge of the map if the range is over 600. If it's under a distance of 600, it will draw inside the map.

Listing 17-2. Drawing a Mini-Map/Radar on Screen to Show Various Objects

```
///draw outline
draw_set_alpha(0.2);
draw_circle(75,600,75,0);
draw_set_alpha(1);
draw_set_colour(c_green);
draw_circle(75,600,75,1);
draw_circle(75,600,10,1);

//set up variables
var d,a,radarX,radarY;
radarX = obj_player.x;
radarY = obj_player.y;

//draw the wall instances that are in range
with(obj_wall)
{
    //how far
    d = point_distance(radarX,radarY,x,y);
    if(d <= 600)  // This is the distance to check for
    {
        d = d/600*75;
        a = point_direction(radarX,radarY,x,y)
        draw_sprite(spr_map_wall, 0, 75 + lengthdir_x(d,a), 600 + lengthdir_y(d,a));
    }
}

//draw the chest on the mini-map
with(obj_chest)
{
    //how far
    d = point_distance(radarX,radarY,x,y);
    //in range
    if( d > 600)  //for long-range chest instances
    {
```

```
        //convert range to draw
        d = 75;
        //angle to target
        a = point_direction(radarX,radarY,x,y)
        //draw relative to center of radar using simplified lengthdir function
        draw_sprite(spr_map_chest, 0, 75 + lengthdir_x(d,a), 600 + lengthdir_y(d,a));
    }
    else if(d <= 600)  // This is the standard distance to check for
    {
        d = d/600*75;
        a = point_direction(radarX,radarY,x,y)
        draw_sprite(spr_map_chest, 0, 75 + lengthdir_x(d,a), 600 + lengthdir_y(d,a));
    }
}
```

That is all for this object.

Next up is **obj_chest**, which has the sprite **spr_chest** and the origin as center. This is the item that the player needs to collect in their mini-quest.

The **Create Event** sets everything up, such as the sprite index and image speed so the subimage 0 is shown. The **has_opened** is used as a flag so we know if the chest is opened or closed, with **false** being closed; see Listing 17-3.

Listing 17-3. Setting Starting Values

```
///set up
image_speed=0;
image_index=0;
has_opened=false;
```

An **Alarm[0] Event** will destroy the instance, as shown in Listing 17-4.

Listing 17-4. Destroying the Instance on Alarm Trigger

```
instance_destroy();
```

Lastly there is a **Collision Event with obj_player**. This checks if the chest is not already opened, and changes the flag for **has_opened** to **true**, changes the subimage, and sets the **Alarm[0]** as shown in Listing 17-5.

Listing 17-5. Opening the Chest, Changing the Image, and Starting an Alarm

```
///open chest, change image, and set alarm
if !has_opened
{
    has_opened=true;
    image_index=1;
    alarm[0]=room_speed*4; //to destroy
}
```

That is all for this object.

Lastly there is the object **obj_clock_and_level_control**. This is used to show a timer that displays how much time the player has to complete their quest. It will also be used as a control object to check whether the player has completed the quest in time or the timer has run out.

It makes use of two sprites: **spr_clock_face** with the origin in the middle of the clock at 73x62, and **spr_clock_hand** with the origin set at 4x38.

obj_clock_and_level_control has the sprite **spr_clock_face**. The Create Event for **obj_clock_and_level_control** is shown in Listing 17-6. This sets the time available and also the initial alarm.

Listing 17-6. Setting the Time and Alarm

```
///set time and alarm
clock_time=360;
alarm[0]=room_speed;
```

An **Alarm[0] Event** reduces the time available and resets the alarm, as shown in Listing 17-7.

Listing 17-7. Restarting Alarm and Reducing Timer

```
///reset alarm and change time
alarm[0]=room_speed;
clock_time--;
```

The **Step Event** checks whether time has run out or the player has completed the quest; see Listing 17-8.

Listing 17-8. Checking Whether Completed or Out of Time and Going to the Corresponding Room

```
///Check if out of time or quest completed
if clock_time==0
{
    show_message("Out Of Time");
    game_restart();
}
if instance_number(obj_chest)==0
{
    show_message("Quest Complete");
    game_end();
}
```

The **Draw Event** just has a comment to prevent default drawing; see Listing 17-9.

Listing 17-9. Preventing Default Drawing

```
///comment to prevent default drawing
```

The **Draw GUI Event** draws the clock face and hand, as shown in Listing 17-10.

Listing 17-10. Drawing the Clock as a GUI Layer

```
draw_self();
draw_sprite_ext(spr_clock_hand,0,x,y,1,1,clock_time,0,1);
```

Figure 17-1 shows an example room layout with **obj_map**, **obj_clock_and_level_control**, and various instances of **obj_wall** and **obj_chest**.

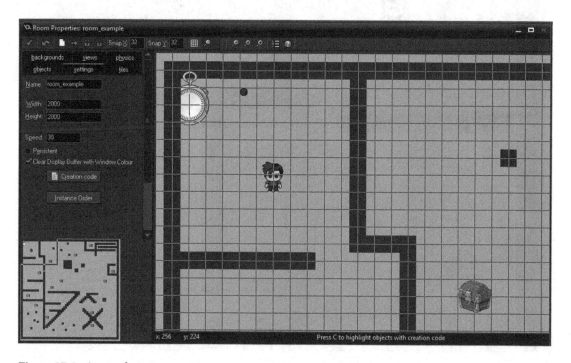

Figure 17-1. *A room layout*

Figure 17-2 shows the element in action.

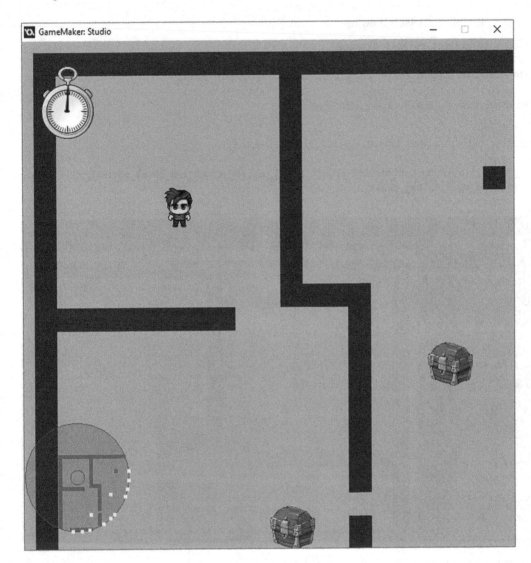

Figure 17-2. *This element in action*

CHAPTER 18

■ ■ ■

Multiple Locations

This example makes use of **Game_Base**.

This element's GMZ is **Multiple_Locations**.

An RPG generally has one large playfield, usually outside, and a number of smaller locations, such as inside buildings.

You'll need some system to transport from one room to another, and then back again. One method is to use separate objects to do this. When the player collides with the object, they are taken to the target location.

At this point, you're probably wondering how the rooms remember what has already happened in them, what's been collected, and what hasn't been collected. Fortunately GameMaker Studio allows you to set rooms as persistent. You can therefore move back and forth between rooms without having to save and load huge amounts of data.

As the rooms remember the x and y positions of all objects, including the player, we'll use a little trick. When the player collides with a door that will take them to another room, we will first move the player away from the door before going to the target room. This prevents infinite looping between target rooms.

First up we'll need some extra sprites and objects.

Create an object named **obj_church** and assign the sprite **spr_church** from the **resources** folder. There is no code for this object.

Next, load in sprite **spr_door** with the origin as center. This is assigned to two objects: **obj_church_enter** and **obj_church_leave**. There is no code for either of these objects.

Next up is **obj_chest** with **spr_chest** assigned. You can set the origin as center for this, and there is no code required.

There are three **Collision Events** to add for **obj_player**.

The first is **Collision Event with obj_church_enter**, with the code from Listing 18-1. Changing the y position is **very important**; it ensures that when you come back to this room the player object is not already touching the door. Failure to make this position change would send you straight back the target room.

Listing 18-1. Moving the Instance Away from the Door and Then Going to the Church Room

```
y+=150; //move away from door to prevent looping
room_goto(room_church);
```

The second is **Collision Event with obj_church_exit** with the code in Listing 18-2.

Listing 18-2. Moving the Player Away from the Church Door and Then Going to the Main Room

```
y+=150; //move away from door to prevent looping
room_goto(room_main_level);
```

Next is a **Collision Event with obj_chest**, with the code from Listing 18-3.

Listing 18-3. Increasing Gold and Then Destroying the Chest

```
global.gold++;
with (other) instance_destroy();
```

Finally, a **Draw Event** has been added for **obj_player**, with the code in Listing 18-4.

Listing 18-4. Drawing the Player's Sprite and How Much Gold

```
draw_self();
draw_text(x,y-100,global.gold);
```

Delete the room that is already present, and create a new room named **room_main_level** and set it as a size of 700x700.

Place one instance of **obj_church**, one of **obj_player**, a few of **obj_chest**, and one of **obj_church_enter**, so that it looks similar to Figure 18-1.

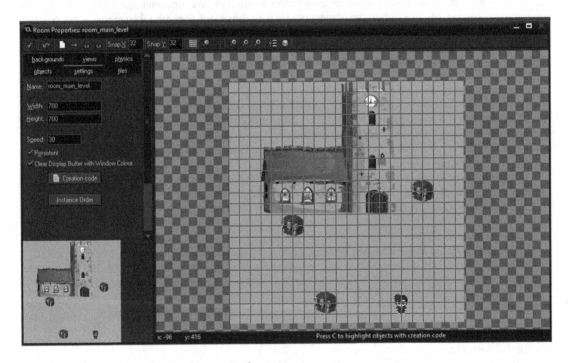

Figure 18-1. *room_main_level with an example setup*

The second room, **room_church**, requires a background named **bg_church**. Load that in now as a background.

Create a new room named **room_church**, set a size of 700x700, and assign this background, as shown in Figure 18-2.

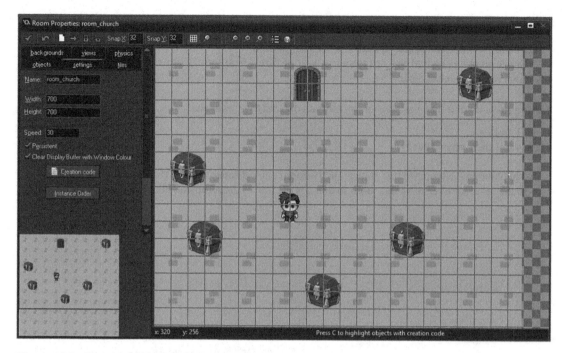

Figure 18-2. *Showing background assigned and objects added*

Go ahead and add objects so the room layout looks similar to Figure 18-2. The door instance shown is **obj_church_leave**.

Now set both of these rooms to persistent, in the settings tab, as shown in Figure 18-3.

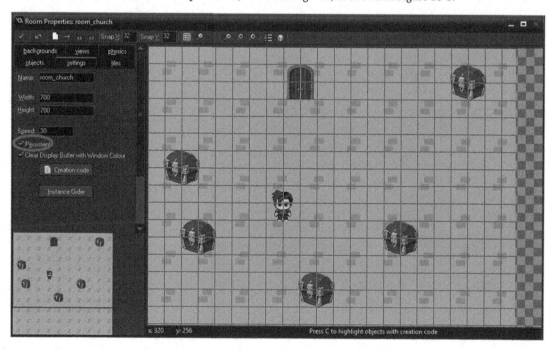

Figure 18-3. *Setting the room as persistent*

Lastly, create a splash screen room to set some initial data. If this was your own game, you'd set up variables or load a save file instead.

Create a room named **room_splash** and set it as 700x700.

Create an object named **obj_splash** with the code from Listing 18-5 in the **Create Event**. This will set the initial value of **global.gold**.

Listing 18-5. Setting Up a Variable for the Amount of Gold the Player Has

```
global.gold=0;
room_goto(room_main_level);
```

Just place one instance of this object into the room named **room_splash**. That is all for this room.

In the resource tree, move this room so that it is the first in the rooms section; this means it will run first.

CHAPTER 19

■ ■ ■

Positional Audio

This example is **Positional_Audio**.

It uses **Game_Base** as a template.

GameMaker Studio has a number of audio effects. One of them allows for positional audio. This plays audio at a volume dependent on the distance and direction between an audio emitter and an audio listener. It plays more through the left channel or right channel depending on the position. If you have surround sound speakers you'll also get front and back audio.

As mentioned before, use audio sparingly because too much can be annoying.

This example is set up to play the audio louder the closer you get to an object, and fade off at a certain distance, leaving just a gentle ambient sound.

This example plays audio for a fire and some water.

This example uses **Game_Base** as a template. There is one change. The **Step Event** of **obj_player** has a new code block, which updates the audio listener each step of the player's x and y location, as shown in Listing 19-1.

Listing 19-1. Noting the Player's Current Location and Updating the Sound Orientation

```
///Update audio position
audio_listener_position(x, y, 0);
audio_listener_orientation(0, -1, 0, 0, 0, -1);
```

There is an object named **obj_fire** with the sprite **spr_fire** assigned. This sprite has six subimages. Set the origin as center.

This object, **obj_fire**, has a **Create Event** with the code shown in Listing 19-2, which will play the fire sound on a loop.

Listing 19-2. Playing the Fire Sound at the Fire's Location

```
///play the sound at position
audio_play_sound_at(snd_fire, x, y, 0, 20, 400, 0.5 , true, 1);
```

The next object is **obj_water** with the sprite **spr_water** assigned, which has 10 subimages. The **Create Event** code again plays audio on a loop, as shown in Listing 19-3.

Listing 19-3. This Code Also Plays a Sound at the Instances Postion

```
///play the sound at position
audio_play_sound_at(snd_water, x, y, 0, 20, 400, 0.5 , true, 1);
```

© Ben Tyers 2017
B. Tyers, *Learn RPGs in GameMaker: Studio*, DOI 10.1007/978-1-4842-2946-0_19

You then need to load in the audio files called **snd_fire** and **snd_water**.
Figure 19-1 shows an example.

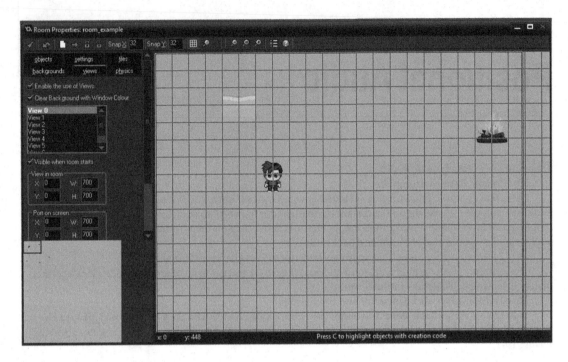

Figure 19-1. *The room setup*

CHAPTER 20

■ ■ ■

Respawn Points

The GMZ for this element is **Respawn_Point**.

This example makes use of **Depth_Based** as a template.

There will be places that you may not want your player to go, such as a bottomless pit or a lava flow. What should you do when the player collides with them?

One answer is a respawn point. You create a variable for both the x and y positions for a respawn point, and just move the player to that location.

This system is pretty simple to put into place. You have a respawn point; in this example, it is a flag. Upon collision with it, you store the location of the player as separate variables. Upon dying, you move the player back to this position.

Where you place these respawn flags is somewhat important. Good places are before and after a difficult point.

This example uses **Depth_Based** as a template.

There is one new object named **obj_water** that has the sprite **spr_water** assigned. There is no code for this object. That is all for this object.

The sprite **spr_flag** needs its collision mask changed, as shown in Figure 20-1.

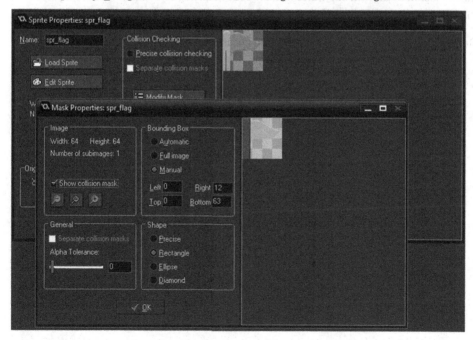

Figure 20-1. *Collision mask changed for sprite spr_flag*

© Ben Tyers 2017
B. Tyers, *Learn RPGs in GameMaker: Studio*, DOI 10.1007/978-1-4842-2946-0_20

The **Create Event** of **obj_player** has been changed. This addition makes an initial starting point for respawning; see Listing 20-1.

Listing 20-1. Additional Code for Storing a Starting Respawn Point

```
///set up
enum player_state {
    idle,
    up,
    down,
    left,
    right
    }

dir= player_state .down;
is_moving=false;
image_speed=0.5;
respawn_x=x;
respawn_y=y;
```

If the player collides with flag pole of **obj_flag**, the respawn points are updated. Open up **obj_player** and make a **Collision Event with obj_flag** with the code shown in Listing 20-2.

Listing 20-2. Updating the Respawn Position

```
respawn_x=x;
respawn_y=y;
```

Finally, add a **Collision Event with obj_water** with the code in Listing 20-3 that will make the player move to the respawn point.

Listing 20-3. Respawning (Moving) the Player to the Saved Location

```
x=respawn_x;
y=respawn_y;
```

Figure 20-2 shows an example room all set up.

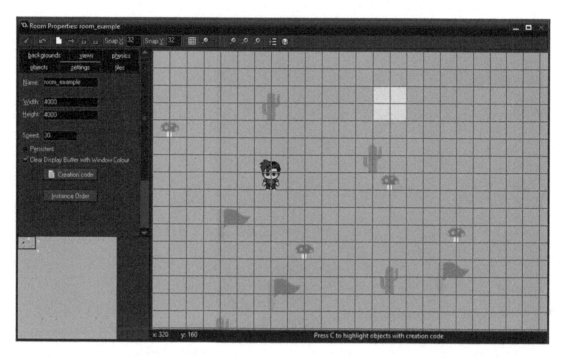

Figure 20-2. *The room all set up*

CHAPTER 21

■ ■ ■

Useable Items

This example's GMZ is **Usable_Items**.

It makes use of **Game_Base** as a template.

This element is almost a clone of the Inventory element, but with some distinct changes. As such, the whole process is shown.

So, your player spends plenty of time filling up their inventory with various items. It would be nice to give them something to do with the items.

Before programming for something like this, you should have already noted down some of the items that the player will need to collect and how they will be used, as shown in Figure 21-1. It's OK to tweak things here and there if you come up with more ideas.

© Ben Tyers 2017

B. Tyers, *Learn RPGs in GameMaker: Studio*, DOI 10.1007/978-1-4842-2946-0_21

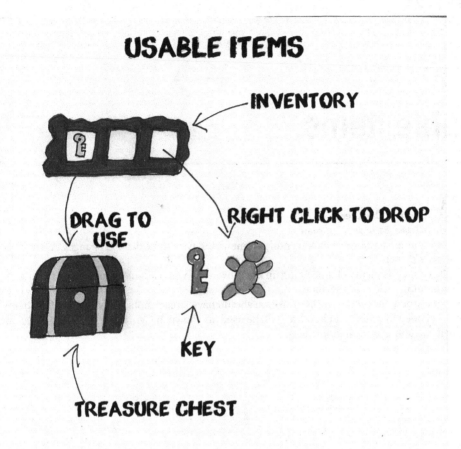

Figure 21-1. *Items and uses*

Each item has a unique reference, **my_id**. This is used to identify whether objects can be picked and held in the inventory. This value also matches the subimage of **spr_items**.

This example shows the use of three keys and three matching chests, each set as a different colour. You can pick up the keys with P and then left-click and drag to use them; you can use the right-mouse button to drop an item.

This element also includes the addition of being able to pick up a new item when the inventory is full. The new item will replace that which is in slot 0.

First up, load in the sprites required. There are quite a few.

The first is **spr_border**. This sprite is 64x64 in size and has a solid border and a transparent middle.

Next up is **spr_items**, which holds the sprites needed for drawing onto the inventory if collected. In this example it's 18x50 in size and consists of four subimages. The first subimage, index 0, is not used. The origin is set as the center. Figure 21-2 shows what this sprite looks like.

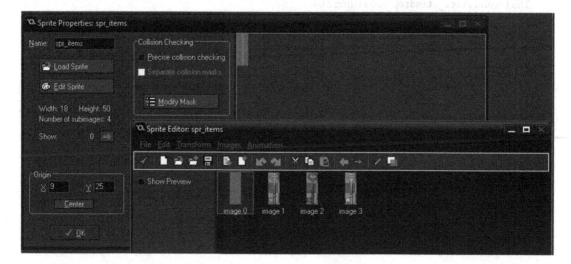

Figure 21-2. *The subimages of spr_items*

The next sprite is **spr_inv_bg**. This sprite is 325x104. This will draw the background of the inventory. The origin is set as 0,0.

Next up are three key sprites, each of which is a different colour. These are the items that the player picks up or puts down. The size of each is 23x64 with the origin as center. They are **spr_brown_key**, **spr_red_key**, and **spr_green_key**.

Next up is **spr_brown_chest**. This sprite has two subimages: index 0 is closed and index 1 is open. It is 64x43 in size and the origin is center. There two more chests, **spr_red_chest** and **spr_green_chest**, which share the same dimensions and origin, with a similar sprite index of 0 for closed and 1 for open. These chests are the items that the player will interact with; specifically she'll open them with the correct colour key.

The final sprite to add is **spr_collision**. This is solid red and has a size of only 1x1 pixel. This sprite will be applied to an object, so we have something to detect a collision between a key and a chest.

That is all the sprites loaded in.

This inventory system needs a few scripts.

The first one, shown in Listing 21-1, is **scr_itemcheck**.

Listing 21-1. Checking If an Item Is Present, and Returning True or False

```
for (var i = 0; i < global.maxItems; i += 1)
{
    if (global.inventory[i] == argument0) //if slot "i" contains argument 0
    {
        return true;
    }
}
return false;
```

The second is **scr_itemdrop**; see Listing 21-2.

Listing 21-2. Checking for Item and Removing It, Returning True or False

```
for (var i = 0; i < global.maxItems; i += 1)
{
    if (global.inventory[i] == argument0) //if slot "i" contains argument0
    {
        global.inventory[i] = -1;
        return true;
    }
}
return false;
```

The third is **scr_itemdrop_slot**, as shown in Listing 21-3.

Listing 21-3. Checking If Not Empty and Making It Empty, Returning True or False

```
//scr_itemdrop_slot(slot);

if (global.inventory[argument0] != -1)
{
    global.inventory[argument0] = -1;
    return true;
}
return false;
```

The fourth is **scr_itempickup_slot**, as shown in Listing 21-4.

Listing 21-4. Checking the Slot for an Empty Space and Adding It If Empty, Returning True or False

```
//scr_itempickup_slot(item,slot);
if (global.inventory[argument1] == -1)
{
    global.inventory[argument1] = argument0;
    return true;
}
return false;
```

The fifth is **scr_itempickup**. This script will check if a slot is available. If it is, it will add the item and return true; otherwise, false is returned, as shown in Listing 21-5.

Listing 21-5. If There's an Empty Slot, Adding to It and Returning True

```
for (var i = 0; i < global.maxItems; i += 1)
{
    if (global.inventory[i] == -1) //if slot "i" is empty
    {
        global.inventory[i] = argument0;
        return true;
    }
}
return false;
```

That's it for scripts.

There is a parent object for the three chests below; it is **obj_chest_parent** with no code or sprite.

The first chest object is **obj_brown_chest** with **spr_brown_chest** applied.

The **Create Event** code is shown in Listing 21-6.

Listing 21-6. Setting Up the Object for Use

```
my_id=1;
image_speed=0;
image_index=0;
```

Next is **obj_red_chest** with **spr_red_chest** applied. The **Create Event** code is shown in Listing 21-7.

Listing 21-7. Setting Up the Object for Use

```
my_id=2;
image_speed=0;
image_index=0;
```

Next is **obj_green_chest** with **spr_green_chest** applied. The **Create Event** code is shown in Listing 21-8.

Listing 21-8. Setting Up the Object for Use

```
my_id=3;
image_speed=0;
image_index=0;
```

As you will notice, the **my_id** values match up with subimages' colour of **spr_items**.

There is a parent object, **obj_pick_up_parent**. This will be used to allow items to be picked up and placed in the inventory, if there is room.

It has a **Collision Event with obj_player**, with the code in Listing 21-9. This will add the picked-up item to the next empty slot if available. If not available, it will place the item in slot 0 into the room and pick up the new item and put that in slot 0 instead.

Listing 21-9. Checking for an Empty Slot and Adding Accordingly

```
///Detect keypress and check for empty slot
if keyboard_check_pressed(ord('P'))
{
    if scr_itempickup(my_id) //if slot available, add to slot
    {
        instance_destroy(); //then destroy instance
    }
    else
    {
        switch (global.inventory[0])
        {
        case 1:
        instance_create(obj_player.x+50,obj_player.y,obj_brown_key);
        break;
        case 2:
        instance_create(obj_player.x+50,obj_player.y,obj_red_key);
        break;
        case 3:
        instance_create(obj_player.x+50,obj_player.y,obj_green_key);
        break;
        global.inventory[0]=-1;
        scr_itempickup(my_id);
        instance_destroy();
        }
    }
}
```

Next up are three keys. The first is **obj_brown_key** with the sprite **spr_brown_key** assigned. This has the **Create Event** code shown in Listing 21-10.

Listing 21-10. This Id Matches the Id of the Chest Colour

```
my_id=1;
```

obj_red_key has the red key sprite, **spr_red_key**, and the **Create Event** code shown in Listing 21-11.

Listing 21-11. This Id Matches the Id of the Chest Colour

```
my_id=2;
```

The last key object is **obj_green_key**, which has the green key sprite, **spr_green_key**, and the **Create Event** code shown in Listing 21-12.

Listing 21-12. This Id Matches the Id of the Chest Colour

```
my_id=3;
```

Set the parent of these three objects as **obj_pick_up_parent**.

Again, you will notice that the variables' **my_id**s match the values of the chests. This is how we're linking them up as useable items.

The next object is **obj_mouseitem** with the sprite **spr_collision**. This will allow the player to move an item from the inventory around the room.

It has a **Collision Event with obj_chest_parent**. This code will check that the colliding object has the same **my_id** as the picked-up item. If it does, it will execute the code, which in this example means changing the chest sprite's image index to 1 (showing it open); see Listing 21-13. In your games, you could do something completely different.

Listing 21-13. Opening the Chest If Possessing Matching Key

```
if other.my_id==global.mouseItem
{
    with (other) image_index=1;
    instance_destroy();
}
```

It also has a **Draw Event**, and the code is shown in Listing 21-14.

Listing 21-14. Drawing Sprite of Currently Held Item

```
var item=global.mouseItem;
if (item != -1)
{
    x = mouse_x;
    y = mouse_y;
    draw_sprite(spr_items,item,x,y);
}
```

The next object is **obj_invbutton**, which draws the appropriate item if present. The **Draw Event** code is shown in Listing 21-15.

Listing 21-15. Drawing the Inventory Items in Slots and Allowing the Right Mouse Button to Drop an Item

```
var item = global.inventory[slot];
var click = mouse_check_button_pressed(mb_left);

if (abs(mouse_x - x) < 30) && (abs(mouse_y- y) < 38)
{
    draw_set_colour(c_white);
    draw_rectangle(x-28,y-28,x+28,y+28,0);
    if (click)
    {
        if (item != -1)
        {
            scr_itemdrop_slot(slot);
        }
        if (global.mouseItem != -1)
        {
            scr_itempickup_slot(global.mouseItem,slot)
        }
        global.mouseItem = item;
    }
    if mouse_check_button_pressed(mb_right)
```

```
    {
        switch (global.inventory[slot])
        {
        case 1:
        instance_create(obj_player.x,obj_player.y,obj_brown_key);
        break;
        case 2:
        instance_create(obj_player.x,obj_player.y,obj_red_key);
        break;
        case 3:
        instance_create(obj_player.x,obj_player.y,obj_green_key);
        break;
        }
        //remove item from inventory
        global.inventory[slot]=-1;
    }
}

if (item != -1)
{
    draw_sprite(spr_items,item,x,y);
}
```

The final object is **obj_inventory**. It has a **Create Event** that sets everything up, as shown in Listing 21-16.

Listing 21-16. Creating the Inventory Slots

///Set up

```
global.maxItems=2; //total item slots

for (var i = 0; i < 4; i += 1)
{
    global.inventory[i] = -1;
    button[i] = instance_create(0,0,obj_invbutton)
    button[i].slot = i;
}

global.mouseItem=-1;
instance_create(0,0,obj_mouseitem);
```

This object also has a **Draw Event**, shown in Listing 21-17.

Listing 21-17. Drawing the Slots and Text Info

///draw the inventory
```
var x1,x2,y1,y2;
x1 = view_xview[0]+75;
x2 = x1 + view_wview[0];
y1 = view_yview[0]+30;
y2 = y1 + 64;
```

```
draw_set_colour(c_black);
draw_set_alpha(0.8);
draw_sprite(spr_inv_bg,0,x1,y1-25);

for (var i = 0; i < global.maxItems; i += 1)
{
    var ix = x1+64+(i * 60);
    var iy = y2-48;

    draw_sprite(spr_border,0,ix,iy)
    button[i].x = ix;
    button[i].y = iy;
}
draw_text(x1+100,y1+200,"P To Pick Up An Item When Touching# Click and Drag To Move & Use #
Right Click To Drop");
```

That's everything done.

Just place one instance of **obj_inventory** and one each of the chest and keys, as shown in Figure 21-3.

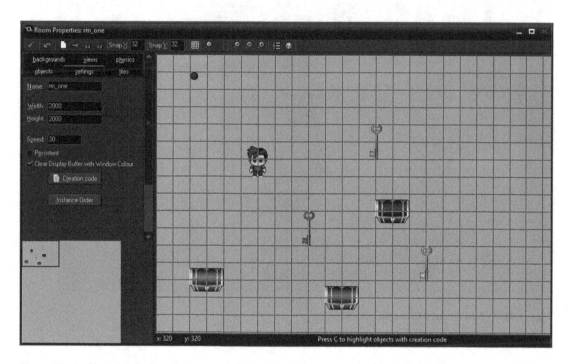

Figure 21-3. *An example room layout*

Figure 21-4 shows this element in action.

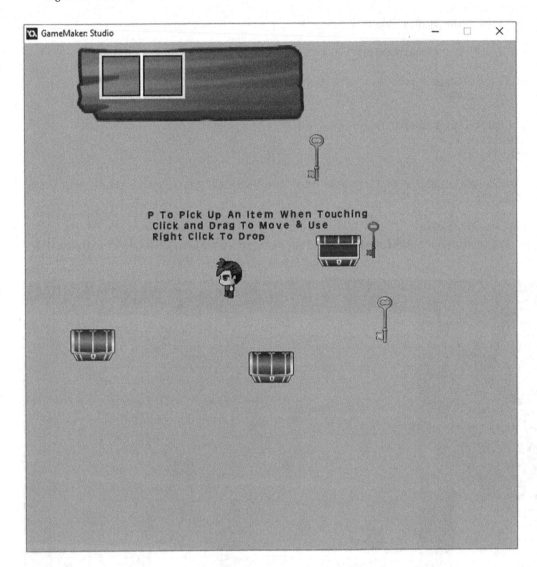

Figure 21-4. This element in action

CHAPTER 22

■ ■ ■

Weapon Control

This example use the **Game_Base** GMZ.

The GMZ for this element is **Weapon_Control**.

There may be quests or interactions that require the use of weapons. This element shows a basic example. It allows you to use a weapon. In this example, it just reduces the weapon count, and collect crates to increase the weapon count. The current weapon in use can be selected by scrolling the middle mouse button up and down.

It doesn't have to be limited to just weapons; it could be used with treasure hunting (element 31).

You could also increase the weapon count in other ways:

- By visiting the shop and buying extra ammo

- By ending a quest or solving a puzzle

- By visiting a secret area

This could easily be incorporated into a save system so weapon stats are saved.

This element uses **Game_Base** as a template.

There are four additional objects.

The first is **obj_hook_crate** with **spr_hook_crate** assigned. There is no code for this object.

The second is **obj_cutlass_crate** with **spr_cutlass_crate** assigned. There is no code for this object.

The third is **obj_gun_crate** with **spr_gun_crate** assigned. There is no code for this object.

All of the above three have the sprite origin as center.

The fourth object is **obj_hud** with **spr_hud_bg** assigned.

The **Create Event** code is shown in Listing 22-1. This will set up the starting values of the data used in this element. If this was your own game, you'd probably load this from an INI file.

Listing 22-1. Creating an Array to Hold Data About Each Weapon and Setting the Starting Weapon

```
///set up, inc array to hold data
global.weapon[1,1]="HOOK";
global.weapon[1,2]=20;
global.weapon[1,3]=spr_hook_hud;
global.weapon[1,4]=snd_hook;

global.weapon[2,1]="CUTLASS";
global.weapon[2,2]=10;
global.weapon[2,3]=spr_cutlass_hud
global.weapon[2,4]=snd_cutlass;

global.weapon[3,1]="GUN";
global.weapon[3,2]=40;
```

```
global.weapon[3,3]=spr_gun_hud;
global.weapon[3,4]=snd_gun;
```

//set selected weapon
```
global.selected=1;
```

The **Step Event** code, which allows selecting the weapon by scrolling the middle mouse button, is shown in Listing 22-2.

Listing 22-2. Allowing the Mouse Wheel to Be Used to Increase/Decrease the Value for a Selected Weapon

///select weapon with mouse wheel
```
if mouse_wheel_up()
{
    global.selected-=1;
    if global.selected==0 global.selected=3;
}

if mouse_wheel_down()
{
    global.selected+=1;
    if global.selected==4 global.selected=1;
}
```

The **Draw Event** code is shown in Listing 22-3.

Listing 22-3. Preventing the Automatic Drawing of a Sprite

///comment to prevent default drawing

The **Draw_GUI Event** code is shown in Listing 22-4.

Listing 22-4. Drawing the HUD and Info

///draw hud
//set alpha at 50%
```
draw_set_alpha(0.5);

draw_sprite(spr_hud_bg,0, 0,550); //background
```

//set up text
```
draw_set_font(drawing_font);
draw_set_halign(fa_center);
draw_set_valign(fa_middle);
```

//draw data
```
for (var loop = 1; loop < 4; loop += 1)
{
    draw_text(200+100*loop,590,global.weapon[loop,1]); //name
    draw_text(200+100*loop,650,global.weapon[loop,2]); //amount
    draw_sprite(global.weapon[loop,3],0,200+100*loop,645); //sprite
    //draw border if selected
    if loop==global.selected draw_sprite(spr_show_selected,0,200+100*loop,645);
}
```

```
//reset alpha to normal
draw_set_alpha(1);
```

```
//info
draw_text(400,50,"Touch Crate To Pick Up#Middle Mouse Button Up / Down To Select#Left
Mouse To Use");
```

There are some additions to **obj_player**.

An additional block of code for the **Step Event** is shown in Listing 22-5. On mouse click, it checks for ammo, plays a sound, and reduces count. Otherwise, it plays a sound to indicate no ammo.

Listing 22-5. On Mouse Click, Checks for Ammo, Plays a Sound, and Reduces Count

```
///use weapon
if mouse_check_button_pressed(mb_left)
{
    if global.weapon[global.selected,2]>0
    {

        audio_play_sound(global.weapon[global.selected,4],1,false);
        global.weapon[global.selected,2]--;
    }
    else
    audio_play_sound(snd_no_ammo,1,false);
}
```

A **Collision Event with obj_hook_crate** uses the code in Listing 22-6 to increase the number of kooks available to use and destroys the other.

Listing 22-6. Increasing the Number of Kooks Available and Destroying Other

```
global.weapon[1,2]+=10;
with (other) instance_destroy();
```

A **Collision Event with obj_cutlass_crate**, via the code in Listing 22-7, increases the inventory for the cutlass and destroys the ammo box.

Listing 22-7. Increasing Inventory for the Cutlass and Destroying the Ammo Box

```
global.weapon[2,2]+=10;
with (other) instance_destroy();
```

A **Collision Event with obj_gun_crate** uses the code in Listing 22-8 to increase the number of guns and destroy the other.

Listing 22-8. Increasing the Number of Guns and Destroying Other

```
global.weapon[3,2]+=10;
with (other) instance_destroy();
```

When you're done, **obj_player** will look like Figure 22-1.

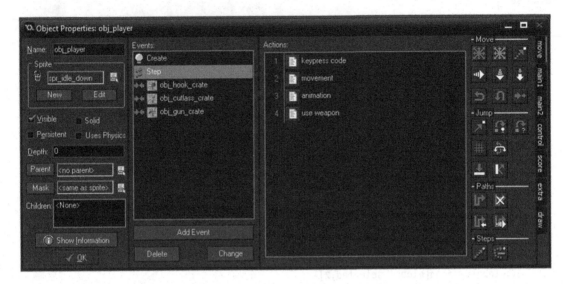

Figure 22-1. *Additions to obj_player*

In addition, there is a font, **drawing_font**, which is Arial size 18.
Figure 22-2 shows the room layout.

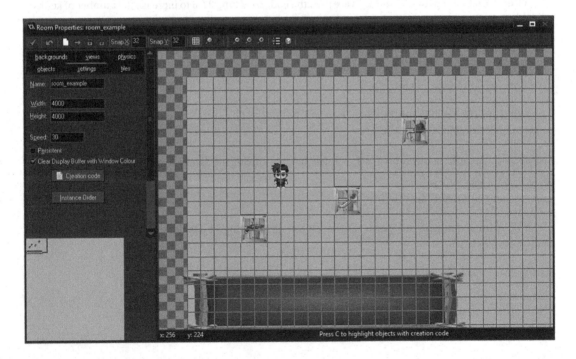

Figure 22-2. *The room layout*

Figure 22-3 shows what this element looks like in action.

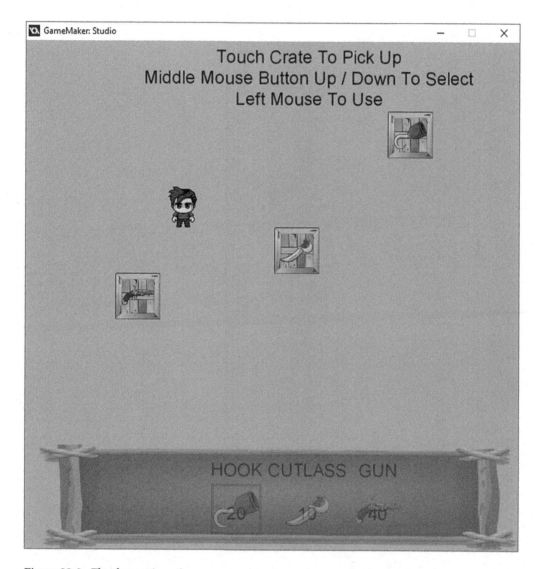

Figure 22-3. *The element in action*

CHAPTER 23

Zooming

This example makes use of **Depth_Based** GMZ.

The GMZ for this element is **Zooming**.

This simple example allows for zooming in and out to the player's position.

It uses keypresses, although you could equally do this in code.

Zooming can be used to create an emphasis of something happening, such as

- When near a special object

- When dying

- When entering/leaving a room

- When starting a boss battle

Effects such as this can add a lot to a game. However, use them sparingly because too many visual effects can be annoying for the player.

There are several additions to **Depth_Based** GMZ.

Listing 23-1 shows a view control object named **obj_view_control** with a **Create Event**.

Listing 23-1. Setting the Initial View and Required Variables

```
view=700;
min_view=50;
max_view=1200;
view_wview[0]=view;
view_hview[0]=view;
zoom_in=false;
zoom_out=false;
```

© Ben Tyers 2017

B. Tyers, *Learn RPGs in GameMaker: Studio*, DOI 10.1007/978-1-4842-2946-0_23

A **Step Event** uses the code in Listing 23-2 to enable the use of keys Z and X to change the zoom within a given range.

Listing 23-2. Allowing the Use of Z and X Keys to Change Zoom Within a Given Range

```
///zoom control
//zoom in
if keyboard_check(ord('X'))
{
    view+=5;
}


//zoom out
if keyboard_check(ord('Z'))
{
    view-=5;
}


//check in range
view = clamp(view, min_view, max_view);


//set view
view_wview[0]=view;
view_hview[0]=view;
```

Finally, Listing 23-2 shows the **Draw GUI Event**.

Listing 23-3. Drawing Info on How to Use This Element

```
draw_text(50,50," Z / X To Zoom In & Out");
```

One instance of **obj_view_control** should be placed in the room. Figure 23-1 shows this element in action.

Figure 23-1. *The zooming element in action*

CHAPTER 24

■ ■ ■

Destructible Terrain

This example makes use of **Depth_Based**.

The GMZ for this element is **Destructible_Terrain**.

Having items that can be built or destroyed is a good idea.

This example allows for the destruction of solid blocks. It will also randomly (1 in 3 chance) create a treasure chest.

A great way of using this approach is to limit how many times the player can use a pick to destroy blocks. You could award picks at other points in the game, so the player needs to come back to the "destroy blocks" section to destroy blocks.

A nice twist would be a maze of some kind that uses solid and destroyable blocks, perhaps with the aim that the player should find the loot hidden within that maze.

Other ideas would be buildings that the player needs to enter but are surrounded by blocks, which the player has to destroy to gain access.

However you decide to use this method, it's bound to make an important contribution to the game play.

There are additions to **Depth_Based** GMZ.

© Ben Tyers 2017
B. Tyers, *Learn RPGs in GameMaker: Studio*, DOI 10.1007/978-1-4842-2946-0_24

obj_block has **spr_block** assigned and it has six subimages, as shown in Figure 24-1.

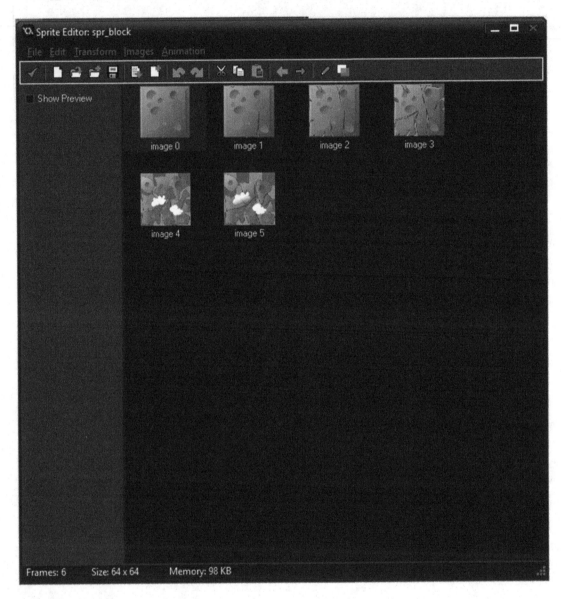

Figure 24-1. *Subimages of spr_block*

The **Create Event** code for **obj_block** is shown in Listing 24-1.

Listing 24-1. Setting Initial Damage and Sprite Frame, Preventing Animation

```
///set up
damage=0;
image_speed=0;
image_index=damage;
```

Next is the **Step Event** code, shown in Listing 24-2, which will test the damage and, if destroyed, will create a treasure chest with a 1 in 3 chance. It also sets the image index to match the damage.

Listing 24-2. Setting Damage and Probability of Creating Treasure

```
///test and set damage
if damage==6
{
    if irandom(3)==1 instance_create(x,y,obj_treasure);
    instance_destroy();
}
image_index=damage;
```

That is all for this object.

obj_treasure has the sprite **spr_treasure** assigned. There is no code for this object.

obj_crate has the sprite **spr_crate** assigned. Also, there is no code for this object.

There are few changes to **obj_player**. The **Create Event** needs to be updated to the code in Listing 24-3.

Listing 24-3. Picking How Many Times a Player Can Damage a Block

```
///set up
enum player_state{
    idle,
    up,
    down,
    left,
    right
    }

dir= player_state.down;
is_moving=false;
image_speed=0.5;
pick=10;
```

The **Step Event** has an additional code block, which will damage the block in the direction the player is pointing if the player has any picks; see Listing 24-4.

Listing 24-4. Looking for a Block in the Direction the Player Is Pointing. If It Is Near, Damage Will Be Applied.

```
///damage block && control
if keyboard_check_pressed(ord('D')) && pick>0
{

    //check for block right
    if dir== player_state.right&& position_meeting(x+34,y-16,obj_block) //see if a block is
    there
    {
            block=instance_position(x+34,y-16,obj_block); //get the id of the block
            block.damage+=1; //damage the block
            pick--;
    }
```

```
//check for block left
if dir== player_state.left && position_meeting(x-34,y-16,obj_block) //see if a block is
there
{
        block=instance_position(x-34,y-16,obj_block); //get the id of the block
        block.damage+=1; //damage the block
        pick--;
}

//check for block down
if dir== player_state.down &&  position_meeting(x,y+16,obj_block) //see if a block is
there
{
        block=instance_position(x,y+16,obj_block);   //get the id of the block
        block.damage+=1; //damage the block
        pick--;
}

//check for block up
if dir== player_state.up && position_meeting(x,y-34,obj_block)  //see if a block is
there
{
        block=instance_position(x,y-34,obj_block); //get the id of the block
        block.damage+=1; //damage the block
        pick--;
}
}
```

In addition there is a **Collision Event with obj_crate**. The code shown in Listing 24-5 will increase the pick count by 10 and destroy the crate.

Listing 24-5. Providing an Additional Pick to Damage Blocks

```
pick+=10;
with (other) instance_destroy();
```

There is also a new **Draw GUI Event** with the code shown in Listing 25-6.

Listing 24-6. Drawing Info and How Many Picks Left

```
draw_text(50,50,"Press D When Facing Block");
draw_text(350,50,"Current Picks"+string(pick));
draw_sprite(spr_pick_hud,0,550,50);
```

That is all.

Set up your room like that shown in Figure 24-2.

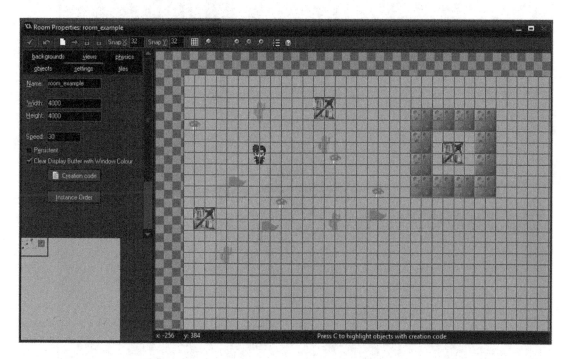

Figure 24-2. *An example room setup*

Figure 24-3 shows this element in action.

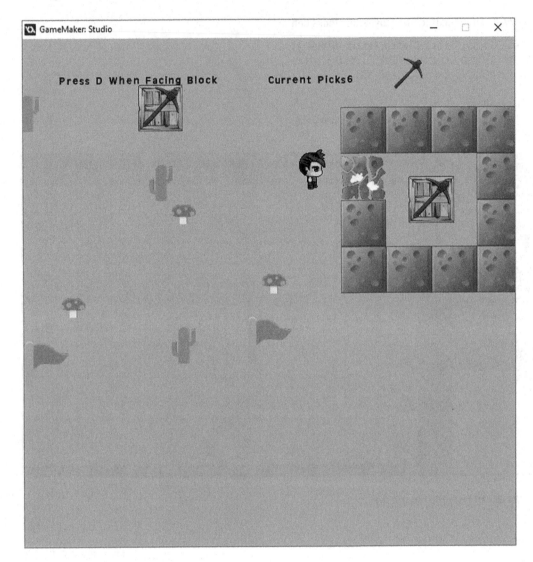

Figure 24-3. *The element in action*

CHAPTER 25

Dashing

This element makes use of **Depth_Based** GMZ.

The GMZ for this element is **Dashing**.

There will be times when you want some variation in player movement. One thing you can add is dashing. This could be used by a player to escape tricky situations, such as avoiding a marauding enemy. You may want to limit how often/much the player can use this ability.

One approach is to use a instance variable that reduces when dashing is used and slowly replenishes over time.

The addition of a graphical effect would add this.

That is exactly what this element does: there is a bar above the player that shows the current dashing energy that is available. It goes down when used and up slowly over time. A simple graphical star effect is displayed when in use.

In your own game, you may want to draw this on your HUD.

You could use this system for things other than dashing, such as

- Faster destroying of blocks

- Ability to walk over lava

- A timing system for a mini-quest

It requires additions to Game_Base GMZ.

The **Create Event** of obj_player needs to change to the code in Listing 25-1, which sets up the additional starting variables needed.

Listing 25-1. Additions to Set a Flag for Dashing, Show How Much Remains, and an Initial Alarm

```
///set up
enum player_state {
    idle,
    up,
    down,
    left,
    right
    }
dir= player_state .down;
is_moving=false;
image_speed=0.5;

dashing=false;
dashing_meter=100;
alarm[0]=room_speed/3;
```

© Ben Tyers 2017

B. Tyers, *Learn RPGs in GameMaker: Studio*, DOI 10.1007/978-1-4842-2946-0_25

You will also need an **Alarm[0] Event** that is used to replenish the dash meter once every 1/3 seconds. It will also keep it at a maximum value of 100; see Listing 25-2.

Listing 25-2. Restarting Alarm and Replenishing Dashing Meter

```
alarm[0]=room_speed/3;
dashing_meter++;
if dashing_meter>100 dashing_meter=100;
```

There is an additional code block in the **Step Event** that takes care of the dashing movement; see Listing 25-3.

Listing 25-3. Allowing Dashing in Direction If Player Has Any Dashing Meter and There Is No Obstacle in the Way

```
///dashing movement
dashing = keyboard_check(ord("D"));
if dashing_meter>1 && is_moving && dashing
{
if dir==player_state.left && !position_meeting(x-8,y,obj_solid_base) && !position_meeting
(x-4,y,obj_solid_base)
{
    effect_create_above(ef_star,x,y,1,c_red);
    x-=8;
    dashing_meter--;
}
if  dir==player_state.right  && !position_meeting(x+8,y,obj_solid_base) && !position_meeting
(x+4,y,obj_solid_base)
{
    effect_create_above(ef_star,x,y,1,c_red);
    x+=8;
    dashing_meter--;
}
if dir==player_state.up &&!position_meeting(x,y-8,obj_solid_base) && !position_meeting
(x,y-4,obj_solid_base)
{
    effect_create_above(ef_star,x,y,1,c_red);
    y-=8;
    dashing_meter--;
}
if dir==player_state.down && !position_meeting(x,y+8,obj_solid_base) && !position_meeting
(x,y+4,obj_solid_base)
{
    effect_create_above(ef_star,x,y,1,c_red);
    y+=8;
    dashing_meter--;
}
}
depth=-y;
```

There is a **Draw Event** to draw the sprite and the dashing meter; see Listing 25-4.

Listing 25-4. Drawing Self and a Meter to Show Remaining Dashing

```
draw_self();
//draw dash_meter
draw_set_colour(c_red);
draw_roundrect(x-51,y-76,x+51,y-69,false);
draw_set_colour(c_green);
draw_roundrect(x-50,y-75,x-50+dashing_meter,y-70,false);
```

Finally you need a **Draw GUI Event**, just for testing; see Listing 25-5.

Listing 25-5. Showing Info on How to Use Dashing

```
draw_text(50,50,"Hold Down D To Dash - Works When You Have Dash Meter HP");
```

Figure 25-1 shows the obj_player set up with the changes.

Figure 25-1. *obj_player with changes made*

Figure 25-2 shows this element in action.

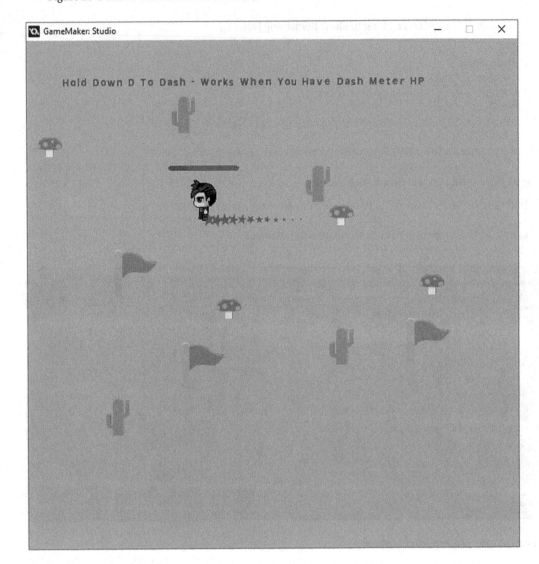

Figure 25-2. This element in action

CHAPTER 26

■ ■ ■

Quest Completion

The GMZ for this element is **Quest_Completion**.

An RPG may have plenty of mini-quests, puzzles, and games.

It's important to track the player's progress in them in an easily accessible way.

Using an array that stores the quest and whether it is completed or not is one approach. By using a global array this data can be accessed, used, and changed as needed. This also allows for easy saving and loading of this data as and when required.

This example demonstrates a basic method for four quests, although the priniciple would remain the same whether it would be ten or a hundred.

In this example, keypresses are used to toggle between completed (true) and not completed (false). You could of course change this at any point within your game, for example when a puzzle game is completed.

This approach could also be used for other things in your game, for example whether a boss has been defeated or not.

Element 40 (saving) demonstrates how to load and save this data.

This element uses just one object. The **Create Event** code sets up the variables needed. If this was your own game, you'd probably be loading this data from an INI file (see element 40, Saving).

The code is shown in Listing 26-1.

Listing 26-1. Setting Up an Array to Hold Four Quests, Setting Them as True or False

```
///Set up data
quest[1,1]="Collect 100 Treasure Chests"; //name of quest
quest[1,2]=false; //whether completed (true) or not completed (false)

quest[2,1]="Defeat All Bosses"; //name of quest
quest[2,2]=true; //whether completed (true) or not completed (false)

quest[3,1]="Puzzle Room"; //name of quest
quest[3,2]=false; //whether completed (true) or not completed (false)

quest[4,1]="Find All Hidden Locations"; //name of quest
quest[4,2]=false; //whether completed (true) or not completed (false)
```

© Ben Tyers 2017
B. Tyers, *Learn RPGs in GameMaker: Studio*, DOI 10.1007/978-1-4842-2946-0_26

The **Step Event** code for testing is shown in Listing 26-2. In your own game, you would probably have other triggers instead of keypresses.

Listing 26-2. Allowing Changing of Flags for Whether a Quest Is Completed

```
///toggle completion true/false
//for example only
if keyboard_check_pressed(ord('1'))
{
    quest[1,2]=!quest[1,2]
}

if keyboard_check_pressed(ord('2'))
{
    quest[2,2]=!quest[2,2]
}

if keyboard_check_pressed(ord('3'))
{
    quest[3,2]=!quest[3,2]
}

if keyboard_check_pressed(ord('4'))
{
    quest[4,2]=!quest[4,2]
}
```

Finally there is the **Draw Event** code (Listing 26-3), which is also for testing. In your own game, you may wish to display the information in your HUD or as a pop-up window.

Listing 26-3. Drawing the Quest and Showing Its State by Using Red or Green

```
for (var loop = 1; loop <= 4; loop += 1)
{
    //set drawing colour based on true/false
    if quest[loop,2]
    {
        draw_set_colour(c_green);
    }
    else
    {
        draw_set_colour(c_red);
    }
    //draw description
    draw_text(10,100+(loop*100),quest[loop,1]);
    //draw completed or not
    if quest[loop,2]
    {
        draw_text(500,100+(loop*100),"Completed");
    }
```

```
    else
    {
        draw_text(500,100+(loop*100),"Not Completed");
    }

}

draw_set_colour(c_black);
draw_text(10,700,"Press 1 2 3 4 To Toggle");
```

Figure 26-1 shows this element in action.

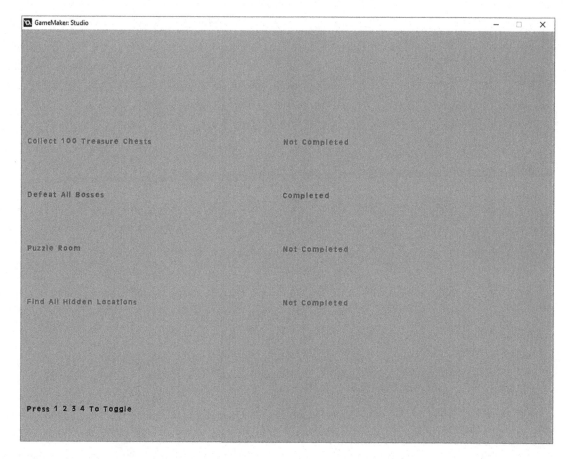

Figure 26-1. *This element in action*

■ ■ ■

CHAPTER 27

Road Builder

The GMZ for this element is **Road_Builder**.

It makes use of the **Game_Base** GMZ.

This element allows for the creation of a road/walkway that the player can walk upon.

This could be used, for example, to make a bridge over some water to an island that would otherwise be inaccessible to the player. This could be combined with a shop where the player has to purchase the road sections using their hard-earned loot.

Systems such as this provide more variation for the player, and to some extent force the player to plan ahead as to what they'll do with their cash.

This element is pretty simple. It allows placing of road instances in empty places, which then link up to other road instances next to it, using a bit of cool math to generate the correct road instance shape, and updating those around it as needed.

If you are using the above example (allowing the player to reach an otherwise inaccessible location and ensuring that their reward is worth their time, effort, and loot, such as an island covered in gold coins and treasure chests, a key to open a door, a treasure map to use elsewhere, etc.) you get the idea.

This makes use of **Game_Base** GMZ, with some changes to **obj_player**.

The first **Step Event** block of **obj_player** has a change to the movement block, as shown in Listing 27-1.

Listing 27-1. Allowing the Player to Move If There Is a Road in the Direction They Want to Go

```
///movement
if is_moving
{
    switch (dir)
    {
        case player_state.up:
        if position_meeting(x,y-4,obj_road) y -= 4;
        break;

        case player_state.down:
        if position_meeting(x,y+4,obj_road)y += 4;
        break;

        case player_state.left:
        if position_meeting(x-4,y,obj_road) x -= 4;
        break;

        case player_state.right:
        if position_meeting(x+4,y,obj_road) x += 4;
        break;
    }
}
```

That is the only change for this object.

Next, **obj_updater** has the sprite **spr_updater** assigned, which needs the *precise collision checking* option on. The **Create Event** code for this object is shown in Listing 27-2. Here you're setting an alarm for one frame to make the next step happen. This is so other objects can interact with it before it's destroyed.

Listing 27-2. Setting an Alarm for One Frame

```
alarm[0]=1; //make it happen in next step
```

The **Alarm[0] Event** code is shown in Listing 27-3.

Listing 27-3. Destroying the Instance

```
instance_destroy();
```

That is all for this object.

Next up is object **obj_road** that has the sprite **spr_road** assigned, which needs *precise collision checking* and *separate collision masks* set. The subimages must look like those shown in Figure 27-1. It is very important to get the correct order.

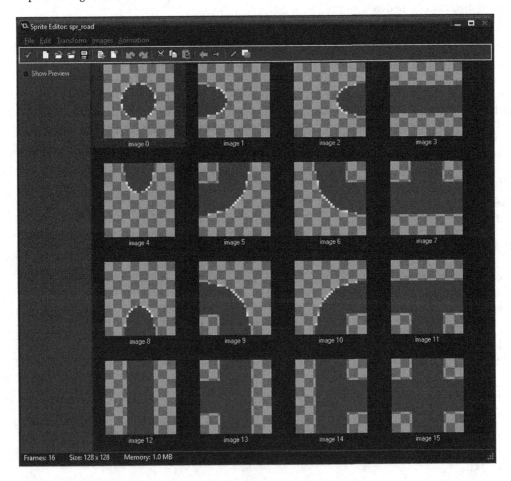

Figure 27-1. *The order of subimages for spr_road*

The **Create Event** for **obj_road** is shown in Listing 27-4.

Listing 27-4. Stopping Auto-Animation

```
image_speed = 0; //we dont want any animation
```

There is a **Collision Event with obj_updater**, the code for which is shown in Listing 27-5.

Listing 27-5. Running the User Event 0

```
event_user(0); //run event
```

Next up for this object is a **Room Start Event**. This is in the **Other** tab, as shown as in Figure 27-2.

Figure 27-2. *Showing where to find the room start event*

The code for this **Room Start Event** is shown in Listing 27-6.

Listing 27-6. Running User Event 0

```
event_user(0); //run event
```

Next up for the same object is a **User Defined 0 Event**. This event can also be found in the **Other** tab.

The code uses some clever math to work out which subimage should be used, based on its neighboring instances. A value is added for each place meeting, and the combined total equals an appropriate subimage. See Listing 27-7.

Listing 27-7. Determining Which Subimage Should Be Drawn

```
// event_user(0) - updates subimage according to surrounding tiles
var t, b, l, r, d, j;
j = object_index;
d = 128;
t = place_meeting(x, y - d, j);
b = place_meeting(x, y + d, j);
r = place_meeting(x + d, y, j);
p = place_meeting(x - d, y, j);
image_index = p + r * 2 + t * 4 + b * 8; //some clever math (based on binary representation)
```

That is all for this object.

The next object is **obj_hud_and_set_up**. This is used for testing this element.

The **Create Event** code is shown in Listing 27-8.

Listing 27-8. Creating Initial Variables

```
///set up
global.amount=100;
global.cash=1000;
```

The **Step Event** code is shown in Listing 27-9.

Listing 27-9. Allowing the Player to Purchase More Road-Building Items

```
///allow buying
if keyboard_check_released(ord('B')) && global.cash>10
{
    global.amount+=10;
    global.cash-=10;
}
```

Finally, there is a **Draw Event**, as shown in Listing 27-10.

Listing 27-10. Drawing the Text Info

```
draw_text(50,50,"Click To Add Road#B To Buy Road + Move With Arrow Keys");
draw_text(50,80,"Amount: "+string(global.amount));
draw_text(50,110,"Cash: "+string(global.cash));
```

That is all for this object.

The final object is **obj_build** with **Global Left Mouse Event**; see Listing 27-11.

Listing 27-11. Creating a Road and Updater Instance If the Mouse Is Clicked in an Empty Space

```
can_build = true; //allow building

if can_build && global.amount>1 && !position_meeting(mouse_x, mouse_y, obj_road) //check if
position free
{
    cx = floor(mouse_x / 128) * 128; //snap to imaginary grid
    cy = floor(mouse_y / 128) * 128;
    instance_create(cx, cy, obj_road); //create pipe
    instance_create(cx, cy, obj_updater); //create updater
    global.amount--;
}
```

Next up you need to load in a background named **back_test**.

Finally, change the room settings so the background **back_test** is tiled, as shown in Figure 27-3.

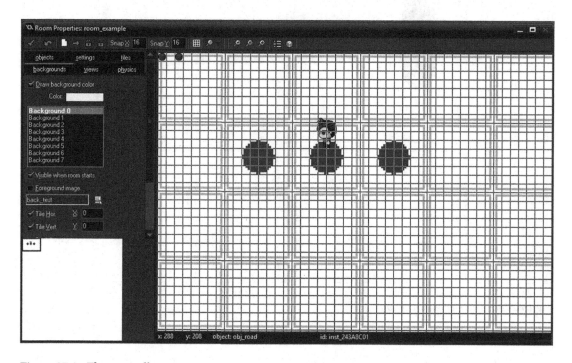

Figure 27-3. *The room all set up*

Place some instance of the objects in the room as shown in Figure 27-3. The two blue circles in the top left of the room editor are **obj_build** and **obj_hud_and_set_up**.

Figure 27-4 shows this element in progress.

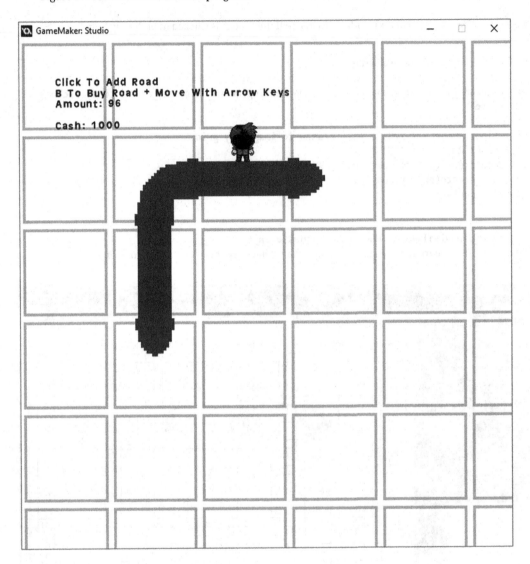

Figure 27-4. *This element in action*

■ ■ ■

CHAPTER 28

Character Progression Upgrade

The GMZ for this element is **Character_Progression_Upgrade**.

Character progression is the development of player characteristics as the player progresses through the game. These can be positive traits, like kindness and charisma, and negative ones, such as evilness. These traits can be updated depending on actions performed within the game.

Positive interactions, which could boost positive characteristics, could be

- Being polite and friendly in character interactions

- Rescuing creatures from rivers

- Giving food/drink to other characters

Negative interactions could be

- Robbing/killing other main characters

- Cutting down too many trees

- Being rude and blunt in character interactions

These traits can be stored as global variables and updated as needed.

You could also base interactions depending on the current values of these traits. This would allow different game progression and outcomes depending on how positively/negatively the player has been so far in the game, such as

- Only allowing access to a church if the player has more kindness than evilness

- A discount in the shop if the player has been kind to other players

- A bonus level for feeding wild animals

This element draws the traits on screen, with buttons to change values. This provides a number of points the player can assign. You could change these values based on anything that the player does within the game.

This element has three objects. The first is **obj_splash** and it sets up the data. If this was your own game, you'd be loading it in from an INI file (see element 40: saving).

The **Create Event** code is shown in Listing 28-1. It employs a simple approach of using a 2D array to hold the data. There are other ways of doing this, but this serves as a great introduction.

Listing 28-1. Setting Up an Array with Various Traits/Abilities and Values for Them

```
///set up stats
//would load from saved data in actual game
global.stats[1,1]="Magic";
global.stats[1,2]=6;
global.stats[2,1]="Kindness";
global.stats[2,2]=8;
global.stats[3,1]="Evilness";
global.stats[3,2]=2;
global.stats[4,1]="Strength";
global.stats[4,2]=3;
global.stats[5,1]="Wisdom";
global.stats[5,2]=0;
global.stats[5,1]="Charisma";
global.stats[5,2]=0;
global.upgrades=6;


//goto main room
room_goto(room_character_progression);
```

There is an additional sprite named **spr_info** that is 32x32 in size. It has two subimages: the first is solid yellow and the second is solid red. The origin for both is center.

Next up is **obj_button**. This **spr_button** has two subimages. Image 0 is green, image 1 is red, and the origin for both is center. The **Create Event** code for this object is shown in Listing 28-2.

Listing 28-2. Preventing Animation and Setting Initial Subimage

```
image_speed=0;
image_index=0;
```

The **Step Event** code, which allows upgrading, is shown in Listing 28-3.

Listing 28-3. Allowing Upgrades If a Player Has Enough Upgrades Remaining

```
///mouse button
if mouse_check_button_pressed(mb_left) && position_meeting(mouse_x, mouse_y, id)
{
    if global.upgrades>0 && global.stats[my_id,2]<10
    {
        //upgrade
        global.upgrades--;
        global.stats[my_id,2]++;
    }
}
```

Finally for this object, a **Draw Event** displays the values visually and whether an upgrade is available or not; see Listing 28-4.

Listing 28-4. Drawing Sprites and Whether Available or Not

```
draw_self();
//draw the text
draw_set_valign(fa_middle);
draw_set_halign(fa_left);
draw_text(50,my_id*100,global.stats[my_id,1]);


//draw red sprite - not the quickest approach, but easy to understange
for (var loop=1; loop < 11; loop += 1)
{
    draw_sprite(spr_info,1,150+loop*40,my_id*100)
}


//draw yellow sprite
for (var loop=1; loop < global.stats[my_id,2]+1; loop += 1)
{
    draw_sprite(spr_info,0,150+loop*40,my_id*100)
}


draw_set_halign(fa_center);
if global.stats[my_id,2]<10 && global.upgrades>0
{
    image_index=0;
    draw_text(x,y,"Available");
}
else if global.stats[my_id,2]==10
{
    image_index=1;
    draw_text(x,y,"Maxed Out");
}
else
{
    image_index=1;
    draw_text(x,y,"Not Available");
}
```

The third and final object is **obj_setup_buttons_and_hud**, which has the **Create Event** that makes the buttons and assigns an instance variable named **my_id**; see Listing 28-5.

Listing 28-5. Creating Buttons for the Player to Use

```
///create buttons
for (var loop = 1; loop < 6; loop += 1)
{
    button=instance_create(700,100*loop,obj_button);
    button.my_id=loop
}
```

Listing 28-6 shows a **Step Event** for testing purposes.

Listing 28-6. Allowing You to Test More Quickly

```
if keyboard_check_released(ord('R'))
{
    game_restart();
}
```

There is also a **Draw Event**, also for testing purposes; see Listing 28-7.

Listing 28-7. Displaying the Player's Remaining Upgrades

```
draw_set_halign(fa_left);

draw_text(100,50,"You Have "+string(global.upgrades)+" Upgrade Points - Press R To Restart
Example");
```

That is all for the objects.

There are two rooms: the first is **room_splash**, which is 1024x768 in size and has one instance of **obj_splash**.

The second room is **room_character_progression** and it has one instance of **obj_setup_buttons_ and_hud**.

Figure 28-1 shows this element in action.

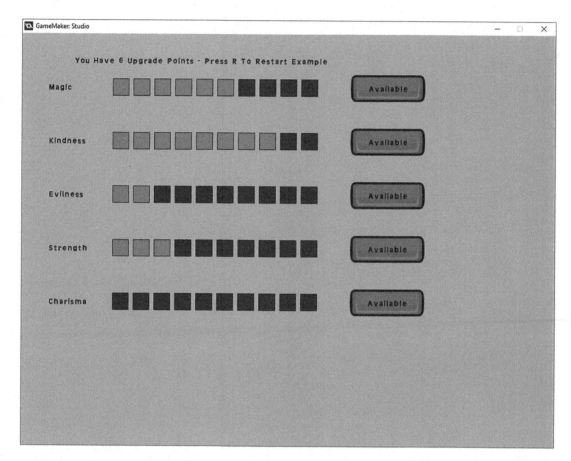

Figure 28-1. *The element in action*

CHAPTER 29

■ ■ ■

Party Mechanics

The GMZ for this element is **Party_Mechanics**.

It uses the **Depth_Based** GMZ as the template.

Party mechanics is the process of being able to switch between characters during the game. This is usually because one character may be better than another at something, such as

- Moving more quickly

- Able to swim

- Better skills at fighting

- Able to climb a mountain

- Quicker at mining/treasure hunting

- Has an appropriate skill set for a mini-quest/puzzle room

In this example, you can switch between characters using keys 1, 2, and 3.

In this example,

- 1 is the main character as normal

- 2 is in red and can move faster

- 3 is green and will chop down trees if she walks into one

In your own game, you would probably give each one more distinctive characteristics, which you set at game start from an INI file or create as new.

This example makes use of the **Game_Base** with some changes to it.

The **obj_player** has been renamed **obj_player_parent**.

There are some changes to this object.

The **Create Event** now contains the code in Listing 29-1.

Listing 29-1. Adding a Variable for How Fast the Instance Will Move

```
///set up
enum player_state {
    idle,
    up,
    down,
    left,
    right
    }
```

```
dir=player_state.down;
is_moving=false;
image_speed=0.5;
global.move_speed=4;
```

The **Step Event** has the three code blocks. The keypress code block is shown in Listing 29-2.

Listing 29-2. Allowing Movement If the Selected Value Matches the ID

```
///keypress code
is_moving=false;
if global.selected!=my_id exit;
if (keyboard_check(vk_left))
{
    dir=player_state.left;
    is_moving=true;
}
else
if (keyboard_check(vk_right))
{
    dir=player_state.right;
    is_moving=true;
}
else
if (keyboard_check(vk_up))
{
    dir=player_state.up;
    is_moving=true;
}
else
if (keyboard_check(vk_down))
{
    dir=player_state.down;
    is_moving=true;
}
else
{
    is_moving=false;
```

The second block is shown in Listing 29-3.

Listing 29-3. Allowing Movement Based on the Move Speed

```
///movement
if is_moving
{
    switch (dir)
    {
        case player_state.up:
        if !position_meeting(x,y-global.move_speed,obj_solid_base) y -= global.move_speed;
        break;
```

```
        case player_state.down:
        if !position_meeting(x,y+global.move_speed,obj_solid_base) y += global.move_speed;
        break;

        case player_state.left:
        if !position_meeting(x-global.move_speed,y,obj_solid_base) x -= global.move_speed;
        break;

        case player_state.right:
        if !position_meeting(x+global.move_speed,y,obj_solid_base) x += global.move_speed;
        break;
    }
}
depth=-y;
```

There is no code change to the third code block, which will allow a tree to be destroyed if player 3 is currently selected.

When done, the object should look like that shown in Figure 29-1.

Figure 29-1. *The object is set up.*

Next, create an object named **obj_player_1**. This has the following **Create Event** code:

```
my_id=1;
event_inherited();
```

It has the sprite named **spr_walk_down** and has **obj_player_parent** as the parent, as shown in Figure 29-2.

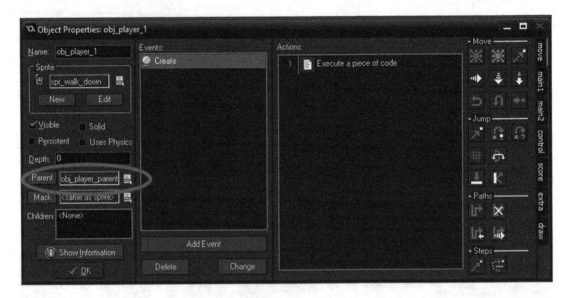

Figure 29-2. *Showing object setup and assigned parent*

The objects **obj_player_2** and **obj_player_3** are set up the same way, with the **Create Event** code for **obj_player_2** as

```
my_id=2;
event_inherited();
```

and for **obj_player_3** as

```
my_id=3;
event_inherited();
```

Note that **obj_player_3** also has a **Collision Event** with **obj_tree** with the code of

///destroy tree
```
with (other) instance_destroy();
```

Figure 29-3 shows an example room, with one instance each of each player object.

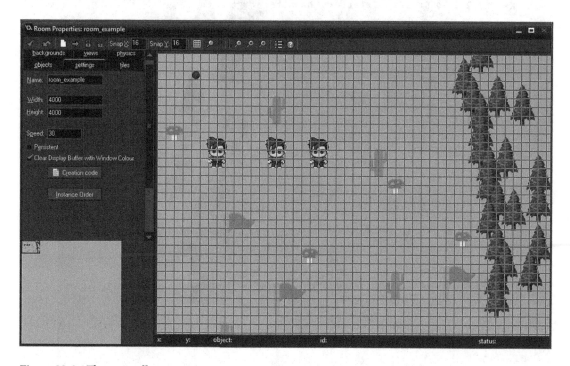

Figure 29-3. *The room all set up*

Figure 29-4 shows this element in action.

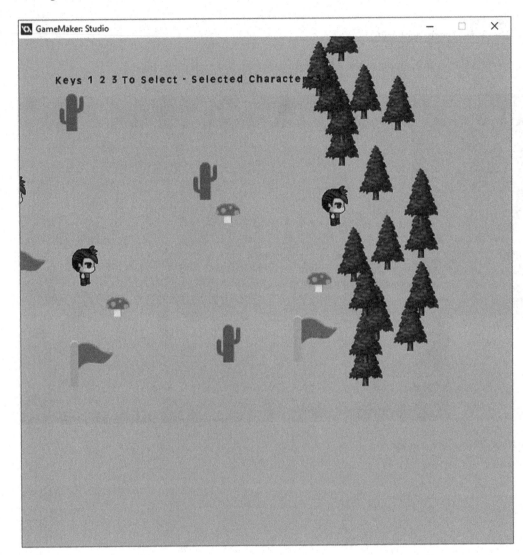

Figure 29-4. This element in action

CHAPTER 30

■ ■ ■

Day/Night Cycle

The GMZ for this element is **Day_Night**.

It uses **Depth_Based** as a template.

Keeping track of how long a player plays your game, and showing this information, is a common aspect of a number of games. Usually time within the game will progress faster than in the real world.

One thing you can do is visually show this progression of time using visual feedback.

This example overlays the room with a coloured rectangle with a set alpha depending on the time of day. This is a simple approach; if you want something visually more stunning, you should look into the use of shaders.

The time of day and the day are displayed on screen.

This uses **Depth Based** GMZ with one additional object.

Create an object named **obj_day_night**.

In a **Create Event**, enter the code in Listing 30-1.

Listing 30-1. Setting Things Up, Including an Initial Alarm

```
time=12;
day=1;
alarm[0]=room_speed*2;
```

In an **Alarm[0] Event**, put the code from Listing 30-2.

Listing 30-2. Increasing Time on Alarm, Adding a Day if Time is 24, and Then Restarting the Alarm

```
time++;
if time==24
{
    time=0;
    day++;
}
alarm[0]=room_speed*2;
```

Add a **Draw GUI Event** with the code in Listing 30-3, which will draw the time as text and set the alpha value depending on the time of day.

Listing 30-3. Drawing a Rectangle in a Colour and Alpha Depending on the Time of Day

```
///drawing
//format and draw text
timestring=string(time);
if string_length(timestring)==1 timestring="0"+timestring;

draw_set_colour(c_white);
draw_text(50,50,"Time "+timestring+":00");
draw_text(250,50,"Day "+string(day));

//draw overlay

draw_set_colour(c_black);
draw_set_alpha(0);
switch (time)
    {
        case 21:
        draw_set_alpha(0.1);
        draw_set_colour(c_yellow);
        break;

        case 22:
        draw_set_alpha(0.2);
        draw_set_colour(c_orange);
        break;

        case 23:
        draw_set_alpha(0.3);
        draw_set_colour(c_blue);
        break;

        case 0:
        draw_set_alpha(0.4);
        draw_set_colour(c_dkgray);
        break;

        case 1:
        draw_set_alpha(0.6);
        draw_set_colour(c_black);
        break;
```

```
        case 2:
        draw_set_alpha(0.8);
        draw_set_colour(c_black);
        break;

        case 3:
        draw_set_alpha(0.6);
        draw_set_colour(c_black);
        break;

        case 4:
        draw_set_alpha(0.4);
        draw_set_colour(c_dkgray);
        break;

        case 5:
        draw_set_alpha(0.3);
        draw_set_colour(c_blue);
        break;

        case 6:
        draw_set_alpha(0.2);
        draw_set_colour(c_orange);
        break;

        case 7:
        draw_set_alpha(0.1);
        draw_set_colour(c_yellow);
        break;

    }

draw_rectangle(0,0,700,700,false);
//reset alpha
draw_set_alpha(1);
```

Just place one instance of this object in the room. Figure 30-1 shows this element in action.

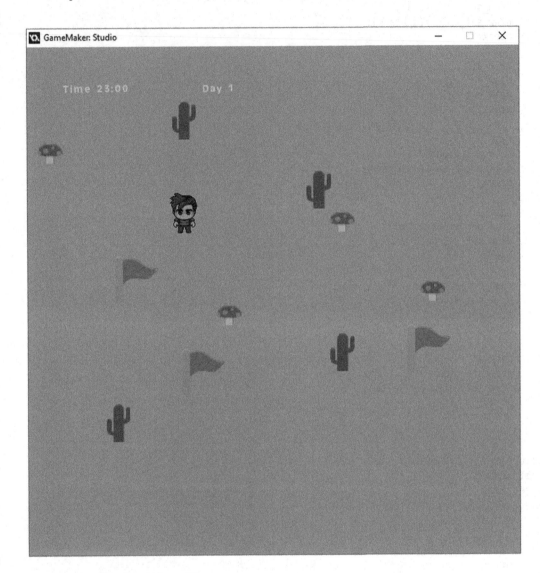

Figure 30-1. *This element in action*

CHAPTER 31

■ ■ ■

Puzzle Room

The GMZ for this element is **Puzzle**.

Having diversity in your mini-games with your RPG is the way to go.

Try to keep the theme relevant to the overall theme of the game.

This example is a classic matching puzzle game, using pirate-themed sprites. The aim is to find all of the matching pairs.

A game such as this could be easily adapted to any theme of your choosing.

If this was your own game, upon completion you would reward your player, possibly with gold or treasure chests.

You may wish to allow the player to revisit this mini-game multiple times. However, it would be a good idea to perhaps limit how often the player can do this.

This is just one puzzle idea. You are free to add any number of mini-games but, as mentioned, keep within the main theme of your game.

This example does the coding within one object. This may be confusing because the coding is quite in-depth. However, there are comments throughout explaining what each part of the code does.

First, you need to load in the sprites. They are **spr_1** through to **spr_18** and they have their origin set as center; **spr_back_med** and **spr_front_med** also have the origin as center.

The first object is **obj_level**, which has the **Create Event** that will create the cards for the game. The code creates a **ds_list** with the cards and then shuffles them. The cards are then dealt out in a grid. The last line declares a **ds_list** to hold the player's selections. The code for this is shown in Listing 31-1.

Listing 31-1. Set Up List And Shuffle, And Create Cards

```
///set up cards

//set random seed
randomize();
deck=ds_list_create(); //create a list
//add 2 of each card to deck:
ds_list_add(deck,spr_1,spr_1);
ds_list_add(deck,spr_2,spr_2);
ds_list_add(deck,spr_3,spr_3);
ds_list_add(deck,spr_4,spr_4);
ds_list_add(deck,spr_5,spr_5);
ds_list_add(deck,spr_6,spr_6);
ds_list_add(deck,spr_7,spr_7);
ds_list_add(deck,spr_8,spr_8);
ds_list_add(deck,spr_9,spr_9);
ds_list_add(deck,spr_10,spr_10);
ds_list_add(deck,spr_11,spr_11);
```

```
ds_list_add(deck,spr_12,spr_12);
ds_list_add(deck,spr_13,spr_13);
ds_list_add(deck,spr_14,spr_14);
ds_list_add(deck,spr_15,spr_15);
ds_list_add(deck,spr_16,spr_16);
ds_list_add(deck,spr_17,spr_17);
ds_list_add(deck,spr_18,spr_18);
//shuffle the deck:
ds_list_shuffle(deck);

//create a grid of cards with this list
var i;
for (i = 0; i <= 35; i += 1)
{
        card=instance_create(70+(i mod 6)*70,70+(i div 6)*70,obj_card);
        card.sprite_index=deck[| i];
        card.xx=i mod 6;
        card.yy=i div 6;
        card.flipped=false;
}

//create a list to hold player's selections
global.selected=ds_list_create();
```

That is all for this object.

The next object is **obj_card**, which is the instance that the player interacts with. It has a **Left Mouse Button Released Event** with the code from Listing 31-2.

Listing 31-2. Flipping the Card If the Player Has Less Than Two Current Selections

```
///allow flipping if only none or one card selected

if !flipped && global.plays<2
{
    flipped=true; //set flag so face can be shown
    ds_list_add(global.selected,id); //add the id to a list
    global.plays++; //mark as a selection made
}
```

This object also has a **Draw Event** with the GML shown in Listing 31-3.

Listing 31-3. Drawing the Back or Front of a Card and the Assigned Sprite

```
///draw front or back of card
if flipped
{
    draw_sprite(spr_front_med,0,x,y);//show back
    draw_self();//show front
}
else
draw_sprite(spr_back_med,0,x,y); //show back
```

The next object is **obj_control**. It has the **Create Event** code shown in Listing 31-4.

Listing 31-4. Setting Things Up

```
///set up
goes=25; //how many attempts the player gets
global.plays=0;
matches=0;
```

An **Alarm[0] Event** contains the code in Listing 31-5.

Listing 31-5. Flipping the Cards Back Over and Allowing Play Again

```
///flip cards back to showing back if not matched
card1.flipped=false;
card2.flipped=false;
global.plays=0; //allow playing again
```

A **Step Event** will compare two cards. If they are the same, it records them as a match. If not, the alarm is started. It then checks if the game has finished. The code for this is shown in Listing 31-6.

Listing 31-6. Comparing Two Cards and Proceeding Accordingly

```
///check cards
if ds_list_size(global.selected)==2 //check if two cards selected
{
    if global.selected[|0].sprite_index == global.selected[|1].sprite_index
    //check if cards face image matches
    {
        //if matched:
        ds_list_clear(global.selected);
        goes--;
        global.plays=0;
        matches++;
    }
    else
    {
        //if not matched
        card1=global.selected[|0]; //these two cards are to store id for alarm event
        card2=global.selected[|1];
        ds_list_clear(global.selected);
        goes--;
        alarm[0]=room_speed;
    }
}

//check for game end
if goes==0
{
    show_message("You Lose");
    game_restart();
}
```

```
if matches==18
{
    show_message("You Win");
    game_restart();
}
```

And finally a **Draw Event** contains the code shown in Listing 31-7.

Listing 31-7. Just Drawing the Remaining Attempts Allowed

```
draw_text(10,10,"Tries remaining "+string(goes));
```

This game has one room, **rm_play**, which is 600x600 in size with one instance each of **obj_level** and **obj_control**.

Figure 31-1 shows this element in action.

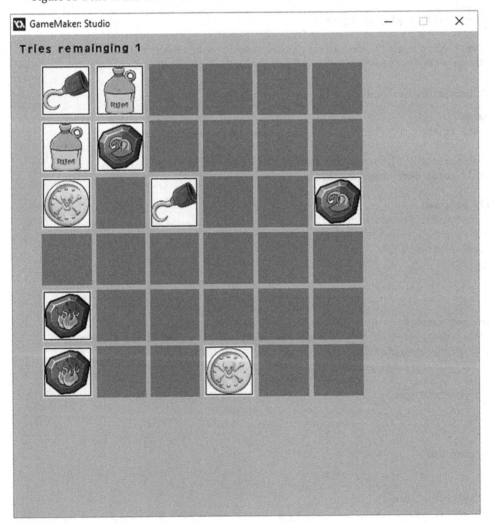

Figure 31-1. *The puzzle game in action*

CHAPTER 32

■ ■ ■

Treasure Hunting

The GMZ for this element is **Treasure_Hunting**.

It uses **Game_Base** as a template.

The main focus of the game we're designing is the collection of treasure/loot that the player needs to collect in order to get off the island they are stuck on.

You just can't have a pirate-themed game without being able to dig for treasure.

This example allows the player to dig for treasure. When they dig, they will be provided with information on the distance to the nearest buried treasure.

In this example, the player has a limited number of digs available. If this was your own game, you could provide these digs as items that can be purchased within a shop or as a reward for completing mini-games/puzzles/challenges.

You could have this buried treasure scattered around the game world so the player could hunt for it if they had digs available.

Little in-game challenges such as this give life and meaning to your game. Your players will thank you if you have more than one such challenge in your game.

This element uses **Game_Base** GMZ as a template.

It has the following additional sprites: **spr_pick**, **spr_treasure**, **spr_treasure_here**, and **spr_no_treasure**. The origin of all of them is center.

© Ben Tyers 2017
B. Tyers, *Learn RPGs in GameMaker: Studio*, DOI 10.1007/978-1-4842-2946-0_32

The first object to add is **obj_treasure_here**, which has **spr_treasure_here** assigned. This object needs the visible option unchecked, as shown in Figure 32-1.

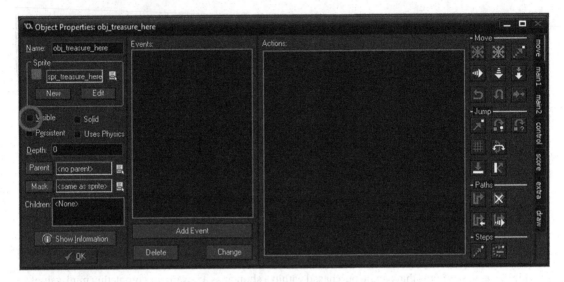

Figure 32-1. *obj_treasure_here with visible unchecked*

There is no code for this object.

The next object is **obj_treasure** with **spr_treasure** assigned. There is no code for this object.

The next object is **obj_x**, which has the sprite **spr_no_treasure** assigned. Set the depth of this object to -50.

The **Create Event** code is shown in Listing 32-1. It will get the id of nearest treasure (**obj_treasure_here**) if an instance of it exists.

Listing 32-1. Getting the Id of the Nearest Instance

```
other_id=noone;
distance=0;
can_show=true;
if instance_exists(obj_treasure_here)
{
    other_id=instance_nearest(x,y,obj_treasure_here);
}
alarm[0]=room_speed*3;
```

It has an **Alarm[0] Event** with the code shown in Listing 32-2, which is used to trigger showing info to nearest treasure.

Listing 32-2. On Alarm Destroys Self

```
instance_destroy();
```

It has a **Step Event** with the code shown in Listing 32-3, which will give the distance to the nearest treasure if it exists.

Listing 32-3. Setting a Variable for the Distance to the Nearest Instance

```
if instance_exists(other_id)
{
    distance=round(distance_to_point(other_id.x,other_id.y));
}
else
{
    distance=0;
}
```

Finally, there is a **Draw Event** with the code in Listing 32-4, which draws itself and the distance to the nearest treasure until **Alarm[0]** triggers.

Listing 32-4. Drawing Self and the Nearest Instance Present

```
draw_self();
if distance!=0 && can_show
{
    draw_set_colour(c_yellow);
    draw_set_halign(fa_center);
    draw_text(x,y-32,"Nearest Buried Treasure: "+string(distance)+"-Meters");
}
```

The next object is **obj_hud**, which has the **Create Event** code shown in Listing 32-5, which sets up starting variables and picks how many attempts a player can make.

Listing 32-5. Setting Up Starting Variables and Picking Number of Player Attempts

```
global.gold=0;
global.picks=50;
```

The **Draw GUI Event** contains the code in Listing 32-6.

Listing 32-6. Drawing the HUD Info and Picks Remaining

```
draw_set_colour(c_black);
draw_set_halign(fa_left);
draw_sprite(spr_pick,0,100,100);
draw_text(100,160,"Z to Dig - Picks Left "+string(global.picks));
```

Finally, **obj_player** has a new code block in the **Step Event**, which allows the player to dig for treasure if any picks remain; this is shown in Listing 32-7.

Listing 32-7. Allowing the Player to Dig for Treasure If Any Picks Remain

```
///dig for treasure
if keyboard_check_pressed(ord('Z')) && global.picks>0
{
    global.picks--;
    instance_create(x,y,obj_x);
    instance_create(x,y,obj_has_dug);
}
```

A final object is **obj_has_dug** with the sprite **spr_has_dug** with an origin of center. This will leave a mark to show where the player has dug. It has a **Collision Event** with **obj_treasure_here** with the GML shown in Listing 32-8.

Listing 32-8. Create Treasure and Destroy Other

```
instance_create(other.x,other.y,obj_treasure);
with (other) instance_destroy();
```

Figure 32-2 shows a room set up with one instance of **obj_hud** and several instances of **obj_treasure_here**.

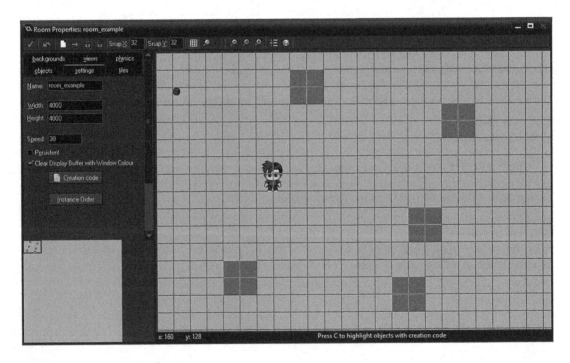

Figure 32-2. *The room is all set up*

Figure 32-3 shows this element in action.

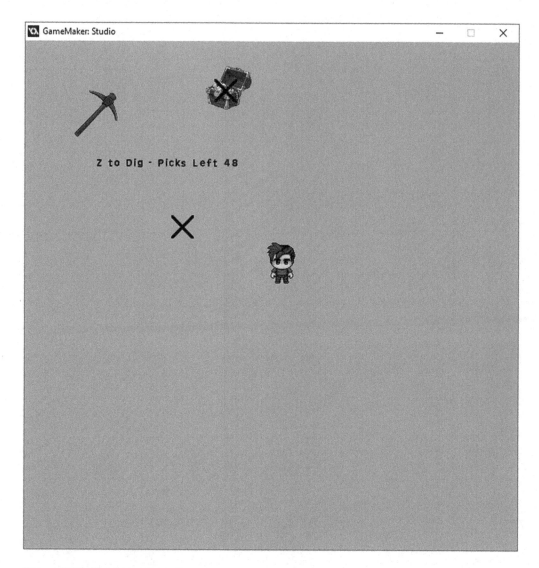

Figure 32-3. *The element in action*

CHAPTER 33

■ ■ ■

Card Battle

The GMZ for this element is **Card_Battle**.

This book covers a number of battle systems: this is another one.

This system uses cards from which a player must choose a stat and try to beat the opposing player (the computer).

This style of game play is used a lot in RPGs.

Some games will have a few systems in place for cohesion, with more variations on the enemies than the system.

For this example, the stats are generated randomly: in your own game, you may want to hard-code the values for each.

For this example, 20 subimages of different characters are used. Stats are held in an array.

All cards have a numerical value, which is added to a **ds_list**. This list is then shuffled, and the player and computer are each dealt 10 cards.

The player's current card and stats are displayed. The player should choose a value that they think will beat the computer's card.

Points are then awarded accordingly, depending on whether the player wins, the computer wins, or it is a draw.

© Ben Tyers 2017
B. Tyers, *Learn RPGs in GameMaker: Studio*, DOI 10.1007/978-1-4842-2946-0_33

First up is a sprite named **spr_characters**. This sprite has 20 images, as shown in Figure 33-1.

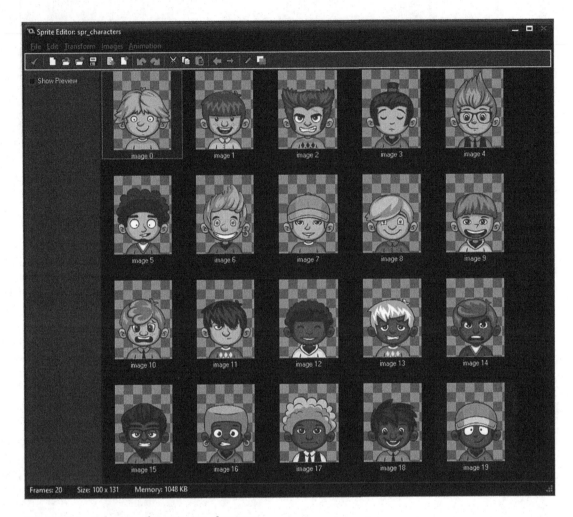

Figure 33-1. *Subimages for sprite spr_characters*

This first object is **obj_setup**, which has the **Create Event** code shown in Listing 33-1. This code will make an array with sprite indexes and random values. It will then deal out cards for the player and enemy into two **ds_list**s. It will then go to the room called **room_game**.

Listing 33-1. Making an Array, Dealing Cards, and Going to the Game Room

```
///set up

//create list and populate
global.cards=ds_list_create();
for (var loop = 0; loop < 20; loop += 1)
{
        global.card[0,loop]=loop; //id - used for sprite
        global.card[1,loop]=irandom_range(1,10); //set strength
        global.card[2,loop]=irandom_range(1,10); //set speed
        global.card[3,loop]=irandom_range(1,10); //set magic
        global.card[4,loop]=irandom_range(1,10); //set gold
        ds_list_add(global.cards,loop); //set up deck
}
ds_list_shuffle(global.cards);
//create player's hand
global.player_hand=ds_list_create();
repeat (10)
{
    ds_list_add(global.player_hand,global.cards[|0]);
    show_debug_message(global.cards[|0]);
    ds_list_delete(global.cards,0) ;
}


//create enemy's hand
global.enemy_hand=ds_list_create();
repeat (10)
{
    ds_list_add(global.enemy_hand,global.cards[|0]);
    show_debug_message(global.cards[|0]);
    ds_list_delete(global.cards,0);
}

global.game_round=0;
global.can_show=false;
global.player=0;
global.enemy=0;
global.draw=0;
room_goto(room_game);
```

Create a room named **room_setup** that is 1024x768 in size and place one instance of this object in it. That is all for this room.

The next object is **obj_play**. It has the **Create Event** code shown in Listing 33-2 to set an initial message.

Listing 33-2. Setting an Initial Message

```
///set starting message
message="Press 1 To Play Stength - 2 For Speed - 3 For Magic - 4 For Gold";
```

An **Alarm[0] Event** has the code in Listing 33-3 to send a message and check if all rounds have been completed.

Listing 33-3. Setting a Flag Back to False, Setting a Message, and Checking for All Rounds Completed

```
/// alarm:
global.can_show=false;
message="Press 1 To Play Stength - 2 For Speed - 3 For Magic - 4 For Gold";
global.game_round++;
if global.game_round==10 room_goto(room_game_over);
```

Next, a **Step Event** has the code in Listing 33-4 to check for a keypress and compare it to the enemy value.

Listing 33-4. Detecting a Keypress and Comparing It to the Enemy Value

```
///compare plays
player=global.player_hand[|global.game_round];
enemy=global.enemy_hand[|global.game_round];

//play 1
if keyboard_check_pressed(ord('1')) && alarm[0]==-1
{
    scr_check_play(global.card[1,player],global.card[1,enemy]);
}

//play 2
if keyboard_check_pressed(ord('2')) && alarm[0]==-1
{
    scr_check_play(global.card[2,player],global.card[2,enemy]);
}

//play 3
if keyboard_check_pressed(ord('3')) && alarm[0]==-1
{
    scr_check_play(global.card[3,player],global.card[3,enemy]);
}

//play 4
if keyboard_check_pressed(ord('4')) && alarm[0]==-1
{
    scr_check_play(global.card[4,player],global.card[4,enemy]);
}
```

And finally a **Draw Event** has two code blocks. The first is shown in Listing 33-5. It displays the score and round number, with 1 added because the variable starts at 0.

Listing 33-5. Displaying the Score and a Round Number

```
///draw score and message
draw_text(500,10,"Player "+string(global.player)+" Enemy "+string(global.enemy)+" Draws
"+string(global.draw));
draw_text(500,20,message);
draw_text(80,10, "Round "+string(global.game_round+1)+" Of 10");
```

The second code block draws the player's current card, and the enemy's current card if the flag is true; see Listing 33-6.

Listing 33-6. Drawing the Player's Current Card, and the Enemy's Current Card If the Flag Is True

```
///draw cards

//draw player

//draw card bg
draw_set_colour(c_teal);
draw_roundrect(40,40,260,500,false);

//draw a border
draw_set_colour(c_white);
draw_roundrect(42,42,258,498,true);

//draw main card
draw_sprite(spr_characters,player,150,150);

//draw stats
draw_set_halign(fa_center);
draw_set_colour(c_black);
draw_text(150,300,"Strength: "+string(global.card[1,player]));
draw_text(150,350,"Speed: "+string(global.card[2,player]));
draw_text(150,400,"Magic: "+string(global.card[3,player]));
draw_text(150,450,"Gold: "+string(global.card[4,player]));

//draw enemy
if global.can_show
{
    //draw card bg
    draw_set_colour(c_green);
    draw_roundrect(340,40,560,500,false);
```

```
//draw a border
draw_set_colour(c_white);
draw_roundrect(342,42,558,498,true);

//draw main card
draw_sprite(spr_characters,enemy,450,150);

//draw stats
draw_set_halign(fa_center);
draw_set_colour(c_black);
draw_text(450,300,"Strength: "+string(global.card[1,enemy]));
draw_text(450,350,"Speed: "+string(global.card[2,enemy]));
draw_text(450,400,"Magic: "+string(global.card[3,enemy]));
draw_text(450,450,"Gold: "+string(global.card[4,enemy]));
}
```

Create a room named **room_game** that is 1024x768 in size, and place in it one instance each of **obj_play**, **obj_draw_player**, and **obj_draw_enemy**.

That is all for this room.

The final object is **obj_game_over** with the **Draw Event** GML shown in Listing 33-7.

Listing 33-7. Drawing the Results of All 10 Rounds

```
draw_text(400,200,"Player "+string(global.player));
draw_text(400,250,"Enemy "+string(global.enemy));
draw_text(400,300,"Draws "+string(global.draw));
```

Create a room named **room_game_over** and place one instance of **obj_game_over** in it.

Listing 33-8. Script for checking plays

```
///scr_check_play(playersvalue,enemysvalue);
//check for player win
if argument0>argument1
{
    global.can_show=true;
    message=("Player Wins");
    alarm[0]=room_speed*4;
    global.player++;
}
//check for enemy win
if argument0<argument1
{
    global.can_show=true;
    message=("Enemy Wins");
    alarm[0]=room_speed*4;
    global.enemy++;
}
```

```
//check for draw
if argument0==argument1
{
    global.can_show=true;
    message=("Draw");
    alarm[0]=room_speed*4;
    global.draw++;
}
```

Figure 33-2 shows this element in action.

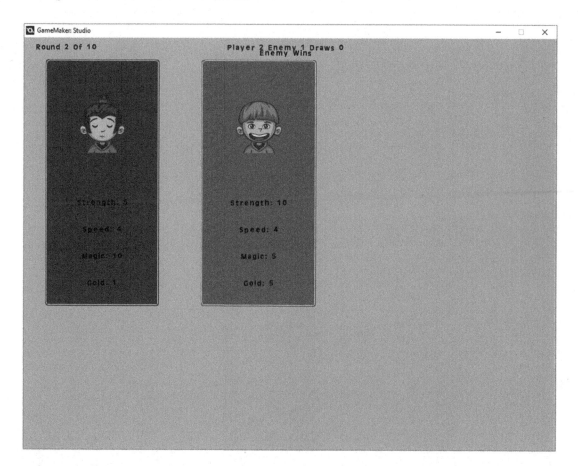

Figure 33-2. *This element in action*

CHAPTER 34

■ ■ ■

Graphical Effects

The GMZ for this element is **Graphical_Effects**.

It uses **Game_Base** as a template.

Graphical effects, as with audio effects, when not overused can make the game more fun to play and make it look more professional.

Little things such as footprints, animals that wander around, and weather effects can contribute to the overall feel of your game.

This element provides a basic effect, but feel free to experiment and diversify within your own game. This element produces the following effects:

- Footsteps when the player moves

- Spinning gold coin

- Wandering chickens

- Flying butterfly

- Rain and snow

If you compare this element with the **Game_Base**, you'll see that these effects instantly make a difference. This element uses **Game_Base** as a template.

There are some additional sprites:

- **spr_butterfly** has 87 subimages. The sprite origin is center

- **spr_chicken** has 24 subimages and an origin of 44,39

- **spr_gold** has 6 subimages and an origin of center

- **spr_foot_step** has a single image with an origin of center

First up is **obj_foot_steps**, which has the sprite **spr_foot_step** assigned. It has the **Create Event** shown in Listing 34-1.

Listing 34-1. Setting Things Up, Including an Initial Alarm

```
image_speed=0;
fading=false;
alarm[0]=room_speed*2;
ia=1;
```

© Ben Tyers 2017

B. Tyers, *Learn RPGs in GameMaker: Studio*, DOI 10.1007/978-1-4842-2946-0_34

An **Alarm[0] Event** fades the flag via the code shown in Listing 34-2.

Listing 34-2. Setting the Flag for Fading

```
fading=true;
```

A **Step Event** reduces the value if fading. It's destroyed when under 0. Then it sets the alpha to **ai** and draws the sprite. It then sets the alpha back to 1 so other objects are not affected; see Listing 34-3.

Listing 34-3. Fades Alpha and Destroys When Under 0

```
if fading
{
    ia-=0.03;
    image_alpha=ia;
}
if ia<0 instance_destroy();
```

That is all for this object.

The next object to create is **obj_chicken**. This has a sprite named **spr_chicken**. The **Create Event** for this object starts moving in one direction, starts an alarm, and adjusts scale so that the sprite points in the correct direction. See Listing 34-4.

Listing 34-4. Starting Movement, Starting Alarm, and Adjusting the Scale

```
motion_set(choose(0,180),1+random(1));
alarm[0]=room_speed*3+irandom(room_speed*3);
if hspeed<0 image_xscale=-1 else image_xscale=1;
```

And an **Alarm[0] Event** with the code in Listing 34-5 restarts the alarm and changes the direction of the sprite.

Listing 34-5. Restarting the Alarm and Changing Direction of Movement and Sprite Direction

```
alarm[0]=room_speed*3+irandom(room_speed*3);
hspeed=-hspeed;
if hspeed<0 image_xscale=-1 else image_xscale=1;
```

That is all for this object.

Next is **obj_butterfly**, which has **spr_butterfly** assigned. It has a **Create Event** with the code shown in Listing 34-6 that starts a path.

Listing 34-6. Starting on a Path That Will Continue in a Loop

```
path_start(path,1+random(2),path_action_continue,false);
```

It also uses a path named **path**, which looks like Figure 34-1.

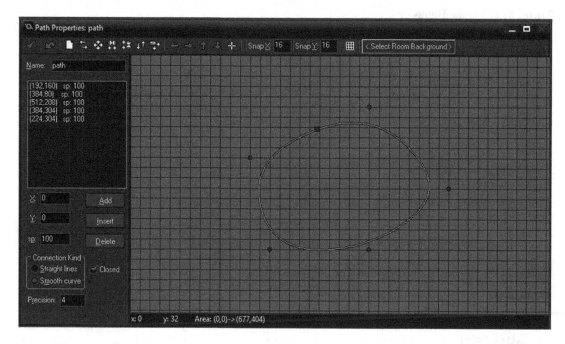

Figure 34-1. *The path*

That is all for this object.

Next up is **obj_control** with the **Create Event** shown in Listing 34-7 that sets the initial flags.

Listing 34-7. Setting Initial Flags

```
snow=false;
rain=false;
```

A **Step Event** with the code in Listing 34-8 changes the flags for rain and snow. If flag is **true**, it will create the effect.

Listing 34-8. Allowing Keypress to Change the Flags for Rain and Snow

```
if keyboard_check_pressed(ord('S'))
{
    snow=!snow;
}
if keyboard_check_pressed(ord('R'))
{
    rain=!rain;
}
if snow effect_create_above(ef_snow,x,y,1,c_white);
if rain effect_create_above(ef_rain,x,y,1,c_blue);
```

Finally, **obj_player** has a change in the **Create Event**, which is shown in Listing 34-9.

Listing 34-9. Setting Things Up

```
///set up
enum player_state {
    idle,
    up,
    down,
    left,
    right
    }

dir=player_state.down;
is_moving=false;
image_speed=0.5;
foot_steps=1;
```

The movement code block in the **Step Event** changes to the code in Listing 34-10.

Listing 34-10. Moving in a Direction and Increasing Footstep Variable

```
///movement
if is_moving
{
    switch (dir)
    {
        case player_state.up:
        y -= 4;
        break;

        case player_state.down:
        y += 4;
        break;

        case player_state.left:
        x -= 4;
        break;

        case player_state.right:
        x += 4;
        break;
    }
}
if is_moving foot_steps++;
```

An additional code block in its **Step Event** is shown in Listing 34-11.

Listing 34-11. Creating a Footstep, Based on Player's Direction State

```
///foot steps
if foot_steps==4
{
    foot_steps=1;
    feet=instance_create(x,y,obj_foot_steps);
    switch (dir)
    {
        case player_state.up:
        feet.image_angle=90;
        feet.image_index=0;
        break;

        case player_state.down:
        feet.image_angle=270;
        feet.image_index=0;
        break;

        case player_state.left:
        feet.image_angle=180;
        feet.image_index=1;
        break;

        case player_state.right:
        feet.image_angle=0;
        feet.image_index=1;
        break;
    }
}
```

Figure 34-2 shows an example room layout, with objects placed including one instance of **obj_control**.

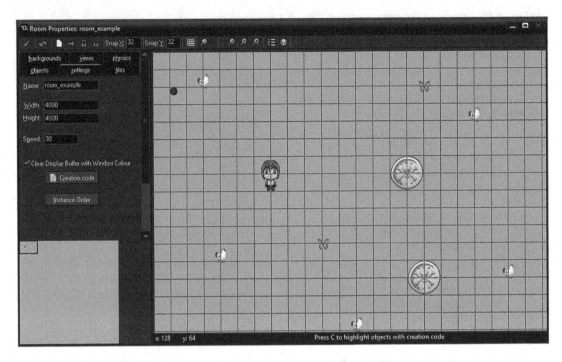

Figure 34-2. *An example room layout*

Figure 34-3 shows this element in action.

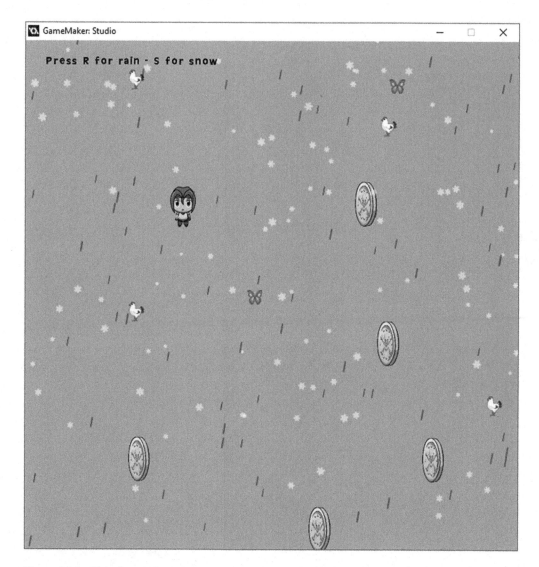

Figure 34-3. *This element in action*

CHAPTER 35

■ ■ ■

Random Level Generation

The GMZ for this element is **Random_Level_Generation**.
It makes use of the GMZ **Depth_Based** as a template.
Randomness allows for diversity within your game. Diversity is good.
Good ways to use this random approach are for

- How much a player gets rewarded for a quest/mini-game completion

- Where items, such as buried treasure, are placed

- How powerful an enemy is

- Initial player stats when playing for the first time

- How enemies and minions move

This example generates random placement of objects within a room.
This is only basic, but it allows you to add additional objects if you so wish.
It uses **Depth_Based** GMZ as a template.
Rename the room to **room_random** and set as 1000x1000 in size. Remove all objects except for
obj_player.
Create an object named **obj_wall** with **spr_wall** assigned, with the origin as center.
Create an object named **obj_water** with **spr_water** assigned, with the origin as center.
Create an object named **obj_road** with **spr_road** assigned, with the origin as center.
Create an object named **obj_generate**. This has the sprite **spr_generate** assigned to allow for collision
detection when the player chooses random empty positions.
In the **Create Event** put the code from Listing 35-1.

Listing 35-1. Setting Things Up

```
randomize();
path=path_add();
alarm[0]=room_speed;
```

© Ben Tyers 2017
B. Tyers, *Learn RPGs in GameMaker: Studio*, DOI 10.1007/978-1-4842-2946-0_35

In **Alarm[0] Event** put the code from Listing 35-2.

Listing 35-2. Creating Wall Object Instances Around the Edge of the Room

```
//place wall borders
size=room_width/32-1;
for (var loop = 1; loop < size; loop += 1)
{
    instance_create(loop*32,32,obj_wall);
    instance_create(loop*32,0,obj_wall);
    instance_create(loop*32,968,obj_wall);
    instance_create(loop*32,1000,obj_wall);
    instance_create(32,32*loop+16,obj_wall);
    instance_create(0,32*loop+16,obj_wall);
    instance_create(968,32*loop+16,obj_wall);
    instance_create(1000,32*loop+16,obj_wall);
}
instance_create(16,16,obj_wall);
instance_create(16,984,obj_wall);
instance_create(984,16,obj_wall);
instance_create(984,1000,obj_wall);
alarm[1]=room_speed;
```

In **Alarm[1] Event** place the code from Listing 35-3.

Listing 35-3. Creating a Path and Drawing a Road Along That Path

```
repeat(5) //do this 5 times
{
    //get two random points at least 100 from room edge
    var xx1=irandom_range(100,room_width-100);
    var yy1=irandom_range(100,room_height-100);
    var xx2=irandom_range(100,room_width-100);
    var yy2=irandom_range(100,room_height-100);
    //add points to a path
    path_add_point(path,xx1,yy1,3);
    path_add_point(path,xx2,yy2,3);
    //get length of path
    var size=floor(path_get_length(path)); show_debug_message(size);
    //divide by 64
    var division=floor(size/64); show_debug_message(division);
    //get total blocks to draw
    total=floor(size/division); show_debug_message(total);
    for (var i = 1; i < total; i += 1)
    {
        var point=(1/total)*i; //get a value based on i
        var placex=path_get_x(path,point); //get x at point on path
        var placey=path_get_y(path,point); //get y at point on path
        instance_create(placex,placey,obj_road); //create a road object
    }
    path_clear_points(path);
}

alarm[2]=room_speed;
```

In **Alarm[2] Event** put the code from Listing 35-4.

Listing 35-4. Creating Some Large and Small Water Bodies

```
//draw some lakes
repeat(12)
{
    do
    {
        xx = random(room_width) div 32*32;
        yy = random(room_height) div 32 *32;
    }
    until (!position_meeting(xx, yy, all))
    instance_create(xx,yy,obj_water);
    instance_create(xx+32,yy,obj_water);
    instance_create(xx+32,yy+32,obj_water);
    instance_create(xx+64,yy,obj_water);
    instance_create(xx+64,yy+32,obj_water);
    instance_create(xx+64,yy+64,obj_water);
}
//draw some square lakes
repeat(12)
{
    do
    {
        xx = random(room_width) div 32*32;
        yy = random(room_height) div 32 *32;
    }
    until (!position_meeting(xx, yy, all))
    instance_create(xx,yy,obj_water);
    instance_create(xx+32,yy,obj_water);
    instance_create(xx,yy+32,obj_water);
    instance_create(xx+32,yy+32,obj_water);
}
alarm[3]=room_speed;
```

In **Alarm[3] Event** put the code from Listing 35-5.

Listing 35-5. Creating Some Cactus and Mushrooms, and Removing the Path from Memory and Destroying Itself

```
//add some cactus and mushrooms

repeat(20)
{
    do
    {
        xx = random(room_width-64) div 32 * 32 +32;
        yy = random(room_height-64) div 32* 32 + 32;
    }
    until (!position_meeting(xx, yy, all))
    instance_create(xx,yy,choose(obj_mushroom,obj_cactus));
}

path_delete(path);
instance_destroy();
```

Place one instance of this object, **obj_generate**, in **room_random**. Figure 35-1 shows this element in action.

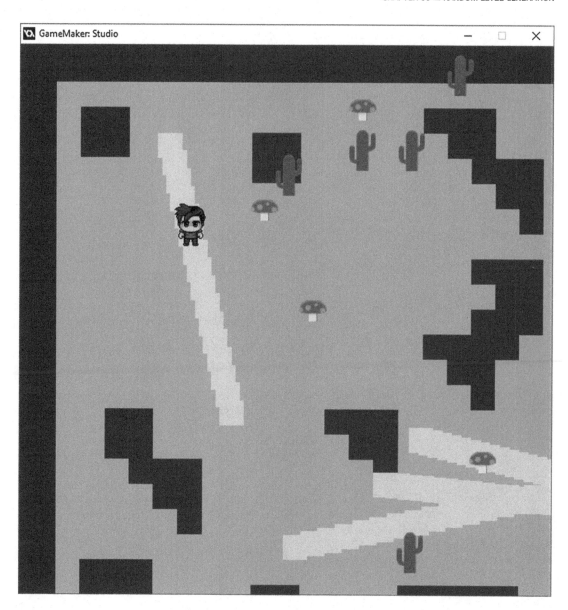

Figure 35-1. *Showing this element in action*

CHAPTER 36

Fishing Mini-Game

This element's GMZ is **Fishing_Mini_Game**.

Here is an example of another mini-game that kind of fits in with the stuck-on-the-island theme.

This is not like any other mini-game in this project, so it avoids the problem of repetition. Having distinct mini-games is the way to go.

For your own mini-games, try to keep them relevant to your game's overall theme.

The aim of this is game is simple enough: get the hook into a fish's mouth in order to gain points. The player's rod and line can be controlled using the arrow keys.

Fish of various size and types are created. The bigger the fish, the bigger the score for catching it. In this example, the player has a limited amount of time in which to catch the fish.

Also, if the hook touches the swimming shark, you will lose points quickly.

You could add additional elements like mines or randomly place treasure chests on the sea bed.

First up are two fonts:

- **font_info_big**, which is Arial size 25

- **font_info_small**, which is Arial size 12

The first object is **obj_splash**, which has the **Create Event** code shown in Listing 36-1.

Listing 36-1. Setting Initial Values and Going to the Game Room

```
score=0;
lives=10;
health=100;
room_goto(room_game);
```

Create a room named **room_splash** that is 800x600 in size and place one instance of **obj_splash** in it. That is all for this room.

Next up are the fish objects.

First up is the fish parent object, **obj_fish_parent**, which has the **Create Event** code shown in Listing 36-2.

Listing 36-2. Choosing a Direction for the Fish and Getting It Moving

```
dir=choose("left","right");
depth=choose(-50,50);
y=irandom_range(120,540);
spd=random_range(1,4);
scale=random(2)+0.3;
if dir=="right"
```

© Ben Tyers 2017
B. Tyers, *Learn RPGs in GameMaker: Studio*, DOI 10.1007/978-1-4842-2946-0_36

```
{
    x=-100;
    direction=0;
    image_xscale=scale;
    image_yscale=scale;
}
if dir=="left"
{
    x=room_width+100;
    direction=180;
    image_xscale=-scale;
    image_yscale=scale;
}
speed=spd;
```

The **Step Event** code is shown in Listing 36-3. It awards points if a hook hits a fish's mouth.

Listing 36-3. If a Hook Hits a Fish's Mouth, Award Points and Destroy the Fish

```
if point_distance(x,y,obj_hook.x,obj_hook.y)<15
{
    score+=size*scale;
    instance_destroy();
}

if x>room_width+200 instance_destroy();
if x<-200 instance_destroy();
```

That is all for this object.

obj_fish_1 has sprite **spr_fish_1** assigned with the origin just above the fish's mouth. The parent is **obj_fish_parent** and the **Create Event** code is shown in Listing 36-4.

Listing 36-4. Setting a Size of Fish (Used for Score)

```
size=10;
event_inherited();
```

obj_fish_2 has sprite **spr_fish_2** assigned with the origin just above the fish's mouth. The parent is **obj_fish_parent** and the **Create Event** code is shown in Listing 36-5.

Listing 36-5. Setting a Size of Fish (Used for Score)

```
size=20;
event_inherited();
```

obj_fish_3 has sprite **spr_fish_3** assigned with the origin just above the fish's mouth. The parent is **obj_fish_parent** and the **Create Event** code is shown in Listing 36-6.

Listing 36-6. Setting a Size of Fish (Used for Score)

```
size=10;
event_inherited();
```

obj_fish_4 has sprite **spr_fish_4** assigned with the origin just above the fish's mouth. The parent is **obj_fish_parent** and the **Create Event** code is shown in Listing 36-7.

Listing 36-7. Setting a Size of Fish (Used for Score)

```
size=5;
event_inherited();
```

obj_fish_5 has sprite **spr_fish_5** assigned with the origin just above the fish's mouth. The parent is **obj_fish_parent** and the **Create Event** code is shown in Listing 36-8.

Listing 36-8. Setting a Size of Fish (Used for Score)

```
size=25;
event_inherited();
```

obj_fish_6 has sprite **spr_fish_6** assigned with the origin just above the fish's mouth. The parent is **obj_fish_parent** and the **Create Event** code is shown in Listing 36-9.

Listing 36-9. Setting a Size of Fish (Used for Score)

```
size=40;
event_inherited();
```

That is all for the fish objects.

Next up is **obj_bubble** which has sprite **spr_bubble** assigned. It has the **Create Event** code shown in Listing 36-10.

Listing 36-10. Declaring Some Variables to Make the Bubble Wobble and Start It Moving from a Random y Location

```
ang=0; //initial angle
sw=0; //for sine wave
move_angle=5+irandom(10);
base=irandom_range(100,700);
x=base;
y=room_height+64;

scale=irandom_range(1,20);
scale*=0.1;
image_xscale=scale;
image_yscale=scale;
motion_set(90,1+scale);
depth=choose(-50,50);
```

There is also a **Step Event** with the code shown in Listing 36-11.

Listing 36-11. Making the Bubble Wobble

```
sw += 0.1; //for sine wave - i.e. speed
angle= sin(sw) * move_angle; //for sine wave
x=base+angle;
```

That is all for this object.

Next is **obj_shark** with the **spr_shark** assigned. It has the **Create Event** code shown in Listing 36-12.

Listing 36-12. Starting a Shark Moving

```
y=irandom_range(200,500);
motion_set(0,2+random(2));
```

A **Step Event** uses the GML shown in Listing 36-13.

Listing 36-13. Making the Shark Turn Around When Off Screen

```
if x>900
{
    x=850;
    y=irandom_range(200,500);
    image_xscale=-1;
    motion_set(180,2+random(2));
}
if x<-100
{
    x=50;
    y=irandom_range(200,500);
    image_xscale=1;
    motion_set(0,2+random(2));
}
```

The next object is **obj_hook**, which has sprite **spr_hook** with an origin of 11,155 assigned to it. The **Create Event** code is shown in Listing 36-14.

Listing 36-14. Setting Initial States

```
verdir="up";
hordir="right";
```

It has a **Step Event** with the code in Listing 36-15.

Listing 36-15. Moving According to Keypresses, Keeping Within the Room

```
///movement
if keyboard_check(vk_left) hordir="left";
if keyboard_check(vk_right) hordir="right";
if keyboard_check(vk_up) verdir="up";
if keyboard_check(vk_down) verdir="down";

if hordir=="left" x-=2;
if hordir=="right" x+=2;
if verdir=="up" y-=4;
if verdir=="down" y+=4;
```

```
if y<96 y=96;
if y>room_height-30 y=room_height-30;
if x<160 x=160;
if x>room_width-100 x=room_width-100;
```

It has a **Collision Event with obj_shark** with the code shown in Listing 36-16.

Listing 36-16. Collison Event Code

```
score--;
```

The code for the **Draw Event** is shown in Listing 36-17.

Listing 36-17. Drawing the Hook, Rod, and Line

```
///draw hook, rod and line
//draw hook
draw_self();
//draw_rod
draw_set_colour(c_maroon);
draw_line_width(96,70,x,90,6);
// draw fishing line
draw_set_colour(c_black);
draw_line_width(x,90,x,y,2);
```

That is all for this object.

Next is **obj_jellyfish** with sprite **spr_jellyfish** for it. It has the **Create Event** code shown in Listing 36-18.

Listing 36-18. Starting the Jellyfish Moving on a Path

```
path_start(path_jelly,3,path_action_continue,true);
```

A **Step Event** has the GML shown in Listing 36-19.

Listing 36-19. Keeping the Instance Pointing in the Direction It Is Moving

```
image_angle=direction;
```

This object makes use of path **path_jelly**. Figure 36-1 shows what this looks like. It doesn't need to be 100% accurate.

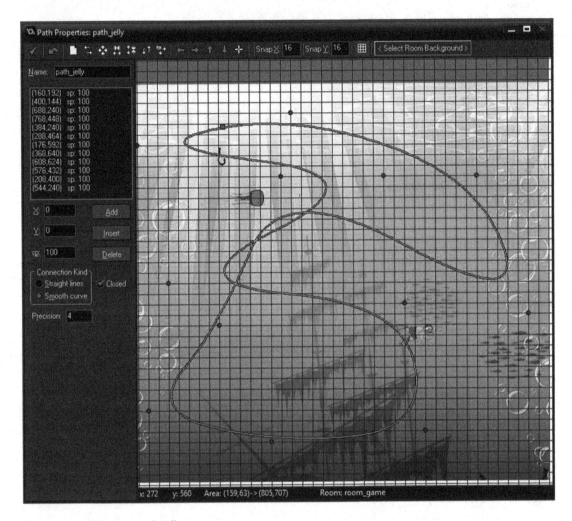

Figure 36-1. Showing path_jelly

Next up is **obj_dock**, which has **spr_dock** assigned. There is no code for this object.

Next is **obj_hud_and_spawn**. There is no sprite for this object. It has the **Create Event** code shown in Listing 36-20.

Listing 36-20. Setting Initial Alarms

```
///alarms
alarm[0]=room_speed*3; //for bubble
alarm[1]=room_speed*4; //for fish
alarm[2]=room_speed*4; //for timer (health)
```

Alarm[0] Event uses the code in Listing 36-21.

Listing 36-21. Creating a Bubble and Restarting the Alarm

```
instance_create(x,y,obj_bubble);
alarm[0]=room_speed*3;
```

Alarm[1] Event is shown in Listing 36-22.

Listing 36-22. Restarting the Alarm and Creating a Random Fish

```
alarm[1]=room_speed*4; //for fish
instance_create(x,y,choose(obj_fish_1,obj_fish_1,obj_fish_2,obj_fish_2,obj_fish_3,
obj_fish_3,obj_fish_4,obj_fish_5,obj_fish_5,obj_fish_6,obj_fish_6))
```

Alarm[2] Event uses the code in Listing 36-23.

Listing 36-23. Restarting Alarm and Reducing Health. If No Health, It Goes to the Gameover Room

```
alarm[2]=room_speed*4; //for timer (health)
health--;
if health<0 room_goto(room_gameover);
```

A **Draw Event** uses the code in Listing 36-24.

Listing 36-24. Drawing HUD Info

```
draw_set_halign(fa_center);
draw_set_valign(fa_middle);
draw_set_font(font_info_small);
draw_text(room_width/2,520,"Left & Right To Extend Rod - Down To Drop Line#Get Hook In Mouth");
draw_text(room_width/2,40,"Score "+string(score));
```

The **Draw Event** has the D&D action for Draw Healthbar, set up as shown in Figure 36-2.

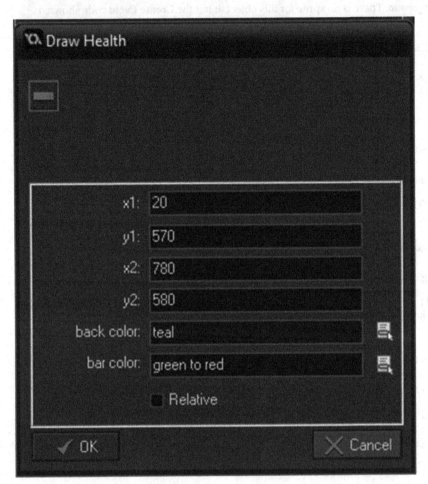

Figure 36-2. *The setup of Draw Healthbar D&D*

Next is **obj_fisher** with **spr_fisher** assigned. There is no code for this.
The last object is **obj_game_over**. It has the **Create Event** code shown in Listing 36-25.

Listing 36-25. Starting an Alarm

```
alarm[0]=room_speed*6;
```

It also has an **Alarm[0] Event**, shown in Listing 36-26.

Listing 36-26. Restarting the Game When the Alarm Triggers

```
game_restart();
```

A **Draw Event** is shown in Listing 36-27.

Listing 36-27. Displaying the Final Score of the Game

```
draw_set_font(font_info_big);
draw_set_halign(fa_center);
draw_text(400,100,"Final Score #"+string(score));
```

Create a room named **room_gameover** that is 800x600 in size and place one instance of **obj_game_over**. That is all for this room.

Next, create a room named **room_game** and set it up as shown in Figure 36-3, including one instance of **obj_hud_and_spawn**.

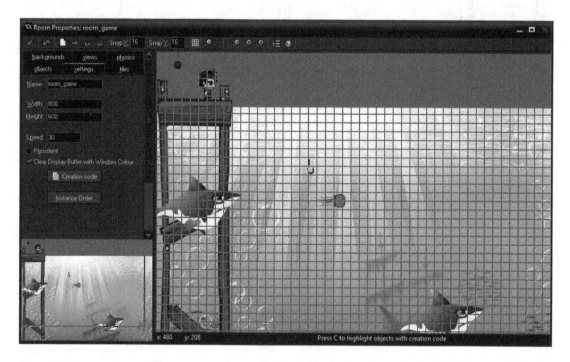

Figure 36-3. *room_game all set up*

Figure 36-4 shows this element in action.

Figure 36-4. This element in action

CHAPTER 37

■ ■ ■

Ship Mini Game

The GMZ for this element is **Ship_Mini_Game**.

Again, this is a mini-game based on the whole lost-on-an-island theme.

For this game you need to navigate a ship around a course without hitting anything. This example is only a small one. If you were using something like this within your own game, you'd probably want a bigger room and more items to collect/avoid.

This example makes use of eight pre-rendered sprites, each for a different direction.

Simple games like this, that the player can participate in, will extend the life of your game and allow them to take a break from the usual RPG mechanics.

This game needs a font named **font_data**, which is Arial size 18.

Next, create the object the player must find: this is **obj_game_end** and has the sprite **spr_flag** assigned. There is no code for this object.

Next, create the object **obj_collision_parent**. There is no code or sprite for this.

Next is **obj_beam_1**, which has sprite **spr_beam_1** with precise collision checking, as shown in Figure 37-1. The parent is **obj_collision_parent**.

© Ben Tyers 2017
B. Tyers, *Learn RPGs in GameMaker: Studio*, DOI 10.1007/978-1-4842-2946-0_37

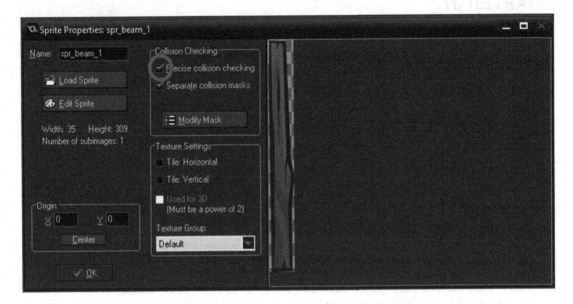

Figure 37-1. Precise collision checking is checked

Next is **obj_beam_2**, which has sprite **spr_beam_2** with precise collision checking. The parent is **obj_collision_parent**.

Next is **obj_beam_3**, which has sprite **spr_beam_3** with precise collision checking. The parent is **obj_collision_parent**.

Next is **obj_beam_4**, which has sprite **spr_beam_4** with precise collision checking. The parent is **obj_collision_parent**.

Next up is **obj_crate_floating**, which has the sprite **spr_crate** assigned. It has the **Create Event** code shown in Listing 37-1.

Listing 37-1. Making a Wobble Effect

```
angle=0; //initial angle
sw=5; //for sine wave
```

A **Step Event** uses the code shown in Listing 37-2.

Listing 37-2. Making the Crate Wobble

```
sw += 0.3; //for sine wave
angle= sin(sw) * 5; //for sine wave
image_angle=angle;
```

The next object is **obj_bubble**, which has sprite **spr_bubble** assigned to it.
It has the **Step Event** code shown in Listing 37-3.

Listing 37-3. Making the Bubble Smaller Each Step and Then Destroying It When Very Small

```
image_xscale*=0.99;
image_yscale*=0.99;
if image_xscale<0.05 instance_destroy();
```

This element's main player object is **obj_ship**.

Create the ship object **obj_ship** and assign the sprite **spr_ship** with precise collision checking set. It has an origin of center.

It has the **Create Event** code seen in Listing 37-4.

Listing 37-4. Setting the Initial Variables and Starting an Alarm

```
///set variables
max_speed=4;
image_speed=0;
direction=0;
bubble=50;
timer=100; //used for timer
alarm[0]=room_speed;
```

Alarm[0] Event is shown in Listing 37-5.

Listing 37-5. Restarting Alarm and Reducing Timer

```
alarm[0]=room_speed;
timer--;
```

The **Step Event** has four blocks. The first block is shown in Listing 37-6. It rotates and moves the player up to maximum speed. It also applies a small amount of friction, keeping speed at 0 or above.

Listing 37-6. Rotating and Moving the Player

```
///movement code

if keyboard_check_pressed(vk_left)
    {
    direction+=45;
    }
if keyboard_check_pressed(vk_right)
    {
    direction-=45;
    }
direction=direction mod 360;
if keyboard_check(vk_up)
    {
    speed+=0.1;
    }
if keyboard_check(vk_down)
{
    speed-=0.2;
}
if speed>max_speed speed=max_speed;
//friction
speed-=0.01;
if speed<0 speed=0;
```

The second block of the **Step Event** is shown in Listing 37-7 and it sets the image angle of the sprite.

Listing 37-7. Setting the Image Angle of the Sprite Depending on the Direction

```
///sprite control

//main sprite control
image_angle=direction;
```

The third block of the **Step Event** is shown in Listing 37-8 and creates a bubble as the player moves.

Listing 37-8. Creating a Bubble as the Player Moves

```
///bubble control
bubble-=speed;
if bubble<0
{
    var scale=random(1);
    bubbles=instance_create(x,y,obj_bubble);
    bubbles.image_xscale=scale;
    bubbles.image_yscale=scale;
    bubble=50;
}
```

The fourth and final block in the **Step Event** is shown in Listing 37-9 and deals with timing issues.

Listing 37-9. If Out of Time, Showing a Message and Restarting the Game

```
///timer check
if timer<1
{
    show_message("You Lose");
    game_restart();
}
```

Next is a **Collision Event with obj_game_end**. The code for this is in Listing 37-10.

Listing 37-10. Showing Winning Message and Restarting the Game If Player Reaches the Flag

```
show_message("You Win");
game_restart();
```

There is a **Collision Event with obj_collision_parent**; the code is in Listing 37-11.

Listing 37-11. If the Player Hits an Object, They Must Restart.

```
show_message("You Died");
game_restart();
```

A **Draw Event** is shown in Listing 37-12.

Listing 37-12. Drawing Ship and Time

```
draw_self();
draw_healthbar(x-50,y-80,x+50,y-75,timer,c_red,c_green,c_blue,0,true,true);
draw_set_halign(fa_middle);
draw_text(x,y-90,"Time");
```

That is all.

Figure 37-2 shows an example room layout.

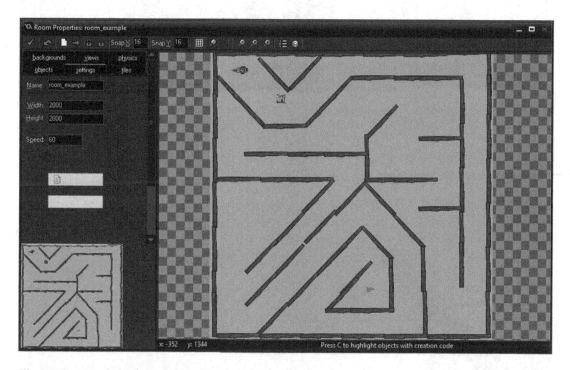

Figure 37-2. *An example room layout*

Figure 37-3 shows this element in action.

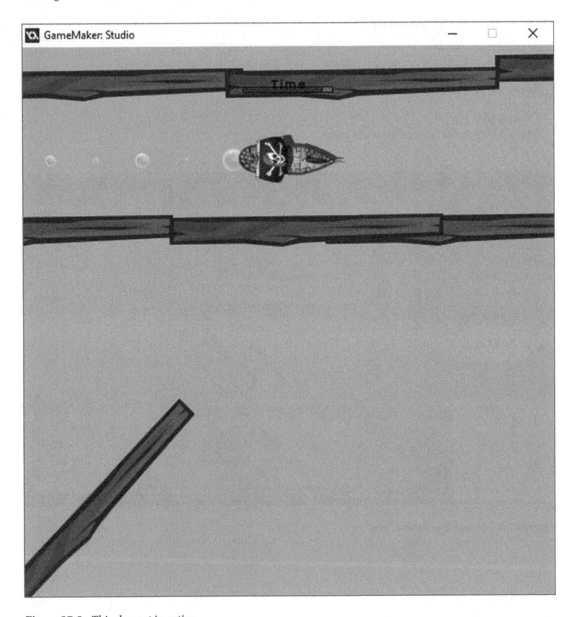

Figure 37-3. This element in action

CHAPTER 38

Dice Rolling

The GMZ for this element is **Dice_Rolling**.

One way to add variety and randomness is rollable dice. Most RPGs will have some kind of non-determined randomness: dice rolling is just one method.

This example rolls two dice and displays the total.

Dice rolling could be used for

- Battle sequences

- Having to throw a double 6 to open a door

- Amount of digs a player gets to hunt treasure

- At the start of game to determine challenge/sub-quest for the player complete

- How strong a weapon attack will be

This example uses two six-sided dice. You could increase the sides on the dice or number of dice to suit your need.

This element uses a sprite **spr_dice**, which has six subimages, each of a dice face.

There is one object, **obj_roll_dice**.

The **Create Event** code is shown in Listing 38-1.

Listing 38-1. Setting Initial Values for the Dice

```
rolling=false;
dice1=1;
dice2=1;
```

There is an **Alarm[0] Event** with the code shown in Listing 38-2.

Listing 38-2. A Flag Used for Whether Dice Are Rolling or Not

```
rolling=false;
```

A **Step Event** has the code shown in Listing 38-3. On press of R, the dice will start rolling. When rolling, it will choose a value between 0 and 5 inclusive, which relates to the subimage. For example, a value of 0 would be the dice with one spot, 5 would be the dice with six spots.

© Ben Tyers 2017

B. Tyers, *Learn RPGs in GameMaker: Studio*, DOI 10.1007/978-1-4842-2946-0_38

Listing 38-3. Choosing the Dice Value

```
if keyboard_check_released(ord('R')) && !rolling
{
    rolling=true;
    alarm[0]=room_speed*4;
}

if rolling
{
    dice1=irandom(5);
    dice2=irandom(5);
}
```

Finally, there is a **Draw Event**, shown in Listing 38-4.

Listing 38-4. Drawing the Dice and Showing R to Roll If the Dice Have Finished Rolling

```
draw_sprite(spr_dice,dice1,200,200);
draw_sprite(spr_dice,dice2,400,200);
if !rolling draw_text(50,50,"Press R to Roll#Last Roll "+string(dice1+dice2+2));
```

Just place one instance of this object in a room.

Figure 38-1 shows this in action.

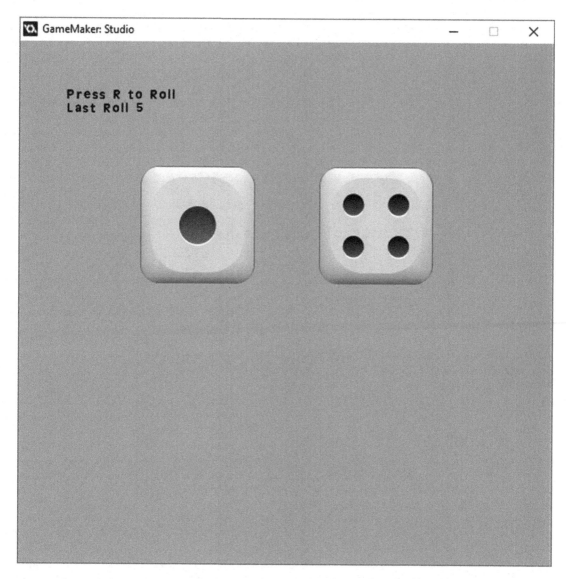

Figure 38-1. This element in action

■ ■ ■

CHAPTER 39

Mini-Game and Dual View

The GMZ for this section is **Mini_Game_Dual_View**.

This element combines a mini-game and dual zooming. This dual zooming keeps both the player and enemy within view, zooming in and out depending on how close they are to each other.

It kind of fits in with the pirate theme that this game follows: I guess pirates may drop bombs!

The aim of this mini-game is to drop bombs and try to hit the enemy with the blast wave.

The enemy has some basic AI: they will seek a bomb crate to replenish their bombs if they have run out. Otherwise, they will either move towards the player's location or a random point in the room. This is achieved using paths. It will drop a bomb at the end of paths and randomly when moving.

Some clever math is used to calculate a point between the player and enemy and to calculate the amount of zoom required to keep both in view.

This zooming approach could be used in other ways when you would like to keep two objects in view at one time. For example, for a maze with treasure in the middle, you could keep the player and treasure both in view at once. See Figure 39-1.

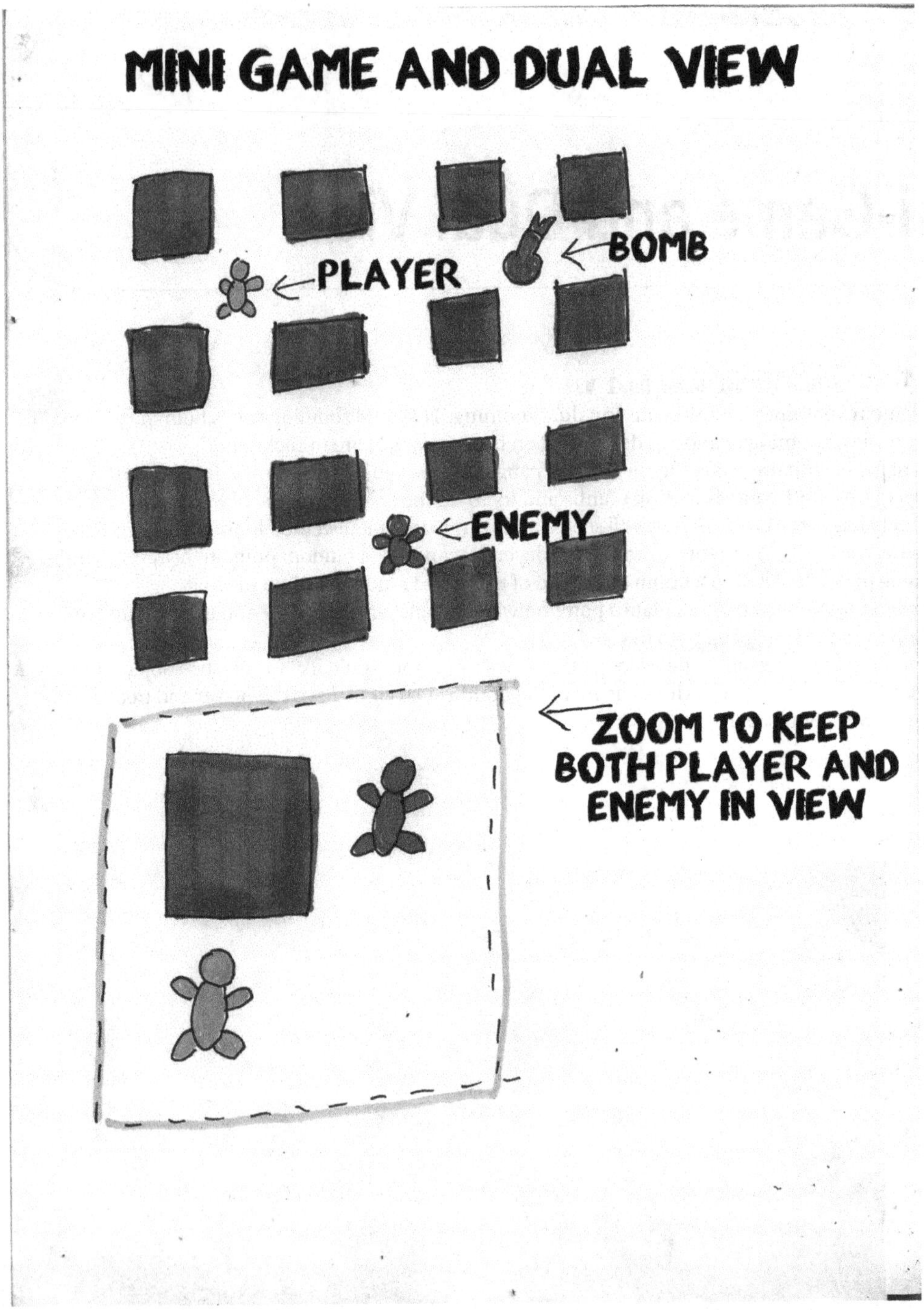

Figure 39-1. Dual views

First up there is a font named **font_hud** that is Arial size 12.

There are two scripts. The first is **scr_sound** with the code shown in Listing 39-1.

Listing 39-1. Script To Play a Sound

```
audio_play_sound(argument0,1,false);
```

The second is **scr_move** with the code shown in Listing 39-2. It works by checking ahead in the direction of movement.

Listing 39-2. Checking Whether the Player Can Move in A Certain Direction and Moving Accordingly

```
/// scr_move(dx, dy)
// attempts to move the current instance, pushing things around as needed.

// calculate new coordinates:
var dx = argument0, nx = x + dx;
var dy = argument1, ny = y + dy;

if (place_meeting(nx, ny, obj_wall))
{
    // if there's a wall there, definitely can't move there
    return false;
}
else if (place_free(nx, ny))
{
    // if there's nothing there, just move there
    x = nx; y = ny;
    return true;
}
else
{
    // otherwise attempt to move every pushable object touched
    with (obj_pushable) if (place_meeting(x - dx, y - dy, other))
    {
        // (if any object fails to move, stop trying to move them)
        if (!scr_move(dx, dy)) return false;

    }
    // if it's now possible to move to the position, do that
    if (place_free(nx, ny))
    {
        x = nx; y = ny;
        return true;
    }
    else return false;
}
```

The next step is to load in the sounds. They are

- **snd_explosion**
- **snd_voice_bonus**
- **snd_ammo**
- **snd_drop_bomb**
- **snd_enemy_1_exp**
- **snd_ouch**

Next up are the objects. First is **obj_splash**. It has the **Create Event** code shown in Listing 39-3.

Listing 39-3. Setting Starting Values and Going to the Room to Play the Game

```
//set up globals and goto game room
global.player_bombs=0;
global.enemy_bombs=0;
health=100;
global.enemy_health=100;
room_goto(room_1_player);
```

Create a room named **room_splash** that is 800x700 in size. Place one instance of **obj_splash** in this room. That is all for this object and room.

Next is **obj_solid_parent**. There is no sprite or code for this object.

Next up is **obj_wall**, which has **spr_wall** assigned with an origin of center. It also has the parent **obj_solid_parent**.

The next object is **obj_explosion**, which has the sprite **spr_explosion** with 48 subimages. The origin needs to be set as center. The **Step Event** code for this object is shown in Listing 39-4. Note that you could also use an animation end event for this.

Listing 39-4. Destroying the Instance When Subimage Is Over 45

```
///destroy at end
if image_index>45 instance_destroy();
```

The next object is **obj_bomb**, which has the sprite **spr_bomb** assigned, with an origin of center. The **Create Event** code is shown in Listing 39-5.

Listing 39-5. Moving to Snap at 32 by 32 (Aligned to Imaginary Grid)

```
move_snap(32,32);
life=5;
alarm[0]=room_speed/4;
```

The **Alarm[0] Event** code is shown in Listing 39-6.

Listing 39-6. Reducing Life and Starting an Alarm

```
life--;
alarm[0]=room_speed/4;
```

It has the **Step Event** code that makes the explosions; this is shown in Listing 39-7.

Listing 39-7. Exploding the Bomb and Creating Explosions in Four Directions, Stopping at a Wall

```
///create explostion
if life==0
{
    scr_sound(snd_explosion);
    //create exp at position
    instance_create(x,y,obj_explosion);

    //create up
    if !position_meeting(x,y-32,obj_wall)
    {
        instance_create(x,y-32,obj_explosion);
        if !position_meeting(x,y-64,obj_wall)
        {
            instance_create(x,y-64,obj_explosion);
            if !position_meeting(x,y-96,obj_wall)
            {
                instance_create(x,y-96,obj_explosion);
            }
        }
    }
    //create down
    if !position_meeting(x,y+32,obj_wall)
    {
        instance_create(x,y+32,obj_explosion);
        if !position_meeting(x,y+64,obj_wall)
        {
            instance_create(x,y+64,obj_explosion);
            if !position_meeting(x,y+96,obj_wall)
            {
                instance_create(x,y+96,obj_explosion);
            }
        }
    }
    //create left
    if !position_meeting(x-32,y,obj_wall)
    {
        instance_create(x-32,y,obj_explosion);
        if !position_meeting(x-64,y,obj_wall)
        {
            instance_create(x-64,y,obj_explosion);
            if !position_meeting(x-96,y,obj_wall)
            {
                instance_create(x-96,y,obj_explosion);
            }
        }
    }
```

```
//create right
if !position_meeting(x+32,y,obj_wall)
{
    instance_create(x+32,y,obj_explosion);
    if !position_meeting(x+64,y,obj_wall)
    {
        instance_create(x+64,y,obj_explosion);
        if !position_meeting(x+96,y,obj_wall)
        {
            instance_create(x+96,y,obj_explosion);
        }
    }
}
instance_destroy();
}
```

We need a **Collision Event with obj_explosion**, which will force a bomb to explode if it is hit by an explosion; see Listing 39-8.

Listing 39-8. Triggering the Bomb to Explode If Hit by Another's Explosion

```
life=0;
```

Finally a **Draw Event** is shown in Listing 39-9.

Listing 39-9. Drawing the Sprite and Timer (Life) Over It

```
draw_set_halign(fa_center);
draw_set_colour(c_red);
draw_self();
draw_text(x,y,life);
```

That is all for this object.

Next up is **obj_ammo**. This has the sprite **spr_bomb_crate**, which has its origin set as center. It has the **Create Event** code shown in Listing 39-10.

Listing 39-10. When Collected by Player or Enemy, Will Jump to an Empty Position

```
//jump to a random free position
do
{
    var _x = (random(room_width) div 32) * 32;
    var _y = (random(room_height) div 32) * 32;
}
until (place_free(_x, _y));
x=_x;
y=_y;
```

That is all for this object.

Next is the controllable player object **obj_player_1**.

It has the sprite **spr_player_1** assigned. Again, the origin is center, and it looks like Figure 39-2. It is important to get the directions correct.

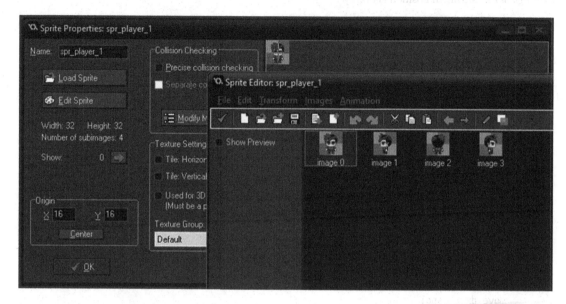

Figure 39-2. *Subimages of spr_player_1*

The **Create Event** code is shown in Listing 39-11.

Listing 39-11. Used for Movement and Damage

```
///setup
move_dx = 0;
move_dy = 0;
move_amt = 0;
image_index=0;
image_speed=0;
can_hurt=true;
```

Alarm[5] Event has the code show in in Listing 39-12.

Listing 39-12. Allow To Be Hurt Again

can_hurt=true;

Next, it has three **Step Event** code blocks. The first is shown in Listing 39-13.

Listing 39-13. Moving If Position Is Empty

```
///MOVEMENT
if (move_amt > 0)
{
    // moving towards destination
    if (scr_move(move_dx, move_dy))
    {
        move_amt -= 1;
    }
    else move_amt = 0; //if hit a wall, stop moving
}
else
{
    var spd = 4; //movement speed (grid size should divide by it w/o remainder)
    move_amt = 32 div spd; //calculate number of steps for movement
    move_dx = 0;
    move_dy = 0;
    if (keyboard_check(vk_left)) && !(position_meeting(x-18,y,obj_wall))
    //move if only 1 block and pos free
    {
        move_dx = -spd;
    }
    else if (keyboard_check(vk_right)&& !(position_meeting(x+18,y,obj_wall)))
    {
        move_dx = spd;
    }
    else if (keyboard_check(vk_up) && (!position_meeting(x,y-18,obj_wall)))
    {
        move_dy = -spd;
    }
    else if (keyboard_check(vk_down))&& !(position_meeting(x,y+18,obj_wall))
    {
        move_dy = spd;
    }
    else move_amt = 0; //don't move if no buttons are pressed
}
```

The second code block in the **Step Event** is shown in Listing 39-14.

Listing 39-14. Dropping a Bomb and Playing a Sound

```
///DROP BOMB
if (keyboard_check_pressed(ord('Z')) && global.player_bombs>0)
{
    global.player_bombs--;
    instance_create(x,y,obj_bomb);
    scr_sound(snd_drop_bomb);
}
```

And the final block in the **Step Event** is shown in Listing 39-15.

Listing 39-15. Changing Subimage Accordingly

```
///sprite control
//move_dx, move_dy
if move_dx>0 image_index=3;
if move_dx<0 image_index=1;
if move_dy>0 image_index=0;
if move_dy<0 image_index=2;
```

Then there is a **Collison Event with obj_ammo** with the code from Listing 39-16.

Listing 39-16. Increasing the Amount of Bombs the Player Has and Playing a Sound

```
///increase number of bombs
global.player_bombs+=5;
with (other) instance_destroy();
instance_create(5,5,obj_ammo);
scr_sound(snd_ammo);
```

A **Collision Event with obj_explosion** reduces the health if hit by an explosion and plays a sound. It also sets an alarm, which prevents being hurt again for 1 second. See Listing 39-17.

Listing 39-17. Reducing Health If Hit and Playing a Sound

```
if can_hurt
{
    health--;
    scr_sound(snd_ouch);
    can_hurt=false;
    alarm[5]=room_speed; //prevent hurting for one second
}
```

When done, **obj_player_1** will look like Figure 39-3.

Figure 39-3. *obj_player_1 all set up*

Next up is **obj_enemy**, which has the sprite **spr_player_2** assigned. The origin should be the center. It has four subimages and the directions are the same as those shown in Figure 39-2, but are a different colour.

The **Create Event** code is shown in Listing 39-18. It creates a grid for the enemy to move on, blocking out places where there is a wall instance. It also sets the initial path to the ammo crate.

Listing 39-18. Creating a Grid for the Enemy and Setting a Path to the Ammo Crate

```
grid=mp_grid_create(0, 0, room_width div 16, room_height div 16, 16 , 16);
mp_grid_add_instances(grid, obj_wall, false);

image_speed=0;
image_index=0;
path=path_add();

mp_grid_path(grid,path,x,y,obj_ammo.x,obj_ammo.y,false);
path_start(path,3.5,path_action_stop,true);

can_hurt=true;
```

It has an **Alarm[0] Event** with the code shown in Listing 39-19.

Listing 39-19. Making a New Path, Either to Player or a Random Position

```
//choose a target
target=choose("player","random");
if target=="player"
{
    mp_grid_path(grid,path,x,y,obj_player_1.x,obj_player_1.y,false);
    path_start(path,3.5,path_action_stop,true);
```

```
    alarm[0]=room_speed*5; //prevent sticking
    exit;
}
if target=="random"
{
    do //find a free place
    {
        var _x = (random(room_width) div 32) * 32;
        var _y = (random(room_height) div 32) * 32;
    }
    until (place_free(_x, _y));

    mp_grid_path(grid,path,x,y,_x,_y,false);
    path_start(path,3.5,path_action_stop,true);
    alarm[0]=room_speed*8; //prevent sticking
    }
```

Alarm[5] Event has the code in Listing 39-20.

Listing 39-20. Allowing Being Hurt Again

```
can_hurt=true;
```

A **Step Event** has two code blocks. The first is shown in Listing 39-21.

Listing 39-21. Setting the Subimage Based on Direction

```
///image control
if hspeed>0 image_index=3;
if hspeed<0 image_index=1;
if vspeed>0 image_index=0;
if vspeed<0 image_index=2;
```

The second code block is shown in Listing 39-22.

Listing 39-22. Randomly Dropping a Bomb, If Available

```
///randomly drop a bomb
rand=irandom(200); //one in 200 chance of dropping a bomb
if rand==1
{
    if global.enemy_bombs>0 //check player has bombs
    {
        global.enemy_bombs--;
        instance_create(x,y,obj_bomb);
    }
}
```

It has a **Collision Event with obj_ammo** and the code is shown in Listing 39-23.

Listing 39-23. Increasing Bombs on Collision with Crate, Destroying the Crate, Making a New One, and Playing a Sound

```
///increase no. of bombs
global.enemy_bombs+=5;
with (other) instance_destroy();
instance_create(5,5,obj_ammo);
scr_sound(snd_ammo);
```

A **Collision Event with obj_explosion** is shown in Listing 39-24.

Listing 39-24. Checking Flag Status, Reducing Health, Playing a Sound, Setting Flag to False, and Setting Alarm

```
if can_hurt
{
    global.enemy_health--;
    scr_sound(snd_ouch);
    can_hurt=false;
    alarm[5]=room_speed; //prevent hurting for one second
}
```

It has an **End of Path Event**, which can be selected by clicking Add Event ➤ Other ➤ End of Path. The code for this event is shown in Listing 39-25. If no bombs are left, it will seek out the bomb crate.

Listing 39-25. Making a New Path Either to the Player or a Random Position

```
///clear and update grid and drop bomb
if global.enemy_bombs>0
{
    global.enemy_bombs--;
    instance_create(x,y,obj_bomb);
}


//grid
mp_grid_clear_all(grid);
mp_grid_add_instances(grid, obj_wall, false);
if global.enemy_bombs<1
{
    mp_grid_path(grid,path,x,y,obj_ammo.x,obj_ammo.y,false);
    path_start(path,3.5,path_action_stop,true);
    alarm[0]=room_speed*5; //prevent sticking
    exit;
}
```

```
//choose a target
target=choose("player","random");
if target=="player"
{
    mp_grid_path(grid,path,x,y,obj_player_1.x,obj_player_1.y,false);
    path_start(path,3.5,path_action_stop,true);
    alarm[0]=room_speed*5; //prevent sticking
    exit;
}
if target=="random"
{
    do //find a free place
    {
        var _x = (random(room_width) div 32) * 32;
        var _y = (random(room_height) div 32) * 32;
    }
    until (place_free(_x, _y));

    mp_grid_path(grid,path,x,y,_x,_y,false);
    path_start(path,3.5,path_action_stop,true);
    alarm[0]=room_speed*8; //prevent sticking
}
```

A **Draw Event** uses the code from Listing 39-26.

Listing 39-26. Drawing Self and Its Path

```
draw_self();
draw_path(path,x,y,true);
```

Finally there is a **Game End Event** with the code from Listing 39-27.

Listing 39-27. Clearing the Memory

```
mp_grid_destroy(grid);
path_delete(path);
```

That is all for this object.
Next up is **obj_hud_1**. This has the **Step Event** code shown in Listing 39-28.

Listing 39-28. Determining Who Won

```
///test  lives
if health<1 or global.enemy_health<1
{
    room_goto(room_game_over);
}
```

And the **Draw GUI Event** code is shown in Listing 39-29.

Listing 39-29. Drawing the HUD Info

```
draw_set_halign(fa_center);
draw_text(400,750,"Player 1 - Arrow Keys Move - Z Drop Bomb");
draw_text(20,20,"Plater Health "+string(health));
draw_text(400,20,"Enemy Health "+string(global.enemy_health));
draw_set_halign(fa_left);
draw_text(20,50,"Player Bombs "+string(global.player_bombs));
draw_text(20,80,"Enemy Bombs "+string(global.enemy_bombs));
```

That is all for this object.

The next object is **obj_view_control**. It has a **Step Event** with the code shown in Listing 39-30.

Listing 39-30. Keeping Both Player and Enemy in View, Zooming In and Out as Needed

```
var x1 = obj_player_1.x; //get x position of player 1
var y1 = obj_player_1.y; //get y position of player 1
var x2 = obj_enemy.x; //get x position of player 2
var y2 = obj_enemy.y; //get y position of player 2
var border = 50; //set a border distance
var vscale = max(1, abs(x2 - x1) / (view_wport[0]- border * 2), abs(y2 - y1) /
(view_hport[0] - border * 2)); //calculte scale needed
view_wview[0] = vscale * view_wport[0]; //apply scale to view port
view_hview[0] = vscale * view_hport[0]; //apply scale to view port
view_xview[0]= (x1 + x2 - view_wview[0]) / 2; //update view
view_yview[0] = (y1 + y2 - view_hview[0]) / 2; //update view
```

Next up is **obj_game_over**.

The **Create Event** code for this object is shown in Listing 39-31.

Listing 39-31. Setting an Alarm for 10 Seconds

```
alarm[0]=room_speed*10;
```

The **Alarm[0] Event** code is shown in Listing 39-32.

Listing 39-32. Restarting Game When Alarm Triggers

```
game_restart();
```

The **Draw Event** code for this object is shown in Listing 39-33.

Listing 39-33. Displaying Text to Show Who Won

```
if health<1
{
    draw_text(100,100,"Enemy Wins");
}
else
{
    draw_text(100,100,"Player Wins");
}
```

An instance of **obj_game_over** goes into a room named **room_game_over**, with a size of 800x700. That is all for this room and object.

Create a room named **room_1_player** and set it up as shown in Figure 39-4.

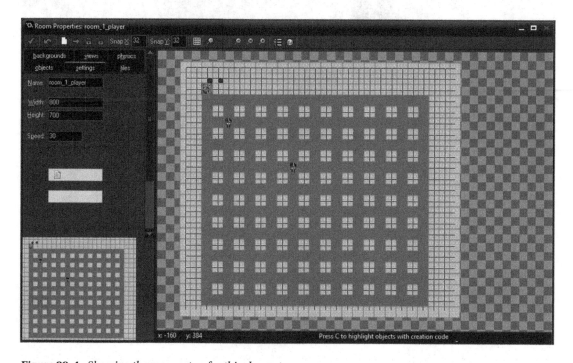

Figure 39-4. Showing the room setup for this element

As you can see, it consists of a border and grid made from **obj_wall**. There is one instance each of **obj_player_1**, **obj_enemy**, and **obj_ammo**. There are also two control objects, **obj_hud_1** and **obj_view_control**. Figure 39-5 shows this element in action.

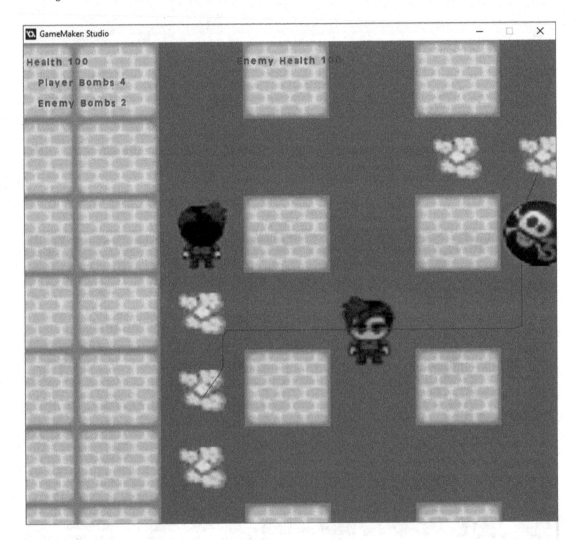

Figure 39-5. *This element in action*

CHAPTER 40

Game End

The GMZ for this element is **Game_End**.

This element makes use of the **Game_Base** GMZ.

By now you should be aware that the aim of this game is to collect enough treasure to get off the island. This basic example checks whether the player has enough to pay the pirate and get off the island.

If they don't have enough, the pirate will ask them to come back when they do.

Upon completion, they'll be rewarded with (a pretty poor) fireworks display.

If this was within your own game, this would be a great time to have another cutscene sequence.

Finishing the story off is important. You may want to end it in another way: perhaps she wakes up in bed and it was all a bad dream, or something with more thought and imagination.

There are a few changes to the **Game_Base** GMZ for this.

First up is a font named **font_message** that is Arial size 16.

Next is a new object named **obj_treasure** with **spr_treasure** assigned.

obj_player has the **Create Event** code shown in Listing 40-1.

Listing 40-1. Setting Up Initial Variables Needed

```
///set up
enum player_state {
    idle,
    up,
    down,
    left,
    right
    }
dir= player_state.down;
is_moving=false;
image_speed=0.5;
global.treasure=0;
```

An additional event, a **Collision Event with obj_treasure**, uses the code in Listing 40-2.

Listing 40-2. Increasing Treasure and Then Destroying It

```
global.treasure++;
with (other) instance_destroy();
```

© Ben Tyers 2017

B. Tyers, *Learn RPGs in GameMaker: Studio*, DOI 10.1007/978-1-4842-2946-0_40

That is the only change for the player object.

There is a new object named **obj_pirate** with sprite **spr_pirate** assigned. This sprite consists of 12 subimages.

The **Create Event** for **obj_pirate** is shown in Listing 40-3. It sets up initial values and a selection of replies if the player doesn't have enough treasure.

Listing 40-3. Setting Up Initial Values and a Selection of Replies

```
///set up text
is_touching=false; //used to check whether colliding with player
text=""; //initial message state
show_text=""; //start the typewriter text as ""
count=0; //location in show_text
pirate_text=ds_list_create(); //create list for text

//add text to list
ds_list_add(pirate_text,
"You Need More Treasure",
"Come Back When You Have 5 Chests",
"Not Enough Treasure",
"It Will Cost More Than That",
"Not Enough",
"I Need More Treasure",
"I Charge More Than That",
"You'll Need 5 Chests",
"My Ship Costs More Than You Have");
```

An **Alarm[0] Event** has the code shown in Listing 40-4.

Listing 40-4. Clearing Any Text and Resetting for Next Collision

```
is_touching=false;
text="";
show_text="";
count=0;
```

There is a **Collision Event with obj_player**, the code for which is shown in Listing 40-5. Basically, if a player has less than 5 treasures, it will display a random message. If a player has more than 5, they go to the end of the game room.

Listing 40-5. Counting Treasure and Determining Player Path

```
if global.treasure<5
{
    if !is_touching
    {
        message=irandom(8);
        show_debug_message(message);
        is_touching=true;
        text=pirate_text[|message];
    }
```

```
alarm[0]=room_speed*5;
}
else
{
    room_goto(room_complete);
}
```

Next is a **Draw Event** with the GML shown in Listing 40-6.

Listing 40-6. Drawing Any Message and Background

```
///drawing stuff

draw_self(); //draw self

//set text to draw
if(string_length(show_text) < string_length(text))
{
show_text = string_copy(text,1,count);
alarm[0] = room_speed*4;
count +=1;
}
if show_text!="" //draw bubble if text present
{
    padding=10;
    //set variables
    width =string_width(text) + padding * 2; // width of message, capped at max_width
    height = string_height(text) + padding * 2;
    border_size=2;

    //draw bits below first to create a border
    //round rectangle first
    draw_set_colour(c_blue);
    draw_roundrect(x-(width/2)-border_size,
    y-90-(height/2)-border_size,x+(width/2)+border_size,y-90+(height/2)+border_size,false);

    //triangle outline for triangle
    draw_line_width(x-(width/4)+border_size,y-90+(height/2)-border_size,x+border_size,
    y-25,border_size);
    draw_line_width(x,y-25,x-(width/2),y-90+(height/2),border_size);

    //draw a the box
    draw_set_colour(c_white);
    draw_roundrect(x-(width/2),y-90-(height/2),x+(width/2),y-90+(height/2),false);
    //draw_triangle to make it look like speech bubble
    draw_triangle(
    x-(width/2)+2,y-90+(height/2),
    x-(width/4),y-90+(height/2),
    x,y-25,
    false);
```

```
//draw a message
draw_set_font(font_message);
draw_set_halign(fa_center);
draw_set_valign(fa_middle);
draw_set_colour(c_black);
draw_text(x,y-90,show_text);
}
```

And finally for this object is a **Game End Event** with the code shown in Listing 40-7.

Listing 40-7. Freeing the Memory

```
ds_list_destroy(pirate_text);
```

Next up is **obj_ship**; it has the **spr_ship** assigned to it. There is no code for this object. The last object is **obj_game_complete** with the **Create Event** code shown in Listing 40-8.

Listing 40-8. Set An Alarm For One Second

```
alarm[0]=room_speed;
```

It has the **Alarm[0] Event** code shown in Listing 40-9 for adding a firework effect.

Listing 40-9. Creating a Firework Effect

```
alarm[0]=room_speed/3;

effect_create_above(ef_firework,irandom(room_width),irandom(room_
height),choose(1,2),choose(c_red,c_green,c_yellow));
```

The **Draw Event** code, in Listing 40-10, shows the final text of the game.

Listing 40-10. The Final Text of the Game

```
draw_set_colour(c_white);
draw_text(350,20,"You Did It!");
```

Figure 40-1 shows an example room layout of **room_end_of_game**.

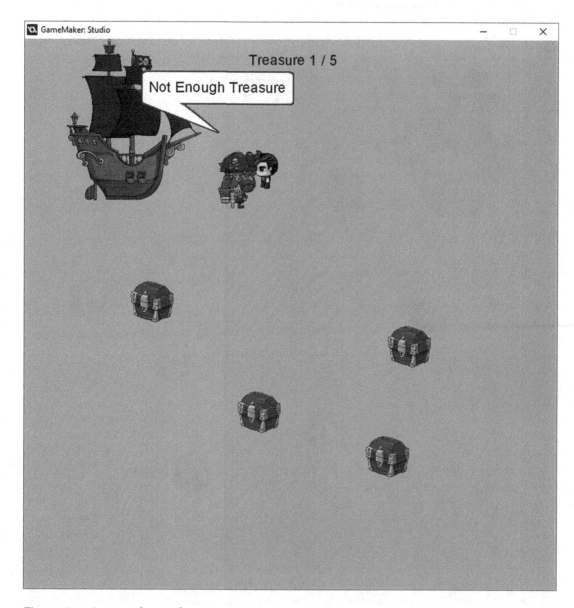

Figure 40-1. An example room layout

room_complete has one instance of **obj_game_complete** in it.
Figure 40-2 shows this element in action.

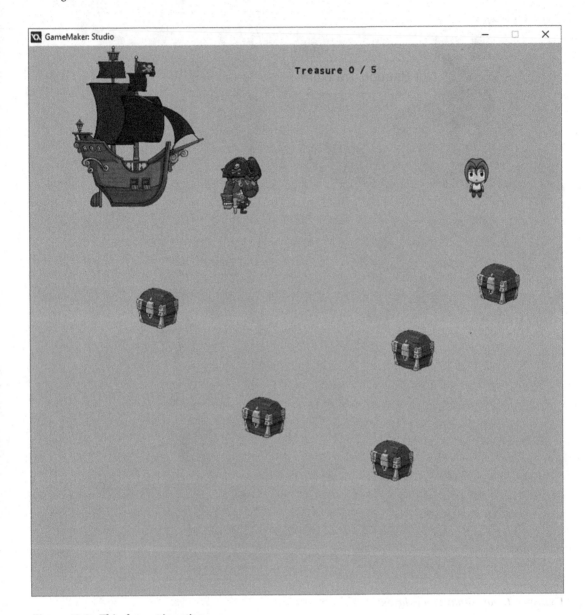

Figure 40-2. *This element in action*

Figure 40-3 shows the end-of-game screen.

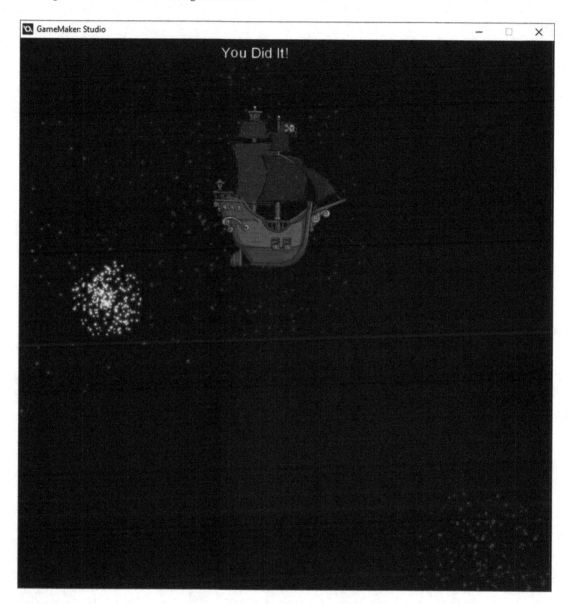

Figure 40-3. *End-of-game screen with some fireworks*

CHAPTER 41

Saving

The GMZ for this element is **Saving**.

Your game will need to hold, save, and load a lot of data. One easy-to-use method is with INI files. You can store and load data to different sections and keys.

In this example, we'll load and save the following: Magic, Kindness, Evilness, Strength, Wisdom, Charisma, Upgrades, Gold, Status of a Quest, and an object's x and y positions. The INI file would look something like:

```
[Stats]
Magic="5.000000"
Kindness="8.000000"
Evilness="5.000000"
Strength="10.000000"
Wisdom="3.000000"
Charisma="3.000000"
Upgrades="2.000000"
Gold="3500.000000"
[Quest]
1="1.000000"
[Pirates]
1x="350.000000"
1y="640.000000"
```

In your game you'll likely have hundreds of variables, although the process remains the same.

The first object is **obj_splash**. This will load any saved data, or set default values if no save file is present (e.g. when starting the game). The **Create Event** code is shown in Listing 41-1.

Listing 41-1. Reading from INI If Present

```
///set up stats
//load data from save
ini_open("save.ini");
global.stats[1,1]="Magic";
global.stats[1,2]=ini_read_real("Stats", "Magic", 4);

global.stats[2,1]="Kindness";
global.stats[2,2]=ini_read_real("Stats", "Kindness", 4);
```

© Ben Tyers 2017
B. Tyers, *Learn RPGs in GameMaker: Studio*, DOI 10.1007/978-1-4842-2946-0_41

```
global.stats[3,1]="Evilness";
global.stats[3,2]=ini_read_real("Stats", "Evilness",2)

global.stats[4,1]="Strength";
global.stats[4,2]=ini_read_real("Stats", "Strength", 4);

global.stats[5,1]="Wisdom";
global.stats[5,2]=ini_read_real("Stats", "Wisdom", 0);

global.stats[5,1]="Charisma";
global.stats[5,2]=ini_read_real("Stats", "Charisma", 1);

global.upgrades=ini_read_real("Stats", "Upgrades", 8);

global.quest1=ini_read_real("Quest", "1", true);

global.pirate1_x=ini_read_real("Pirates", "1x", 350);
global.pirate1_y=ini_read_real("Pirates", "1y", 640);

global.gold=ini_read_real("Stats", "Gold", 200);

ini_close();
//goto main room
room_goto(room_saving);
```

Let's look at one part:

```
global.stats[1,1]="Magic";
global.stats[1,2]=ini_read_real("Stats", "Magic", 4);
```

This sets **global.stats[1,1]** to "Magic". The second line loads the appropriate data held in the INI file. If the section and key are not present, it will set the default value, in this case 4.

There is a sprite named **spr_info** that has two subimages, 32x32 in size with the first in solid yellow and the second in red. The origins are center.

The next object is **obj_button**, which will allow for testing, allowing you to increase stats. The sprite for this is **spr_button**.

It also has two subimages with the origins as center, as shown in Figure 41-1. A different subimage will be displayed depending on whether an upgrade is available or not.

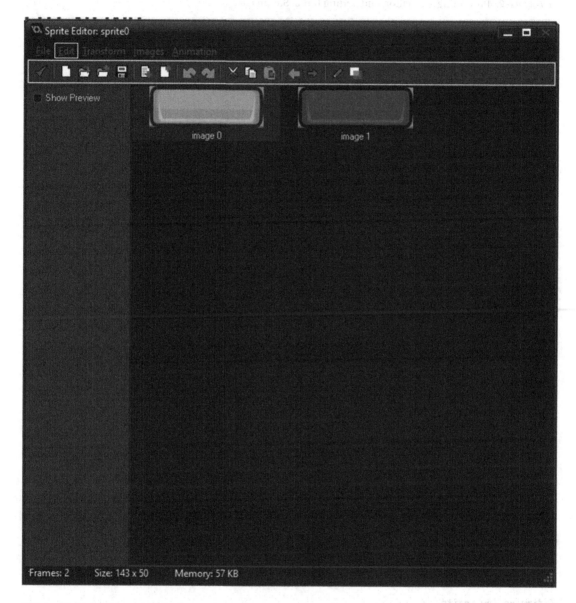

Figure 41-1. Subimages of obj_button

The **Create Event** code for this object is shown in Listing 41-2.

Listing 41-2. Preventing Animation and Setting Initial Subimage

```
//set up
image_speed=0;
image_index=0;
```

The **Step Event** code checks for a left mouse button click over the object, and will then update the values if this is available; see Listing 41-3.

Listing 41-3. Allowing Upgrading of a Stat

```
///mouse button
if mouse_check_button_pressed(mb_left) && position_meeting(mouse_x, mouse_y, id)
{
    if global.upgrades>0 && global.stats[my_id,2]<10
    {
        //upgrade
        global.upgrades--;
        global.stats[my_id,2]++;
    }
}
```

The **Draw Event** code draws the appropriate text that was created in the splash room object. It also draws a red or yellow rectangle depending on the stats; see Listing 41-4.

Listing 41-4. Drawing the Buttons and Text

```
//draw button
draw_self();
//set text drawing
draw_set_halign(fa_center);
draw_set_valign(fa_middle);
//draw the text
draw_set_halign(fa_left);
draw_text(50,my_id*100,global.stats[my_id,1]);

//draw red sprite - not the quickest approach, but easy to understand
for (var loop=1; loop < 11; loop += 1)
{
    draw_sprite(spr_info,1,150+loop*40,my_id*100)
}

//draw yellow sprite
for (var loop=1; loop <= global.stats[my_id,2]; loop += 1)
{
    draw_sprite(spr_info,0,150+loop*40,my_id*100)
}
```

```
//draw button text
draw_set_halign(fa_center);
if global.stats[my_id,2]<10 && global.upgrades>0
{
    image_index=0;
    draw_text(x,y,"Available");
}
else if global.stats[my_id,2]==10
{
    image_index=1;
    draw_text(x,y,"Maxed Out");
}
else
{
    image_index=1;
    draw_text(x,y,"Not Available");
}
```

The next object is **obj_setup_buttons_and_hud**. The **Create Event** code is shown in Listing 41-5.

Listing 41-5. Creating the Buttons on Screen

```
///create buttons
for (var loop = 1; loop < 6; loop += 1)
{
    button=instance_create(700,100*loop,obj_button);
    button.my_id=loop;
}
```

The **Step Event** code is shown in Listing 41-6.

Listing 41-6. Keyboard Shortcuts to Make Things Happen

```
///for testing
if keyboard_check_pressed(ord('R'))
{
    show_message("Saved - Restaring");
    game_restart();
}

if keyboard_check_pressed(ord('S'))
{
    scr_save_data();
    show_message("All Data Saved");
}

if keyboard_check_pressed(ord('Q'))
{
    global.quest1=!global.quest1;
}
```

```
if keyboard_check_is_pressed (ord('G'))
{
    global.gold+=100;
}
if keyboard_check_pressed (ord('X'))
{
    global.upgrades+=5;
}
```

The **Draw Event** code is shown in Listing 41-7.

Listing 41-7. Drawing Upgrade Points, Whether a Quest Is Completed, and Current Gold

```
///for testing
draw_set_halign(fa_left);

draw_text(100,50,"You Have "+string(global.upgrades)+" Upgrade Points - Press R To Restart
Example#Arrow Keys To Move Character#S To Save Data - A D move pirate - Q Toggle Quest -#G
For More Gold  X For More Upgrade Points");

if global.quest1 draw_text(400,700,"Quest Completed");
else
draw_text(400,700,"Quest Is Not Completed");

draw_text(400,720,"Gold "+string(global.gold));
```

The final object is **obj_pirate**. The **Create Event** code is shown in Listing 41-8.

Listing 41-8. Setting Up a Pirate

```
x=global.pirate1_x;
y=global.pirate1_y;
```

The **Step Event** code is shown in Listing 41-9.

Listing 41-9. Some Basic Movement

```
if keyboard_check(ord('A'))
{
    x--;
}
if keyboard_check(ord('D'))
{
    x++;
}

if x<64 x=64;
if x>room_width-64 x=room_width-64;
```

There are two rooms. The first is **room_splash**, which is 1024x768 in size and has one instance of **obj_splash** in it.

This element make use of a script to save data, named scr_save_data with the code:

Listing 41-10. Save Data To INI File

```
///Save Data
ini_open("save.ini");

ini_write_real("Stats", "Magic", global.stats[1,2]);

ini_write_real("Stats", "Kindness", global.stats[2,2]);

ini_write_real("Stats", "Evilness",global.stats[3,2])

ini_write_real("Stats", "Strength", global.stats[4,2]);

ini_write_real("Stats", "Wisdom", global.stats[5,2]);

ini_write_real("Stats", "Charisma", global.stats[5,2]);

ini_write_real("Stats", "Upgrades", global.upgrades);

ini_write_real("Quest", "1", global.quest1);

ini_write_real("Pirates", "1x", obj_pirate.x)
ini_write_real("Pirates", "1y", obj_pirate.y);

ini_write_real("Stats", "Gold", global.gold);

ini_close();
```

The second room is **room_saving** and it is also 1024x768 in size and has one instance of **obj_setup_buttons_and_hud** and one of **obj_pirate**.

Figure 41-2 shows what this element looks like in action.

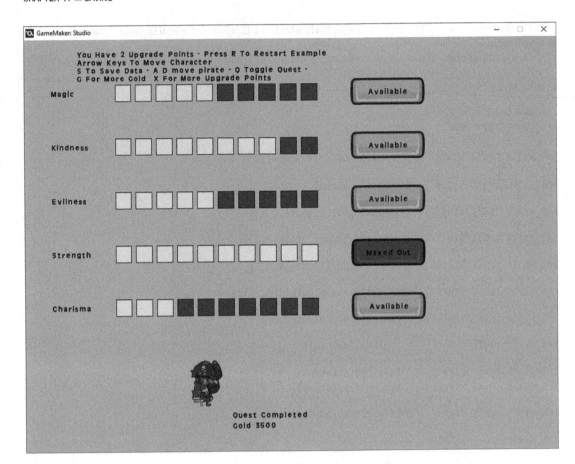

Figure 41-2. *The element in action*

Index

B. Tyers, *Learn RPGs in GameMaker: Studio*, DOI 10.1007/978-1-4842-2946-0

Get the eBook for only $5!

Why limit yourself?

With most of our titles available in both PDF and ePUB format, you can access your content wherever and however you wish—on your PC, phone, tablet, or reader.

Since you've purchased this print book, we are happy to offer you the eBook for just $5.

To learn more, go to http://www.apress.com/companion or contact support@apress.com.

Apress®

Printed in the United States
By Bookmasters